Pathways to Asia

Pathways to Asia

The politics of engagement

Edited by Richard Robison

ALLEN & UNWIN

First published in 1996 by
Allen & Unwin Pty Ltd
9 Atchison Street, St Leonards, NSW 2065 Australia
Phone:(61 2) 9901 4088
Fax:(61 2) 9906 2218
E-mail:100252.103@compuserve.com

National Library of Australia
Cataloguing-in-Publication entry:

Pathways to Asia.

ISBN 1 86448 102 1.

1. Australia—Foreign relations—Asia. 2. Asia—Foreign
relations—Australia. I. Robison, Richard, 1943– .

327.9405

Set in 10/11 Times by DOCUPRO, Sydney
Printed by KHL Printing Company (Pte) Ltd, Singapore

10 9 8 7 6 5 4 3 2 1

Contents

**Part IV   Strategies for engagement: industry policy and labour
policy**

Contributors

Chua Beng Huat is currently a Senior Lecturer, Department of Sociology, National University of Singapore. His most recent book, *Communitarian Ideology and Democracy in Singapore* (Routledge, London, 1995) deals with the political and ideological trajectories of contemporary Singapore. In addition he has also published extensively on issues of urban development and public housing within the peculiar welfare systems of Singapore.

Robert Fagan is Professor of Human Geography, School of Earth Sciences, Macquarie University. His recent research has focused on industrial change in Australia; the economic, social and political implications of globalisation; and the impacts of restructuring on production and employment in Australian cities and industrial regions. His most recent book, with Michael Webber, is *Global Restructuring: The Australian Experience* (Oxford University Press, Melbourne, 1994) and he is currently writing a book on restructuring in the Australian food industry.

Kevin Hewison is Professor of Asian Studies and Languages at the University of New England and a Fellow of the Asia Research Centre. With a PhD from Murdoch University, he has held positions at universities in Australia, Papua New Guinea and Thailand and has been a consultant to a number of agencies in Thailand and the Lao PDR. His publications include *Bankers and Bureaucrats* (Yale), *Power and Politics in Thailand* (Journal of Contemporary Asia Publishers), (with Seri Phongphit) *Village Life in Thailand: Culture and Transition in the Northeast* (Moolban Press), and the edited collections, *Southeast Asia in the 1980s* and *Southeast Asia in the 1990s* (Allen & Unwin).

Rob Lambert is a Senior Lecturer in the Department of Organisational and Labour Studies at the University of Western Australia. He is currently researching labour developments in Indonesia and is also working on the globalisation of Australian manufacturing. He has been responsible for organising several international conferences on labour in the Asian region.

Stephanie Lawson is a Fellow in the Department of International Relations, Research School of Pacific and Asian Studies, Australian National University. She has published numerous articles on politics in the South Pacific Region as well as a book, *The Failure of Democratic Politics in Fiji* (1991) for which she was awarded the Crisp Medal in 1992, by the Australasian Political Science Association. Her most recent book is *Tradition Versus Democracy in the South Pacific: Fiji, Tonga and Western Samoa* (Cambridge University Press, forthcoming). She is also the current editor of the *Australian Journal of International Affairs*. Her present research interests include the politics of culture and democratisation in Southeast Asia.

Trevor Matthews is an Associate Professor in the Department of Government in the University of Sydney. He is also the co-author of *The Japanese Connection: Australian Leaders' Attitudes Towards Japan and the Australia-Japan Relationship* (Longman Cheshire, 1988). His recent publications have dealt with business interest groups in Australia, Australia's trade policy and the use of trade and technology policy by the Japanese and South Korean governments.

John Ravenhill is a Senior Fellow in the Department of International Relations, Research School of Pacific and Asian Studies, Australian National University. His most recent publications are *Pacific Cooperation: Building Economic and Security Regimes in the Asia-Pacific Region* and *The Political Economy of East Asia*. He is the editor of the Cambridge University Press series, *Cambridge Asia-Pacific Studies*.

Richard Robison is Professor of Southeast Asian Studies and Director of the Asia Research Centre at Murdoch University. He is the author and editor of several books on political and economic change in the Asian region, including *Indonesia: The Rise of Capital* (Allen & Unwin) and most recently, *Southeast Asia in the 1990s: Capitalism, Authoritarianism and Democracy* (with Kevin Hewison and Garry Rodan).

Garry Rodan completed his PhD in 1986 at Murdoch University, where he is a Lecturer in Politics in the School of Social Sciences, and a Senior Fellow of the Asia Research Centre. He is the author of *The Political Economy of Singapore's Industrialization* (Macmillan and St Martin's Press) and editor of *Singapore Changes Guard* (Longman Cheshire) and Southeast Asia in the 1990s: Capitalism, *Authoritarianism and*

Democracy. His forthcoming book, *Opposition Without Civil Society: Politics in Industrializing Asia*, will be published by Routledge.

Peter Searle is presently a Lecturer in Politics at University College, University of New South Wales, Australian Defence Force Academy. He is the author of *Politics in Sarawak: The Iban Perspective* (1983) and has recently completed a PhD entitled 'Rent-Seekers or Real Capitalists? The Riddle of Malaysian Capitalism'. He is currently working on a book about Australia's relations with Malaysia.

Linda Weiss (PhD London) is Senior Lecturer in Comparative Politics at the University of Sydney. Dr Weiss specialises in comparative government–industry relations. Her most recent book, *States and Economic Development* (co-authored with John Hobson), is being translated into Korean. She is currently completing a book on state capacity, comparing the institutions of public–private coordination in East Asia and Northern Europe. Dr Weiss is a research associate of the Asia Research Centre and is on the Editorial Board of the *Australian Journal of International Affairs* and founding co-editor of the *Journal of Industry Studies*.

Tables and figures

Tables

Figures

Introduction

Until the 1970s, Australia's economic prosperity rested on a commodity-based export sector complemented by a heavily protected domestic manufacturing industry. Within this shell, and sanctioned by both major political parties as well as by powerful industry cartels and trade unions, a vigorous and in some ways corporatist social democracy emerged replete with an extensive social welfare system. In the post-war era, protection, jobs and high living standards came to be considered a normal condition of Australian life.

With the oil shocks of the 1970s and the substantial declines in commodity prices that followed, as well as the emergence of the EC and major structural shifts in the global economy, this system could no longer be sustained in its existing form. Thatcherism, Reaganism, structural adjustment and fiscal retrenchment were the new courses charted in the UK and US. In this environment, the ideological and policy agenda in Australia shifted dramatically towards a mix of economic rationalism and an instrumentalist form of corporatism, particularly in labour relations. Coming to power in the early 1980s, the new Labor government immediately undertook a fundamental structural reordering of the economy, dismantling the old protectionist frameworks and seeking to construct in their place an economic regime focused upon the task of deregulating economic life as a means of achieving a new international competitiveness.

Most important, a deliberate 'look north' policy was adopted, identifying Asian economies as the engine room of world growth for the next few decades and placing Asian markets at the heart of Australia's new strategy for internationalising its economy and its world view. While the degree to which this new northward vision has been actually reflected in the pattern of Australia's exports and investments lags behind the rhetoric, there is no doubting that a remarkable metamorphosis in Australia's view of the importance of Asia has been achieved. Indeed, in many quarters it has assumed almost the status of a cargo cult.

It is now a decade since these efforts to internationalise and engage with Asia were commenced. It is time to reflect upon the ideological and strategic assumptions that have driven policy and the ways in which 'Asia' and the dynamics of engagement have been understood. Most important, however, is the question of the implications of the engagement for Australian society; in particular, for its social, democratic and egalitarian ideals and traditions, however flawed they may have been in practice. Whether social democracy in its present form can be combined with achieving a new competitiveness in the world economy is perhaps the central question facing Australia. In what some see as a Darwinian struggle for the economic survival and competitiveness of nations, does the social democratic framework place an untenable burden upon Western economies in their contest with the sleek new industrial predators of the Asian region? Can the West avoid adopting the structures that appear to have underpinned the Asian miracle: a seemingly contradictory world of markets and pervasive state control, where the interest of economic growth is portrayed as the collective public interest and where the state smooths the way for the corporate or family agenda in an ironic reversal of the rhetoric of 'Asian values'?

Australia's political leaders are sending out confusing messages on this question. On the one hand, Prime Minister Paul Keating is confident that an economic metamorphosis involving engagement with the Asian economic dynamo can be achieved without sacrificing its basic principles and traditions of social and political life. In the inaugural 'Weary' Dunlop Asialink lecture in December 1993, Keating argued that, 'Australia is not and never can be an "Asian nation" . . . and can only relate to our friends and neighbours as Australian'. He expressed confidence that Australia's values and institutions were strong enough to enable restructuring to be undertaken within the prevailing democratic traditions. In apparent contradiction, he has expressed the view that Asian culture and values would begin to make an impact on Australian culture while Foreign Minister Evans has talked of Australia thinking of itself as an Eastern hemisphere nation.[1]

Within Asia, there is less equivocation. A range of leaders, led by former Prime Minister Lee Kuan Yew of Singapore and Prime Minister Mahathir of Malaysia, argue that Western society is in a process of social and moral disintegration where rampant individualism, laissez faire and the legal obsession with individual rights overwhelms the broader communal interest, and where the decline of the family accompanies a loss of individual commitment to achievement. In contrast, they argue, the Asian model is built upon cooperative rather than individualistic principles and upon sets of moral values that ensure that individual behaviour is responsible to the larger interest of social cohesion and economic progress.[2] Hence, the social interest and the private interest, and, it might be added, the market and the state, are reconciled. It is to this formula that Asia's success in the international economic markets is attributed. In Mahathir's view, and that of his Trade Minister, Rafidah Aziz, successful engagement with Asia is not possible for Australia until it moves away from its Western roots and towards these Asian values.[3]

That important structural changes are under way in Australian society, economy and culture is indisputable. It is also evident that much of this change is being driven by the process of internationalisation. Engagement with Asia, in particular, brings Australia into direct competition with countries free of the fiscal burden of large social welfare systems and able to provide low tax regimes; where investment is relatively unconstrained by distributional coalitions such as organised labour and environmental movements, and where endless reserve armies of labour continuously pour on to the labour market, all orchestrated by powerful systems of industrial mercantilism. Quite clearly, social democratic attempts to address collective interests and maintain the public sphere and a social wage come under severe pressure in these circumstances. These pressures are amplified by elements within Australian business. The Australian government has been urged to match the Asian investment environment in such areas as tax, the labour market, regulatory controls on investment, in work conditions, quality controls and environmental safeguards. The threat to move offshore has been invoked as the natural consequence of failure to address these issues.

As the economic balance shifts and Asian economies become increasingly important as markets and as sites and sources of investment, greater leverage is delivered into the hands of Asian political leaders. The threat of exclusion from markets and from the emerging regional political community has been an important expression of the way in which Western nations approach Asia. Asian nations have shown a willingness to threaten economic retaliation in response to Western press criticism or other perceived political slights. In response, some Western political and business elites as well as liberal academics have increasingly embraced the notions of cultural relativism and 'Asian values'. These justify constraints on behaviour and policies that might threaten commercial interest.[4]

This new situation has strengthened the political position of conservatives and neo-liberals within Australia. Both agree that a radical change in Australian social and political life is precisely what is needed and take selective inspiration from the Asian model. For conservatives, what is perceived as an Asian emphasis on hierarchy, order and authority in Asian political regimes as well as the priority given to the 'national interest' are particularly attractive features.[5] For neo-liberals it is the freedom accorded investors through a deregulated labour market, an absence of powerful distributional coalitions and the absence of a social welfare system that is attractive about the Asia 'model'. In their view, Asian economic success ironically confirms the appropriateness of the American liberal model so despised by the ideologues of the Asia model.

The resolution of this critical watershed is, therefore, partly a process of domestic political struggle for control of the policy agenda within Australia between social democrats, conservatives and neo-liberals. But it is a struggle that has also taken place within sets of concrete constraints imposed by the very dynamics of the global economy Australia is seeking to enter and by the Asian economies whose markets Australia seeks to capture. It is the intention of this volume to examine the way in which competing ideological and economic interests in Australia and the West seek to define 'Asia' and the nature of engagement and to capture the agenda of structural change.

In the first chapter this task is explained in detail, the central issues and questions are identified and the framework for the book established. Chapters 1 and 2 examine aspects of the nature of engagement. To what extent is engagement a question of reconciling contending cultures? Does Asia offer to the West a cohesive and superior model of economic and political organisation for the twenty-first century? Are the problems between Asia and the West over questions of trade, investment, human rights and the press simply questions of different cultural values? Is cultural sensitivity and willingness to adapt to 'Asian' values a prerequisite for successful engagement for Australia and the West? Garry Rodan and Kevin Hewison argue that, on the contrary, Asian societies are divided by the same ideological schisms that fracture societies in the West. So-called 'Asian' values are, in this interpretation, an expression of the dominance of conservatism in Asia, sharing most of its views with conservatism in the West. Rather than a clash of civilisations, what is taking place is an internationalisation of ideological conflict. Peter Searle's chapter develops these investigations in the context of the crisis in Australian–Malaysian relations that followed Paul Keating's 'recalcitrant' remarks about Mahathir in 1993. Notions of contending cultures, cultural sensitivity, cultural relativism and 'Asian' values are discussed in relation to the intense contests that took place in Australia over the interpretation of these events and the desirable responses. It is the ideological and social interests of the contending positions within countries rather than the cultural divides between Australia and Asia that appear to be the most revealing and helpful tools of analysis. One of the implications of such interpretations is that the rise of conservatism in Asia may tilt the global balance against liberalism and influence the contest within the West itself.

The second section deals with some of the difficulties of defining and claiming concepts. Lee Kuan Yew, Mahathir and others are able to point to gross inconsistencies in the practice of democracy and human rights in the West which undermine Western proprietorial claims to these concepts. Such observations may, on the one hand, lead to propositions that 'naming' is simply a question of power. Democracy, in this view, is not a universal concept but a relative one: anybody's definition is as good as anyone else's. Another view is that revealing the clay feet of Western democracies does not destroy universalist notions but, simply, points to hypocrisy in much of the Western rhetoric. In her chapter on political myths about Asia and the West, Stephanie Lawson investigates some of these complex questions. However, juxtaposing cultural relativism to universalism may obscure a possibility that universal principles may be achieved in a range of institutional and ideological forms. Chua Beng Huat's chapter raises this question in his exploration of some aspects of Singapore's political culture. To counter the view that liberal or social democracy is inimical to vigorous and sustained economic growth he sees the task for Australia as building a system in which these two are combined.

One of the central questions in the debate has been whether the rise of the Asian industrial economies has been constructed upon strategies that give priority to markets. Do the Asian examples point the direction for policy reform in Australia and the West? The chapters by Trevor Matthews and John Ravenhill and by Linda Weiss in the third section of the book address these questions. They examine in detail how industrial growth has been achieved in the most successful of the Asian industrial exporting economies and challenge the neo-liberal mythologies about the policies and institutions that produced such 'miracles'. Instead of liberal markets and regulatory states they find policies and institutions whose function is to manage and coordinate rather than facilitate any naturally self-regulating market. Revealing the real dynamics of industrialism in these prominent Northeast Asian examples is a major step towards securing accuracy and honesty in the Australian debate. It raises new questions. Why have neo-liberals been so resistant to admitting this aspect of Asian economic organisation? What can Australia learn from these industrial mercantilist models? Given its social and political history, can Australia borrow from these Northeast Asian examples? Or, are these state-centred models transitionary phenomena that are not relevant to advanced industrial society? These are concerns that are much more sophisticated in their perspective of the dynamics and options of economic and policy change than simply worrying about how liberal reforms can be achieved.

The final section deals with economic policy in Australia. A view that the dynamics of investment decisions are driven by the forces of international competition leads naturally to strategies that seek to identify international competitiveness and make appropriate structural adjustments. Plunging into the world of deregulation and structural adjustment confronts two problems. First, the labour markets and tax and regulatory regimes of Asian economies claimed to constitute frameworks in competition with those in the West are not the products of neutral policies. They are the products of particular sets of power relationships. Hence, policy switches involve much more than different choices on the part of policymakers. They imply fundamental shifts in the structure of social and political power in the West. This issue is pursued by Rob Lambert in his chapter. Bob Fagan, in his chapter, looks at a further issue. To what extent are investment decisions actually driven by international dynamics? Fagan proposes that the pattern of much investment is still decided within the national arena and that the global location of investment is not always determined by such factors as international competitiveness, comparative labour costs or tax rates. Indeed, most of the Asian industrialisers have combined open, outward-looking sectors with protected domestic sectors in their economic strategies. It is the exercise of power, the forging of deals and the building of institutions and coalitions, as much as international market forces that have been critical in shaping investment and pricing decisions. While many national industry policies are little more than crude featherbedding of vested interests, the costs of which have been borne by the poorer sections of society, the recognition that there is good industry policy as well as bad and that market outcomes can often be disastrous is important. Such recognition opens the door for options not imagined by neo-liberals.

This book is the outcome of a cooperative research project designed and coordinated within the Asia Research Centre at Murdoch University. Such projects are an important part of the Centre's activities, bringing together Australian and Asian researchers to tackle questions central to the public debate in Australia and the region. The emphasis is upon innovation, imagination and relevance. The focal point of these projects are workshops intended to draw individual research interests into a central theme through cooperation and to give the opportunity for refinement and focus of the papers through discussion and debate. All of this is costly, as is the time of the editor and other staff. The financial support of the Australian Research Council, Murdoch University and of other private sponsors has been critical. The executive officer of the Asia Research Centre, Del Blakeway, secretary, Nanette Adams, publications officer, Helen Bradbury and publications assistant, Neena Mairata, have provided a highly efficient and skilled service, organising the workshop, preparing material and assisting with editing. As editor, I found a normally grinding task to be a stimulating experience largely because of the enthusiasm with which contributors approached the central problem and because of the quality of work I was to deal with.

Richard Robison
October 1995

Notes

1 Paul Keating, The Inaugural Sir Edward 'Weary' Dunlop Asialink Lecture, Melbourne, 8 December 1993. On Keating's 1995 remarks see, Greg Sheridan, 'Lure of the East', *Weekend Australian*, 25–26 March 1995, p. 24. Gareth Evans, 'Australia in Asia and the Asia Pacific: Beyond the Looking Glass' Fourteenth Asia Lecture to the Asia–Australia Institute, 20 March 1995.

2 Zakaria, Fareed, 1994, 'Culture is Destiny: Interview with Lee Kuan Yew', *Foreign Affairs*, vol. 73, no. 2, pp. 109–26.

3 *Australian Financial Review*, 19 November 1993; *Australian* 17 & 18 May 1995, p. 1–2.

4 Indonesian and Australian response to David Jenkins' criticism of the Soeharto family's business activities in the *Sydney Morning Herald* (10 April 1986), is dealt with in detail in Richard Robison (ed.), *The Australia-Indonesia Relationship: A Current Assessment* (special issue of *Australian Outlook*, 40 (3), 1986). The Recalcitrant debate was treated in a range of publications. See, for example; Greg Sheridan, 'War of the Words' *Australian,* 4–5 December 1993, p. 19; Richard Woolcott, 'Asia—Can't Live With it or Without it', *Bulletin,* 14 December 1993, pp. 24–28; Clive Kessler, 'Keating's Blunder: three lessons', *Asian Studies Review*, 17 (3), April 1994, pp. 125–31. More recently, the burning of the Indonesian flag by protesters in Australia provoked threats of a trade boycott by the Indonesian Importers Association (*Australian*, 18–19 August 1995, p. 1).

5 For a survey of this see: Gabriel Lafitte, 'Reorientations', *Arena*, August–September 1994, pp. 13–15. The chapter in this volume by Garry Rodan and Kevin Hewison, 'A Clash of Cultures or the Convergence of Political Ideology?' also deals with this issue.

Part I

The politics of engagement

1

Looking north: myths and strategies

Richard Robison

As individual countries are drawn into the new global markets and financial networks and into new international communications, media and information systems they are subjected to pressures for structural change. Much of the focus has been upon the pressures imposed upon 'Asia' by the 'West' for predictable and transparent systems of regulation law and accountability of the state and its officials. Emerging capital markets seeking the funds of international financial institutions have been forced to move toward these requirements. The long struggle between the US and various Asian and Latin American governments over the issue of intellectual property rights has recently seen some important victories for those pushing regulation.

However, with the emergence of the East Asian industrial exporters, important pressures for change are being brought to bear upon liberal economies. Rather than relying upon the free market and the much vaunted cold winds of competition to achieve international competitiveness, the most successful Asian industrialisers have developed cohesive national strategies to organise powerful state and corporate institutions for the purposes of creating international economic ascendancy in a range of sectors. Central to this process has been the role of the state as coordinator, organiser, facilitator and, at times, surrogate for the bourgeoisie. While the particular experience of each country is different the following characteristics have been the common ingredients of success.

- The state has played a critical role in clearing political and social obstacles to the development of corporate power within the framework of policies of outward-looking economic growth. In particular, it has constrained organised labour, environmental groups and even elements of capital whose interests lie contrary to those of the manufacturing exporters.

- The state has been a central player in the construction of international competitiveness through trade and industry policies that shape markets to a framework of strategic targeting.
- Within such frameworks of industrial mercantilism, the emergence of corporate conglomerates in the region has been generally assisted in the initial stages by rent-seeking activities in which monopolies, subsidies, access to credit and other preferences are allocated by specific power-holders and institutions within the state apparatus to selected firms and capitalists rather than by the state to business in general. This pattern continues to prevail in Indonesia, Malaysia, Thailand and the Philippines. As China emerges from socialism it also appears to be taking this path.
- The foreign policies of the most successful exporters, their education systems and other state resources have been deployed in an intensively instrumental fashion to serve the immediate needs of building competitiveness and economic growth.

In many ways, then, the engagement of the West and Asia involves contradictions between economic liberalism and industrial mercantilism. The central question is: on what grounds should the engagement be fought?

Conservative Asian leaders, most prominently Lee Kwan Yew, Mahathir and Soeharto, have argued that 'Asian' models of political and social organisation embody the principles of harmony, hierarchy and consensus. This they contrast to the confrontation, individualism and decay that characterises Western liberalism.[1] To some extent these claims can be regarded as self-serving. By claiming an immutable and discrete Asian set of values, conservative leaders are able to deny legitimacy to domestic opponents, who can be dismissed as opposing the national interest or simply being un-Asian. The cultural relativism implicit in their claims can be used to deny the validity of any non-Asian (or even non-national) judgements upon such issues as human rights. However, whether such values are imposed upon the populace by conservative dictatorships or are part of a natural 'Asian' culture, the outcome is a system of economic and political order orchestrated by the state. What is more important from the perspective of this study are the claims that these characteristics transcend phases and stages of social and economic change, representing a fully developed alternative to the liberal/social democratic models of the West rather than a stage in the evolution towards these paradigms.

Implicit within this view, there are some very specific propositions about the way Australia should handle the process of engagement with Asia and about the sorts of changes in Australian society and politics required to achieve successful engagement. It is implied that, when dealing with Asia, Australia must suspend many of the normal criteria upon which it bases political relationships with other countries in the interests of 'cultural sensitivity'. In other words, the principles of social and political life can be considered culturally relative rather than universal. Hence, 'Asian' practices in the areas of freedom of speech, human rights, citizenship and the environment, to name a few, are hardly legitimate arenas for criticism. Prominent Australian conservatives, including former Chief Justice, Anthony Mason, academic, Owen Harries and former Prime Minister, Bob Hawke have publicly criticised what they regard as Australia's practice of forcing its cultural values on Asia and suggested that we could do well to learn from the Asian example. In all cases 'Asian' culture was conflated with the authoritarian views of regional dictatorships; in the case of Bob Hawke, with Burma's SLORC.[2] It is also claimed by Australian conservatives and business figures that the political and economic regimes of Asia offer some generic advantages both for the regulation of markets and the integration of an orderly industrial society. The presence of a social welfare system in Australia is seen to be a critical structural disadvantage for Australia.[3] In both cases there are reasons for accepting Mahathir's proposition that Australia must become more like 'Asia' if it is to successfully engage.

As Asian industrial economies, increasingly capable of producing sophisticated consumer manufactures and capital goods, began to compete seriously within the markets of the West, the debate over strategic responses assumed increasing political significance. While some elements among domestic manufacturers, often in league with labour unions, attempted to confront the new Asian industrial exporters with protective trade agendas, this strategy was to fail. So, too, were attempts by Western governments to bring pressure to bear on the political and legal arrangements that exist in Asia to assist in maintaining low wages, poor conditions, low domestic consumption and high savings rates by pressing for reforms in the political and legal frameworks, in labour policy and in human rights. This was a strategy attempted by the Clinton Presidency in its early years. US business clearly indicated what they thought of this strategy. Both were defeated by those elements of business integrating with the new global economy. Fearing the loss of Asian markets, US business lobbyists brought pressure to bear on President Clinton to end his reformist policies in the region by disconnecting trade and investment policies from issues of human rights and labour reform.[4] Western business clearly signalled that it would prefer to resolve the trade and investment tensions between Asia and the West by means of conservative and neo-liberal reforms in the West rather than by social democratic reforms in Asia.

What is clear is that Western conservatives and neo-liberals have found much to admire in the so-called 'soft authoritarianism' or 'developmental authoritarianism' that has prevailed in the industrialising Asian economies. For neo-liberals, such authoritarianism is distinguished by its capacity to enable government decisions in the national interest, eschewing ideology and politics in favour of pragmatic, scientific, technocratic principles.[5] In reality this means implementing successful policies of economic growth and removing constraints upon the private sector. The no-nonsense approach of many of these governments to reformist critics, organised labour and other opposition groups can, in this view, be interpreted as necessary moves to resist the pressures of distributional coalitions and vested interests at a critical time of economic progress. For conservatives, the capacity of such regimes to achieve national integration and a stable, hierarchical, social order is the most impressive element.[6]

The willingness of Western business to play, at least selectively, by rules set by various Asian governments is also driven by commercial interest. This is perhaps best illustrated in the area of disputes over press freedom and responsibility. In some Asian countries, including Indonesia, Singapore, Malaysia and China, the media are regarded as having a responsibility to the 'national interest'. This means, in effect, considerable government control and censorship. As the Asian market becomes more important and as the media industry becomes increasingly internationalised, what were previously Western media companies have to deal with political restrictions upon news and information by Asian governments. The Malaysian government has shown a willingness to respond to outside government and media criticisms by invoking economic sanctions, and the threat of sanctions, on both British and Australian investors. In the 1980s, Indonesia had also reacted with hostility to comment in the domestic Australian press and universities, at one stage threatening to cease a range of contacts between the two countries.[7] Singapore prohibits publication and distribution of media products that do not adhere to its censorship requirements. As the recent case of the *International Herald Tribune* in Singapore illustrates, Western media are increasingly prepared to conform to local constraints where markets are at stake.[8]

In the race to build international media outlets in Asia, including satellite transmissions, there is an increasing awareness by proprietors of the need to produce what is commonly called 'government friendly' programs; meaning no content that contravenes the moral and political order and hierarchies imposed by local regimes.[9] It is ironic that Rupert Murdoch's success in gaining access to China with his Star TV came as he shed the BBC news. Contrary to his earlier claim that no dictatorship is safe in the age of mass electronic media, it would appear that the trend might be in the opposite direction: the liberal mass media may not be safe in the era of dictators.

Accommodation to political authoritarianism in such instances is a product of increasing economic ties with the region and the increasingly active role played by business in the policy debate. This new force is driven by a sensitivity to criticisms of their Asian operations and fears of commercial retaliation by some of the more authoritarian or nationalist governments of Asia in response to attacks from Western press and academics. Some Australian businessmen have even evinced a willingness to constrain media and government criticism where these threaten investment and trade.[10] In other words, Western business interests are in conflict with Western political and social institutions, including both the media and universities. The latter are under increasing pressure to accommodate in their activities a utilitarianism related to the trade and investment agenda.

But the pressures are not simply those for the accommodation to authoritarian political regimes. Economic regimes in the region represent a somewhat different genre to the model of liberal markets. They are regimes in which economic ascendancy is sought through what Amsden calls 'getting the prices wrong' or creating comparative advantage. If there is any lesson to be learnt from the Asian experience it is that international competitiveness has been achieved on a basis of national strategic planning in which the state plays a key role.[11] What Australia is confronting in international competition is not simply more efficient competitors with lower costs but competitors working within different trade and political regimes often able to deliver cheap finance, compliant labour forces, high saving rates, low taxes, and access to the resources of international trading houses and powerful planning agencies.[12] Australia confronts economies where trade regimes allow efficient export industries to coexist with large and highly protected, inefficient domestic industries which ensure high rates of employment and the avoidance of the destabilising influence of structural adjustment.

Just as institutional and political factors underpin the competitiveness of capital among the major Asian industrial exporters, so they underpin the competitiveness of labour. While some neo-liberals have chosen to portray labour relations in Asia as the product of a superior work ethic and a 'free' labour market, it is not just low wages that overseas investors seek in countries like China, Indonesia and Thailand. What is critical is the long working hours, the relative absence of such overheads as long service leave, superannuation, medical insurance, the relative lack of safety regulation and the general absence of powerful labour unions. These advantages are the consequence of the political and social circumstances in which labour operates.

Australian firms and workers find themselves in the position of having to compete with labour markets where governments play a major role in enforcing the conditions necessary for low wages, child labour and poor conditions. While wages and conditions in Asia are undoubtedly depressed by the nature of the labour market itself, they are also influenced by policies intended to prevent the free organisation of labour. In other words, these are not labour markets that can be characterised as free.[13]

What is important is how these structural pressures interact with existing ideological and political forces in Australia to shape new policy agendas. It is no exaggeration to say that social democrats have been unable to develop a strategy response when the political and fiscal costs of their project appear to constrain the potential to compete in markets where instrumentalism in the service of economic growth and private sector profits are so well developed. In comparison, conservatives and neo-liberals have made substantial claims to providing new frameworks.

The conservative revival and Australia's engagement with Asia

The evolution of capitalist society in the West has seen the relative decline of political conservatism at the hands of liberal and social democratic forces. In much of Asia, by contrast, the central role of the state in the process of capitalist transformation has allowed conservative perspectives to remain influential within the context of ideologies that view society as embodying a single organic interest of which the state is the guardian. The political influence of both the middle classes and labour which underpinned the rise of liberalism and social democracy in the West has been much weaker in Asia.

The conservative agenda in the West has been re-activated by the breakup of inward looking economies and the accelerating process of engagement with a global economy. For conservatives, this process is associated with a moral and social disintegration of Western society, manifest in the corporate excesses of the 1980s, rising crime rates, urban decay, the drug problem and the breakdown of the family. In their view, both social democracy and neo-liberalism as the harbinger of a new and unconstrained form of market capitalism are to blame for this situation.[14] State-funded social welfare programs, public education and other policies based upon redistribution of wealth have, in their view, little place in a world of natural hierarchies.[15] On social issues, crime and disintegration are seen as a moral, behavioural question rather than one evolving from poverty or social alienation. Hence, policy prescriptions focus on law and order, punishment and the separation of social deviants from the law-abiding communities rather than strategies of social and economic reform or new social welfare measures. In the US, where this conservative social agenda is most advanced, the building of prisons spearheads the law and order program and the public works budgets. On the other hand, conservatives also reject the liberal emphasis on the self-interest of the individual and the self-regulating market as the primary mechanisms for achieving social prosperity. Instead, they have a clearly defined concept of the 'national interest' and of the responsibility of the state for social cohesion.

It is in the area of social policy that Western conservatives find the purported Asia model most attractive. The views of Lee on social welfare, law and order, discipline, social hierarchy and dissent invoke considerable resonance. Lee has argued that, 'Man needs a certain sense of right and wrong. There is such a thing called evil, and it is not the result of being the victim of society. You are just an evil man prone to doing evil things, and you have to be stopped from doing them. Westerners have abandoned an ethical base for society, believing that all problems are solvable by a good government, which we in the East never believed possible.'[16] The Singaporean approach towards welfare is nicely illustrated in recent legislation enabling children to be sued by parents for financial support. With a rapidly ageing population this is clearly a move aimed at protecting state budgets as well as achieving an ideological goal.[17] The recent caning of the American juvenile, Michael Fay, also evoked considerable support in the West. In this sense, conservatives are pointing to Asian examples as evidence of the technical superiority of their social prescriptions for structural dilemmas now confronting Western society, quite independent of the process of engagement with Asia.

In the sphere of economic policy as well, the Asian experience is attractive to Western conservatives. The fact that government intervention and coordinated national strategies, rather than unconstrained markets, have been central to Asian economic development reinforces the conservative belief that economic policy should serve broad social goals; in this case those of maintaining social cohesion. In matters of Australian economic policy, for example, we find the Australian conservative Santamaria protesting against the excesses of financial deregulation, the destructive nature of the international money market and the derivatives trade, arguing for a stronger central bank.[18]

Yet there is a critical difference between the conservatism of developmentalist Asian governments and the Western conservative model. Although hierarchical in nature, the ordering of privilege and authority in places like Singapore is not based (at least not yet) on tradition but on a fairly crude utilitarian criteria. The market, albeit

managed or governed, as well as economic growth, is central to the
Asian conservative agenda. Society is geared to the process of international economic competitiveness. And it is this pressure for constant
struggle to improve and compete in economic terms as the process of
engagement with the world economy and with Asia progresses that is
incompatible with important aspects of Western conservatism.

The fatal weakness of the conservative agenda is not specifically
that it only partially accords to the sort of conservatism that has
provided a shell for the process of industrial growth in Asia and its
international competitiveness, but it confronts processes of structural
change in Australia and provides no alternative agenda for dealing with
the challenges of engaging with the international economy. In this it
is ironically in much the same position as the social democrats.
However, as I will argue below, elements of the conservative position
are being drafted into a revised neo-liberalism. The idea of order and
authority is being fused with the notion of free markets to produce a
neo-conservative position.

The neo-liberal ascendancy

In the past decade, neo-liberals have gained an ascendancy in the
Australian policy agenda. This ascendancy was driven in part by
increasing fiscal crisis of the state and by declining competitiveness
in international markets. These factors made it more difficult for
Western economies to finance social democratic economic programs
and to maintain inward-looking economic policies. Neo-liberals
brought with them claims of a technically superior economic solution
which involved the progressive withdrawal of the state from the economy through privatisation as well as the retrenchment of welfare
programs, economic deregulation and structural adjustment. Such
policy agendas fitted well with the pressures at work.

The neo-liberal vision differs from the conservative approach in
several important ways. It sees the individual and the market as
cornerstones of prosperity and the state as a neutral arbiter of largely
self-regulating market mechanisms. It opposes the natural social hierarchies central to conservative philosophy, preferring hierarchies built
on performance in the market by individuals. Neo-liberal policy objectives include small government, structural adjustment, deregulation of
finance and trade as well as the internationalisation of national economies.[19] The opening of Australia to engagement with the global
economy and, in particular, with the emerging Asian industrial societies
could be best achieved, it was argued, by removing the constraints on
trade, and reforming the microeconomy, especially the labour market.

By allowing prices to respond to scarcity and market demand, allocative efficiencies would be achieved to allow the Australian economy to become competitive. Structural adjustment would force offshore industries not suited to Australia's natural competitive niches. It was precisely these market strategies, neo-liberals argued, that underlay the Asian miracle.[20]

These neo-liberal interpretations and prescriptions are not new. Lower taxes, smaller government, less union power, less regulation and more discipline have been part of this agenda for decades. But their calls have attained a degree of potency in recent times because of the increasing pressure on fiscal resources, growing foreign debt and rising unemployment being experienced in many Western countries. Deregulation and the retreat of the state becomes an attractive option for governments in such times. Consequently, the neo-liberal agenda has become dominant in policy institutions since the early 1980s. As well, the rise of the global economy and the emergence of Asian industrialism has given Western business the opportunity to escape the strictures of vigorous domestic civil societies and democratic political systems, and gain access to social and political environments long since superseded in the West where capitalism is either unconstrained or in uncontested alliance with governments. Their increased mobility has added weight to their veto power and given them greater leverage to press for restructuring in Western economies.[21] It is these structural pressures in the international economy that have driven the neo-liberal agenda.

The attractions of Asian models of capitalism for business in the West are illustrated in a recent special edition of the *Far Eastern Economic Review* on the topic of twenty years of Asian growth. In the lead article, the editors of this publication, now an evangelical instrument of free market values, propose that the so-called Asian Miracle has been due to four simple factors: hard work, low taxes, high savings rates and minimal government.[22] Hard work and the work ethic is contrasted with ' . . . government handouts or make-work programmes or social "benefits" that destroy jobs in so many Western countries'. This ideological emphasis upon moral values and individualism is combined with the practical advantage that such a regime obviates the need for a social welfare system and thus clears the way for low taxes and higher savings. Asia is being used in this discourse to protest the constraints that the labour movement and social democracy have forced upon the efficient operation of the market as well as to offer confirmation of the correctness of neo-liberal prescriptions.

But the assumption by Western business that the investment environment in Asia has been achieved by liberal deregulation of markets is a misreading of the situation. For many market-oriented advocates in the West, the realisation that neo-liberalism is not simply a technical economic solution but a broad political and social ideology has led to greater acceptance of a central role in the shaping of markets by the state.

This recognition that free markets require strong government is being developed by influential US theorists who propose that the free operation of markets in Western economies is being politically obstructed by excessive democracy. It has been argued that the liberal democracies have been captured by powerful distributional coalitions seeking access to public funds and influence upon state policy, thereby forcing higher levels of state expenditure and revenue raising. In the process, they crowd out the private sector, restrict savings and investment and, therefore, the velocity of economic growth upon which all prosperity ultimately rests. This view is held by the new school of public choice or rational choice theorists but perhaps best expressed by Mancur Olson.[23] It is a view that has entered the public arena via the business-oriented conservative press. The *Asian Wall Street Journal* has given considerable space to views that attribute low rates of growth and savings in the West with policies of social redistribution.

> The likely explanation is that political democracy has offsetting effects on economic incentives. In the one-person/one-vote system of present day Western democracies, popular governments tend to pursue Robin Hood-style policies. Redistributions from rich to poor—which include welfare transfers and high rates of taxation on successful businesses and individuals—often command majority support. Regardless of one's views about Robin Hood's merits, it is clear that such policies hamper economic performance.
>
> A different force that flourishes under Western democracy is the political power of concentrated interest groups, such as agriculture, environmental lobbies, defence contractors, the elderly and the handicapped. These groups generate policies that redistribute resources in favour of themselves, a transfer that typically does not benefit the poor over the rich, but tends to hamper economic growth.[24]

The clear message of such analyses is not only that social democracy is incompatible with economic growth and international competitiveness but that the democratic political systems of the West also restrain the mechanisms of economic efficiency and, in the long run, the creation of economic growth. The obvious implication is that democracy must be restricted. Public choice theorists advocate a variety of constraints on the power of elected governments to tax and spend as well as a more intense system of checks and balances upon the power of legislative majorities.[25]

While neo-liberals have been prepared to accept that the development of markets may require the exercise of state authority to clear away distributional coalitions and to impose an instrumental restructuring on the labour market and on educational institutions, they have been less willing to accept arguments that Asian industrialising economies have emerged via nationally coordinated trade and industry policies rather than by the free operation of the market mechanism.[26] Such an admission would contradict one of the basic tenets of neoliberal theory: that the private sector is naturally efficient and its problems emanate predominantly from constraints and inefficiencies directed from outside, including high taxes, protective trade regimes, unresponsive education systems. Hence, market failure is a largely unreported phenomenon. Since the industry plans of the 1980s Australian policymakers have studiously avoided and even denied those dimensions of Asian economic development involving planning in industry and trade and institutional cooperation between government and business.[27] Upon this conclusion they confirm that the appropriate policy for engagement with the new global economy and with Asia is one of deregulation of the Australian economy. In other words, their interest in the Asian experience is primarily aimed at substantiating an existing agenda.

However, while some neo-classical economists continue to deny the importance of state-led economic strategies in Asia, the evidence has become so overwhelming that more recent neo-liberal assessments seek to accommodate or explain this in some way. One means of reconciling markets with state intervention has been to explain the undeniable intrusion of the state in the economies of the major Asian industrial powers as being market-facilitating rather than market-constraining. This is a position recently taken by the World Bank itself in a half-hearted attempt to explain the undeniable role of state power in the rise of the Asian NICs without destroying the whole neo-classical paradigm.[28]

The idea of selective state intervention to promote national interests in trade and other aspects of competition has long been attractive to Western business where market ideology is mixed with a good dose of practical self-interest. Hence, the *Far Eastern Economic Review* also delivers the market-facilitating message to a business readership. 'There you have it. Rather than trying to second guess the market, Singapore and other governments around the region got out of the way and let the markets do what markets are supposed to do. In other words, governments acted to promote wealth, not destroy it'.[29] It might be cynically observed that the only real means of distinguishing market facilitating intervention from other kinds is whether it is successful and/or is approved by influential elements of the private sector.

What we have, therefore, is a tendency for some neo-liberals to develop a vision combining free markets with authoritarian politics: a shift to a neo-conservative agenda. The idea that the state should address itself to the task of bringing other sectors of society into line with the 'national interest' in achieving international competitiveness is an attractive one for state bureaucrats in Australia. Intervention has proceeded in the name of the removal of constraints to what is accepted as the natural efficiency of the private sector. Hence, the expansion of certain elements of the public sector is justified in terms of achieving greater utility and market efficiency. The rapid growth of some of Australia's largest Federal Government departments in the era of economic rationalism has been justified on these very instrumental grounds.[30] In the case of higher education it is assumed that the poor performance of the private sector has been in part due to the poor quality and inappropriateness of products delivered by universities. The particular direction taken by the reforms of the late 1980s was to place a new priority upon solving the technical problems of trade and investment as already defined rather than advancing the frameworks themselves through critical scrutiny. For quite independent reasons Australia is beginning to replicate the forms of utilitarianism and instrumentalism so prevalent in the way knowledge is regarded in many of the industrialising regimes of Asia.

Thus, the new neo-conservatism embodies the neo-liberal focus upon markets but with a greater recognition that there is a central role for the state in guaranteeing markets beyond the traditional neo-liberal view of the ideal state as neutral arbiter of naturally self-regulating markets. Hence, in the name of markets, the neo-conservative state constrains distributional coalitions and other special interest groups, may intervene economically to facilitate the free working of markets, and may establish extensive bureaucratic apparatus to ensure a technical utilitarianism within the administrative and educational systems.

The most recent neo-classical move to come to grips with the dilemma has been that of Paul Krugman.[31] He accepts that the state has played a central role in the rapid industrialisation of the industrialising countries of Asia but argues that the sort of growth achieved has been that generated by increased inputs of labour and capital. Strong and interventionist states are suited to such strategies. However, he sees these strategies as historically limited. He doubts these new Asian industrial economies can shift to a new stage based upon higher levels of productivity entrenched by knowledge and technology. What Krugman's thesis does is to confirm the correctness of neo-liberal prescriptions: that for the West and for Asian economies hoping to move into the post labour/capital era, the most important policy achievement is to get the economic macro-fundamentals right.

Unravelling the myths

To what extent does the Asian experience point to directions that the West might follow in its attempts to successfully engage with the Asian engines of economic and industrial growth? For conservatives, the major problem in the West is social disintegration and the overwhelming of the social interest by liberal individualism. Asian countries show the way in terms of political systems that guarantee social order and discipline and take a team approach in which the 'national interest' is enshrined. While neo-liberals rely on the extension of free markets to open a new world of prosperity for all, this vision is also implicitly reliant upon the capacity of the state to guarantee free markets. This relates not only to the 'orthodox paradox' that economic deregulation requires increased instruments of regulation but to the increased requirement for state intervention to clear away distributional coalitions that may divert resources from savings, investment and production. However, difficulties in understanding the Asian experience are generated when they are interpreted within conservative and neo-liberal paradigms. More important are the problems generated by a tendency to see selective aspects of Asian political and economic regimes, taken out of their social and economic context, as generically superior technical instruments in the pursuit of specific moral or economic orders.

Rather than seeing the various Asian political and economic regimes as either superior economic mechanisms or immutable cultural products, they are better understood as regimes characteristic of late industrialising economies where the state rather than the bourgeoisie or the middle classes has played the leading role in financing, managing and planning the industrial transition. There are two theoretical points to be made. First, the current authoritarian ascendancy in some Asian countries is not a natural condition but one forged in the framework of specific conjunctures of social and political power in the period of transition to industrial capitalism. The emergence of capitalist authoritarianism in Europe as well as Asia has generally been characteristic of transitions where strong states and bureaucratic strata are already dominant over relatively poorly formed civil societies. Further, it is the political mechanisms of coercion and co-option rather than any inbuilt social harmony or culturally derived affinity with consensus or submission in the 'Asian' character that underpins those Asian political regimes built upon systems of hierarchy and authority. In this they are similar to the sorts of political systems Gerschenkron saw emerging from instances of 'late industrialisation in Bismarck's Germany or pre-revolutionary Russia'.[32]

Second, rather than being immutable and monolithic, Asian

political systems are characterised by change and diversity. Significantly, the soft or developmental authoritarianism of Asia so admired by Western neo-liberals and conservatives is coming under pressure for change in some important instances. The very problems that confronted Western capitalism and led to political and economic reforms are emerging in the Asian region and leading to similar accommodations. Among these is the pressure upon narrow political and bureaucratic elites to accommodate increasingly autonomous and powerful social forces outside the state and to develop mechanisms that allow mediation and resolution of conflicting interests. Bureaucratic elites are also being progressively integrated into emerging bourgeoisie and middle classes, building political and economic alliances outside the state apparatus. Emerging social forces seek mechanisms for achieving orderly transition from one government to another.[33]

This places in perspective the conservative enthusiasm for Asian authoritarianism and its assumption that a good dose of the same medicine would benefit the West. It neglects the historical specificity of politics. Authoritarian systems in Asia have been sustained in societies experiencing the typical rapid growth characteristic of early industrial capitalism where middle classes and business are able to trade off frustration with the arbitrary nature of political rule, corruption and incompetence against rising levels of prosperity and the protection afforded them against revolutionary and reactionary populism. The capacity of such regimes to deal with the conditions of mature capitalism where lower rates of growth tend to apply, where greater diffusion of social and economic power exists and where the hegemony of capitalism is less reliant on coercive state power is less certain.

Conveniently neglected by conservatives in the West, liberalism, communism and social democracy have all played important roles in modern Asian history along with the sort of Hegelian authoritarianism claimed by Asian conservatives to embody the essence of Asia.[34] Major democratic reforms have occurred in Taiwan, Korea and Thailand in the past decade, representing significant shifts in power towards the institutions of parliament, parties and elections and transforming the political systems of those countries.[35] Perhaps most significantly, the one-party system in Japan, the most mature of the Asian industrial economies, appears to be confronting quite new economic and political dilemmas. The reality is that Asian political systems are moving rapidly along the various paths trodden in the West, driven by the same set of social and political dynamics even if the outcomes are not all the same.

Such movement and diversity within Asia undermines the claims of Lee, Soeharto and others about Asian values. Their caricature of an

'Asian' press is a case in point. Rigorous control of information and media is not a general Asian phenomenon. The Philippines, Japan, Taiwan and Korea boast presses relatively free of government constraints. As media groups become increasingly corporate in nature the pressure to integrate with international consortia and to access global programming increases even in the most controlled environments. In Indonesia, for example, the Ministry of Information's brief to ensure a press responsible to the tasks of political control, integration and development is counterbalanced by the commercial needs of the growing corporate media empires. CNN, for example, is beamed directly into Indonesia via satellites partly owned by Bambang Trihatmojo, the President's second son.[36] Despite the recent crackdown of press freedom, involving the banning of three magazines, *Tempo, Detik* and *Editor,* this general tendency towards conflict remains. As media empires become corporatised they must seek the advertisers' dollar and the burgeoning markets of the new middle classes which demand provocative and interesting news rather than the dull fare of state-controlled media.

Similar logic also applies to neo-liberal and conservative enthusiasm for the much touted absence of social welfare systems in most Asian economies as if these situations were technical policy choices. Nowhere is business resentment of social democracy more intense than on the issue of social welfare. Increasing rates of entrenched and structural unemployment and the shift to casual and part-time employment have been combined in most Western countries with a decreasing state capacity to sustain the social welfare budget. This circumstance has opened a new debate on the welfare issue in which neo-liberals and conservatives are urging major changes. For the former, social welfare can distort market mechanisms and reduce incentives, dulling the entrepreneurial drive; opportunity should, in this view, be shaped by the self-reliant efforts of individuals maximising their options through the rational decisions they make. For conservatives, state-funded social welfare programs have little place in a world of natural social hierarchies. These ideological positions are driven by real structural pressures for lower taxes and reduced government demand on domestic savings, and from pressures on currencies and persistent balance of payments deficits.

An increasing number of Asian economies held up in the West as examples in fiscal restraint are confronting the same social–structural changes that precipitated social welfare systems in the West a century ago. Yet social welfare has existed through such institutions as family structures and life-long employment systems. As populations age and as the family and enterprise structure begin to change there is increased pressure upon the state to accept the responsibility for care of the

elderly, the sick and the unemployed.[37] Despite initial resistance, of
which one notable case is the previously mentioned Singapore legislation allowing parents to take legal action against children who fail
to support them adequately in retirement, the writing is clearly on the
wall. Either large sections of society are to be abandoned as in the
American model so detested by proponents of 'Asian' values, or some
public welfare mechanism must be put in place in which the state must
necessarily play an important role.

Recognising that regimes are constructed within historical processes
of political and social conflict provides a very different perception of
authoritarianism in Asia. It contradicts the claims that the ascendancy
of these regimes can be attributed to a *sui generis* functional superiority
in facilitating economic growth or social integration and stability and
challenges the implicit claims to the inherent superiority of conservative and neo-liberal political prescriptions that are the real message of
that analysis. As societies change so do the policy options. The capacity
of governments to exclude civil society from the political process and
to ensure high levels of saving, partly by keeping social welfare out
of the government sphere and maintaining low rates of taxation, is a
condition specific to certain historical experiences and conjunctures of
state and social power. Embarking on these policy directions is not
simply a matter of technical choice. While such forms of state power
may have been useful in enforcing labour discipline and mobilising
resources in the early years of 'late' industrialisation, they rapidly
become counterproductive as capitalist society matures. In other words,
these are historically specific sets of state–society relations which
cannot be transplanted and replicated easily.

Asian governments themselves are recognising the need to move
away from many of the conditions that underpinned the early stages
of industrial growth. Ironically, these are the very factors that have
appealed to Western conservatives and neo-liberals. For example, low
tax regimes have often been maintained by neglecting investment in
physical and social infrastructure. Growth based solely upon massive
injections of cheap labour and capital has its limits and the neglect of
collective goods is now becoming a constraint to investment and to
prospects for escaping from the low-wage manufacturing trap.
Throughout Asia the sudden surge of investment in infrastructure has
been considerable.[38] While it is hoped that much of this surge can be
financed by the private sector, there is no doubt that the bulk of the
burden must be sustained by the public sector and will involve a
broadening of the revenue base.[39]

Similarly, the sort of political environment that has been frequently
touted as giving freedom to so-called entrepreneurs, in contrast to the
constraints of regulation in the West, has proven also to be an oppor-

tunity for political and military elites to engage in widespread predatory behaviour; reneging on contracts, defaulting on loans, plundering
state budgets, filling family coffers and engaging in widespread piracy
of intellectual property. While the sheer size of the growth surge has
allowed such depredations to be sustained for long periods in some
cases, the impact on the fiscal health of many of these countries, not
to mention international business and investor confidence, has been
damaging. The World Bank is becoming increasingly involved in
developing what it calls 'good governance' in addition to its project
aid and its concern for market reforms.[40] China is the latest country
to confront such a situation. Western business, so loud in its condemnation of regulation in the West and so initially embracing of the free
rider spirit in China, has discovered that some set of laws guaranteeing
the common interests of all capital is not such a bad idea and that
regulation is a necessary requirement of the market economy. As Asia
becomes increasingly involved in international financial systems and
investment flows, procedures and guarantees are becoming increasingly subject to international standards of regulation and law governing
economic and business activity.[41]

This does not mean that both the advanced industrial economies
of the West and the newer industrial economies of Asia are simply on
different points of the same linear paths to liberal democratic and free
market destinations. Even though the social and political situations of
Asian industrialising societies are changing this may be towards different varieties of political regimes. Just as Germany, Italy, France and
Russia have trodden very different paths to Britain and the US, so we
can expect divergence within Asia. Singapore has developed a model
radically distinctive, even from other states supposedly propelled by
the same Confucian ideals. Taiwan and Korea have moved in quite
different ways towards systems of parliamentary government.

Finally, Krugman's point about the relevance of Asian economic
regimes for the twenty-first century must be considered. As leading
Asian economies move out of a period of economic history requiring
high rates of investment and savings and low wages, are the various
regimes of industrial mercantilism redundant? Will we begin to see
Asian economies stumble as they attempt to enter the post-industrial
stage?[42]

If the varieties of Asian authoritarianism are interpreted as specific
and changing political constructions, the whole construct of 'Asia'
begins to crumble. There is no reason to accept that Lee Kuan Yew
speaks for a monolithic Asian spirit any more than Ronald Reagan
might be considered to have spoken for the 'West'. Indeed, Lee Kuan
Yew's lectures, tolerated in Australia, receive short shrift in other Asian
countries not constrained by demands for 'cultural sensitivity'.[43] 'There

is no more 'natural' incumbency upon Australia to become 'Asian' in order to engage with Asia than there is upon Germany or Argentina, or even Japan.

Perhaps the most important difficulty in framing a policy agenda lies in the confusion over the nature of the new global economy.[44] The Asian experience illustrates that the liberal notion of competitiveness cannot explain the surge of industrial power in that region. Nor do decisions about investment lead firms in an endless journey around the globe in pursuit of markets and labour. As Bob Fagan argues (in Chapter 8) only some firms operate in the true international economy, shifting capital and other resources rapidly in response to global market signals. National and regional markets and financial circuits remain important and discrete arenas for investment and production. In the food industry, the assumed imperative to access Asian markets is not automatic. Balancing this, competitive advantage and international best practice are often not the determinants of decisions whether to remain national or expand into global markets.

Expectations that Western economies might claim the niches of high-tech post-industrial economic activity based on service and knowledge-based industries via policies of deregulation within the West itself, intended to sweep away inefficiencies and constraints to trade and investment, are therefore to be viewed with caution. On the contrary, what is happening is that a range of hierarchies is being established within most countries, from high-tech to low-wage. Ironically, it has been the attempt to make labour in the West more competitive through deregulation of the labour markets that has perhaps been the strongest facet of restructuring. Deregulated labour markets in the West are producing labour forces increasingly based on casual and part-time work and where the price of labour is competitive with that in the more advanced economies of Asia. Indeed, the deregulation achieved in Britain and the US, involving new mechanisms of wage negotiation and the decline of the power of organised labour, has transformed the labour market to the point where Asian manufacturers, in an ironic twist, are seeking to invest there, particularly in the industrially devastated Britain, citing low labour costs as well as market access as the primary incentives. Workers and governments within the West have had little option but to compete for investors on entirely new terms.[45]

Hence, a prime objective has been to achieve lower labour costs through labour market deregulation and 'down-sizing' in Australia or by relocating to take advantage of labour conditions prevailing in the region. These are clearly strategies that substitute for the more difficult and imaginative tasks of creating new products with new technologies and within new organisations, reinforcing the legendary unwillingness of Australian business to invest in R&D and the continued absence of an innovative, self-reflective business culture. Transfer of investments overseas in low-wage industries such as whitegoods or textiles cannot be assumed to indicate that industry in Australia is restructuring into higher value-added industries or into knowledge or technology-intensive activities. Nor can we draw firm conclusions that Australian manufacturing investments in Asia are drawing exports of higher value-added goods from Australia.[46] Regarded as naturally efficient in this context there is little systematic scrutiny of the performance of the private sector.[47]

Both 'Asia' and the new 'global economy' are therefore politically and ideologically contested notions. The various contending images embody agendas and interests already in train in the West and in Asia itself.

Conclusion: Directions for Australia

The current strategy for engagement with Asia and with the global economy is based on neo-liberal principles. It is a pathway in which an optimum environment for investment and trade is sought through deregulation of the financial sector and of trade and the labour markets, fiscal retrenchment and minimal taxation. Contrary to claims that it is the very technical superiority of the neo-liberal prescription that has sustained its ascendancy, it is its utility to governments in the context of a particular set of structural pressures that is critical. The neo-liberal pathway offers solutions to governments increasingly unable to fund traditional social democratic budgets or to insulate economies from international pressures, particularly on the price of labour.

The significance of the strategy debate is not only related to questions of policy effectiveness but to those of social organisation. The neo-liberal position is based upon the proposition that the choices made by rational individuals within free markets will achieve the greatest general levels of prosperity. In the global economy of the late twentieth century, however, free-market strategies have resulted in the disengagement of large sections of the population from the core of society and economy. Such outcomes can be considered functional. They have given the US an important tool in securing international competitiveness in the form of a huge underclass of underemployed, unemployed and dispensable people able to be absorbed and shed as economic conditions change and increasingly able to compete with low-wage Asian workers.

The neo-liberal ascendancy is not only propelled by structural factors but by a series of associated political victories throughout the

Western world. It has been institutionalised in the policy community, in both the major political parties as well as in the universities and the media. New constituencies in the bureaucracy have flourished and expanded as the enforcers of market instrumentalism. Within Australia, opposition to this neo-liberal surge was initially dominated by a relatively unreconstructed protectionist line from critics within the trade union movement and the manufacturing sector as well as from theorists within academia who followed a dependency line.[48] The policy implications of their work were a return to protectionism and inward-looking strategies. Out of touch with the realities of structural change in the world economy, without real institutional power and chasing unrealisable political goals, these were easy targets for neo-liberal snipers, serving only to feed the latter's overweening hubris and to stifle serious debate.

What is perhaps unique about the shift to neo-liberalism in Australia is that it has been done in the name of preserving social democracy. Australian Labor governments of the past decade have proposed that social democratic traditions can only be sustained by abandoning the old protectionist frameworks that were leading clearly to economic decline and the deterioration of the state's fiscal capacity to provide collective goods and welfare nets. Reinvigorating the economy through a neo-liberal restructuring, it is claimed, will create the wealth to include all Australians in the benefits of the new prosperity. Whether the natural dynamics of a liberal economy can be diverted from their usual outcomes of social and labour fragmentation and the disintegration of the public sphere and concern for collective goods, is one of the fundamental questions of the coming decade and one now being vigorously debated in Australia.[49]

In terms of securing an international market niche, Australian policy has proceeded with a strategy of deregulation domestically and within the region. Asian countries are urged to enter this win–win formula through APEC, established as the primary instrument of international reform and designed to introduce regimes of free trade progressively into the Asia–Pacific region (an ironic contradiction in itself of the neo-liberal insistence that it was the workings of the market that lay at the heart of the industrial miracles of Asia in the past decades). There are two problems with this approach. First, that some Asian economies will be unwilling to progress along this path where they consider that strategic domestic industries and interests will be damaged. Prime Minister Mahathir has already stated this.[50] Second, that trade deregulation is a leap of faith insofar as securing any particular niches for Australia in the engagement. Trade represents only the tip of the iceberg among the factors that contribute to constructing niches in the global economy. Nor is deregulation an easy concept to enforce when the very concept of 'cheating' according to the neo-liberal liturgy is foreign to the operation of industrial neo-mercantilism in Asia and, indeed, it may be argued, to the way in which the US's own industrial ascendancy was achieved and is maintained. But are there other options for both domestic social policy and for policies of international engagement? The idea that the engagement should be crafted within the framework of national strategic objectives rather than in the terms of an ideological commitment to the market is one that is beginning to re-emerge. Recent US trade policy toward Japan has been propelled by the so-called revisionists (notably Chalmers Johnson, James Fallows, Karel Van Wolferen and Clyde Prestowitz), who argue that because Japan does not play by market rules, so trade imbalances have to be secured by bilateral pressures to change the very environment in which Japanese trade policy is made.[51] Unlike Australia, the US did not purge its political, academic and bureaucratic institutions of opposition to the neo-liberal agenda. Hence, the debate is vigorous and the policy options intensively argued.[52] Signs of some reassessment in Australia are much weaker. The Minister for Trade, Bob McMullan, has begun to take some preliminary soundings in the direction of regional and bilateral discriminatory trade arrangements.[53] Sicklen[54] has signalled some interesting proposals. Nevertheless, the topic of strategic trade and industry policy is yet to be established in the public debate.

At one level the primary task of social democrats is to fuse an economic system that is vigorous and innovative with a political system that secures collective interests. Within capitalist systems there is a natural set of contradictions at work insofar as this objective is concerned. Powerful corporate and social interests will tend to push for economic regimes that minimise the diversion of resources to collective social enterprises. While it is only in the context of strategic policies that address broader collective and social interests that social democracies may be secured, strategic policies are also potentially dangerous options. Their employment in Australia in the pre-neo-liberal period was precisely to enable business and labour to avoid restructuring rather than facilitating it. It was a cocoon that could not be economically sustained. Nor, for all the rhetoric, was equality of opportunity as enshrined in reality as claimed in social democratic mythology. Strategic policies are also potential shells for the sort of authoritarian, technocratic and bureaucratic *dirigisme* that characterises many of the Asian industrial economies. The nature of strategic policies is therefore determined by processes of political conflict. Quite apart from the domestic considerations it must be asked whether a small economy such as Australia can, in any case, sustain strategic trade and industry policies against strong tides of international economic restructuring dominated by the big players.

Notes

1 While these claims are often associated with Mahathir and Lee, they are commonly resorted to by most Asian leaders. In Indonesia, Soeharto and leading politicians regularly compare disintegrative, confrontational liberalism with the order, stability and community/family values of *Pancasila*, the state ideology. See, for example, Soeharto, *Pidato Kenegaraan*, Presiden Republik Indonesia, Jakarta, Departement Kenegaraan Republik Indonesia, 1990, p. 16; and comments on this in *Tempo*, 25 August 1990, p. 25. See also Kishore Mahbubani, 'Dangers of Decadence: What the Rest Can Teach the West', *Foreign Affairs*, September/October 1993.

2 This cultural relativism was particularly evident in the wake of the problems between Australia and Indonesia in the mid-1980s. Letter from Sir Keith Shann to *Age*, 8 May 1986, p. 12; H.D. Anderson in *Canberra Times*, 27 January 1983; Blanche d'Alpuget in *West Australian*, 3 May 1986, p. 17; John Holloway, 'Australia–Indonesia: Managing the Relationship', *AFAR* 56 (6) 1985; Peter Jeanes, *West Australian*, 24 July 1985, pp. 9 and 10. More recent plays on the same theme have been made by Hawke (*Canberra Times*, 9 February 1995, p. 10); Harries (*Weekend Australian*, 8–9 April 1995, p. 26); Mason (*Australian*, 7 April 1995, p. 15).

3 Michael Parkinson, 'How Asia Delivers the Goods', *Australian Financial Review*, 23 January 1995, p. 17; Robert Gottleibson, 'Australia Could Get Lucky Again', *Business Review Weekly*, 27 March 1995, p. 6; Kevin Blackburn, 'Does the West Need to Learn Asian Values?' *IPA Review*, 7 (2), 1994, pp. 35, 36; Special Review, 'Asia-Australia: Where will the Future Take Us?' *West Magazine*, 18 February 1995, pp. 16–22.

4 See Barry Wain, 'Asia Strains to Pat Itself on the Back', *AWSJ*, 27–28 May 1994, p. 8; Clinton Renews China's MFN Privileges, Severs Link of Trade and Human Rights', *AWSJ*, 27–28 May 1994, p. 1.

5 This has been a long-standing belief. See, for example, Heinz Arndt's enthusiastic welcome of Indonesia's New Order as a pragmatic government willing to shed ideology for economic facts (Heinz Arndt, 'Economic Disorder and the Task Ahead' in T. K. Tan (ed.), *Soekarno's Guided Indonesia*, Brisbane, Jacaranda, 1967, p. 130.

6 See Chapter 2 by Rodan and Hewison.

7 Robison, Richard, 'The Australian Indonesian Relationship: A Current Assessment', *Australian Outlook*, vol. 40, no. 3, 1986.

8 The *International Herald Tribune* was even prepared to make an embarrassing apology for an oblique reference in one of the stories it carried to the use of the judicial system by some Asian governments to silence opposition. The apology was not accepted and the Singapore government has proceeded with legal action. See: *New York Times*, 12 December 1994; Garry Rodan, 'Singapore Picks its Ground for Showdown over Western Values', *Australian*, 17 January 1995, p. 13.

9 *Australian Business Asia*, 22 June–5 July 1994; Parker, Jeffrey, 'Murdoch's Star TV Bolsters Shaky Chine Foothold', *Reuters*, 24 Nov.

1994; Stein, Janine, 'Robert Chua Tells Why His Pan-Asia Service will Work', *Electronic Media International*, 1 Dec. 1994.

10 *Australian Financial Review*, 6 Dec. 1993.

11 Wade, Robert, *Governing the Market: Economic Theory and the Role of Government in East Asian Industrialization*, Cambridge University Press, Cambridge, 1990; Amsden, Alice, *Asia's Next Giant: South Korea and Late Industrialization*, Oxford University Press, New York, 1989; Rodan, Garry, *The Political Economy of Singapore's Industrialization: National State and International Capital*, Macmillan, London, 1989; Haggard, Stephen, *Pathways from the Periphery: The Politics of Growth in the Newly Industrialized Countries*, Cornell University Press, Ithaca, 1990.

12 See Chapter 6, by L. Weiss.

13 See Chapter 9.

14 *Australian*, 11–12 March; 10–11 June 1995.

15 Palmer, Tom G., 'Britain's Costly Lesson in Welfare', *Asian Wall Street Journal*, 26 October 1994, pp. 8.

16 Zakaria, Fareed, 'Culture is Destiny: A Conversation with Lee Kuan Yew', *Foreign Affairs*, vol. 73, no. 2, 1994, p. 112.

17 Woon, Walter, 'Honor Thy Father and Mother', *Asian Wall Street Journal*, 28 June 1994, p. 10.

18 *Australian*, 4–5 March 1995; Carroll, John, 'Economic Rationalism and its Consequences', *Shutdown: The Failure of Economic Rationalism and How To Rescue Australia*, eds J. Carroll & R. Maine, The Text Publishing Company, Melbourne, 1992.

19 World Bank, World Development Report, Washington, 1983, Chs 6, 7 and 8; for an excellent overview of the rise of the neo-liberal position in relation to developmental questions, see John Toye, *Dilemmas of Development*, Oxford, Basil Blackwell, 1987, Chs 3 (on Peter Bauer), and 4 (on Little, Lal and Balassa).

20 Garnaut, Ross, *Australia and the Northeast Asian Ascendancy*, AGPS, Canberra, 1990.

21 See Chapter 7.

22 *FEER*, 24 November 1994.

23 Olson, Mancur, *The Rise and Decline of Nations*, Yale University Press, New Haven, 1982.

24 Barro, Robert J., 'Pushing Democracy is No Key to Prosperity', *Asian Wall Street Journal*, 27 December 1993, p. 6.

25 For a summary of this portion see Gabriel A. Almond, 'Capitalism and Democracy', *PS: Political Science and Politics*, vol. XXIV, no. 3, September 1991, p. 471

26 It is interesting to note that many of the best-performing Australian export industries of the 1990s are those that underwent industry plans in the 1980s. See Derek Sicklen, *National Industry Policy: The Key to Job Growth and Industry Structure,* Australian Economic Analysis Pty Ltd, 1993, p. 6. See also, Malcolm Fraser's comments in *Australian Financial Review*, 22 March 1993, p. 15.

27 See Chapters 6 and 5.

28 World Bank, *The East Asian Miracle: Economic Growth and Public Policy*, Oxford University Press, New York, 1993.

29 *FEER*, op. cit.

30 Robison, Richard & Rodan, Garry, 'Economic Restructuring and the Reform of the Higher Education Sector', *Politics*, vol. 25, no. 1, 1990, pp. 21–36.

31 The mythology of superior productivity has been challenged in a recent article by Jong-Il Kim and Laurence Lau, *The Role of Human Capital in the Economic Growth of the East Asian Newly Industrialised Countries*. According to their findings, the US, West Germany and France topped an index of productive efficiency, followed by Japan, Britain and, well behind, Hong Kong, Singapore, Taiwan and South Korea (*Sydney Morning Herald*, 1 October 1994). Similar conclusions have been made by Paul Krugman ('The Myth of Asia's Miracle', *Foreign Affairs*, November/December 1994, pp. 62–78 and *International Herald Tribune*, 4 November 1994, p. 15), who proposes that Asian industrial growth was driven by extraordinary growth in inputs of labour and capital rather than by gains in efficiency and productivity. It is interesting to note that Paul Keating has been quick to draw attention to the superior productivity of the Australian construction industry over that of Singapore (*Weekend Australian* 1994, p. 4).

32 Kurth, James, 'Industrial Change and Political Change: A European Perspective', *The New Authoritarianism in Latin America*, ed. D. Collier, Princeton University Press, Princeton, 1979, pp. 319–62.

33 Robison, Richard,'Economic and Political Liberalisation in Southeast Asia: Inexorable Force or Red Herring?', Paper presented to the workshop on Political and Economic Liberalisation, Center for International Studies, 21 March, University of Southern California, 1995

34 Kim Dae Jung, 'Is Culture Destiny?: The Myth of Asia's Anti-Democratic Values', *Foreign Affairs*, vol. 73, no. 6, 1994, pp. 189–94.

35 Hewison, Kevin,'Of Regimes, State and Pluralities and Thai Politics Enters the 1990s', *Southeast Asia in the 1990s: Authoritarianism, Democracy and Capitalism*, eds K. Hewison, R. Robison & G. Rodan, Allen & Unwin, Sydney, 1993; Tun-jen Cheng, 'Democratizing the Quasi-Leninist Regime in Taiwan', *World Politics*, vol. 61, no. 4, 1989, pp. 471–99.

36 *Asian Wall Street Journal*, 15 April 1993

37 Asher, Mukul, 'Social Security Systems and Regional Challenge', *Bangkok Post*, 18 May 1995, p. 16.

38 At the recent World Infrastructure Forum, sponsored by the World Bank and held in Jakarta, Asian nations outlined plans for infrastructure investment. Indonesia announced plans for US$19.2 billion, India, US$3.3 billion, China, US$230 billion, Vietnam, US$12.8 billion and Philippines, US$13.5 billion (*Australian Business Asia,* 2 November 1994, p. 14.

39 For an analysis of problems confronting Indonesia as a result of poor infrastructure and the investment priorities in this sector see, World Bank, *Indonesia: Sustaining Development*, Jakarta, May 1993,

pp. 105–23. This report also emphasises the need for continued heavy public investment, anticipating that public sector investment in infrastructure will rise to Rp. 73–77 trillion for 1994/5–1998/99 compared with Rp. 37–38 trillion for the private sector (see Table 4.3, p. 111).

40 World Bank, *Managing Development: The Governance Dimension*, Washington D.C., 1991.
41 In Indonesia the struggle to regulate is a long-standing one. The latest arena for contest has been the banking sector where massive loans to politically connected individuals have blown out the bad debt burden of state banks and placed a strain on the capacity of the state budget to support them. This has been a very public battle (for an overview of this issue see; Richard Robison, 'Organising the Transition: Indonesian Politics in 1993/94' in Ross McLeod (ed.), *Indonesia Update 1994*, Singapore, Institute For Southeast Asian Studies, 1995). Perhaps the latest example is China where widespread predatory behaviour by Chinese businesses, many of them government-owned or operating in cooperation with local and regional governments, has provoked a backlash by the very US businesses that had hoped to profit from the lack of regulation and had so recently opposed President Clinton's attempts to link trade to human rights behaviour (Thomas L. Friedman, 'American Business is Seeing the Light about Rule of Law in China', *International Herald Tribune*, 9 January 1995; Yungeng Hu and Jeffrey Sweet, 'Dealmaking in China Must Go Back to Fundamentals', *Asian Wall Street Journal*, 5 January 1995, p. 6). See also the *AWSJ* editorial, 'China Inc. on Trial' of the same issue.
42 Chong, Florence, 'Growing Pains: Is Asia's Boom Headed for Bust?', *Australian*, 14 June 1995, p. 37.
43 President Ramos of the Philippines, for example, was not at all impressed with Mr Lee's comments about the need for more discipline and less democracy in the Philippines. *Far Eastern Economic Review*, 10 December 1992, pp. 4, 29.
44 Krugman, Paul, 'Competitiveness: A Dangerous Obsession', *Foreign Affairs*, vol. 73, no. 2, 1994, pp. 28–44; Holloway, John, 'Global Capital and the National State', *Capital and Class*, vol. 52, Spring 1994.
45 *AWSJ*, 27 Oct. 1994.
46 Yetton, Philip, Davis, Jeremy & Swan, Peter, *Going International: Export Myths and Strategic Realities*, Report to the Australian Manufacturing Council, 1991.
47 *Australian Financial Review*, 20 September 1994.
48 David, Abe & Wheelwright, Ted, 'The Third Wave', *Australia and Asian Capitalism*, Left Book Club, Sydney, 1989.
49 One current focus of discussion in Australia is whether structural change is producing greater social inequality. See R. G. Gregory and B. Hunter, 'The Macro-Economy and the Growth of Ghettos and Urban Poverty in Australia', Discussion Paper no. 325, April 1995, Economics Program, Research School of Social Sciences, Australian National University.
50 *AFR*, 19 November 1993.
51 *AWSJ*, 9–10 June 1995.

52 Reich, Robert, *The Work of Nations: Preparing Ourselves for 21st Century Capitalism*, Simon & Schuster, New York, 1991; Tyson, Laura D'Andrea & Zysman, John, 'Developmental Strategy and Production Innovation in Japan', *Politics and Productivity: The Real Story of Why Japan Works*, eds C. Johnson, L. D. Tyson & J. Zysman, Ballinger, USA, 1989.
53 See *Winning Markets: The Next Steps*, Circulated by Senator McMullan, Minister for Trade, 15 February 1995. See also the neo-liberal response from Alan Wood in *Weekend Australian*, April 8–9 1995, p. 28.
54 Sicklen, Derek, 'National Industry Policy: The Key to Job Growth and Industry Structure', *Australian Economic Analysis Pty Ltd* 1993, p. 6.

Further References

Asher, Mukul, 'Present Social Security Arrangements in Southeast Asia: Can They Be Sustained?', Paper presented to the Asia Research Centre, 14 June, Murdoch University, 1995.
Santamaria, B.A., 'Speculation Fuelled by Laissez-faire', *Australian*, 4–5 March 1995, p. 30.
——'Fall Guy in Comic Opera', *Australian*, 11–12 March 1995, p. 28.
——'When Governments No Longer Call the Tune', *Australian*, 10–11 June 1995, p. 22.

2

A 'clash of cultures' or the convergence of political ideology?

Garry Rodan and Kevin Hewison[1]

The controversial 'clash of civilisations' thesis elucidated by Samuel Huntington sees global ideological conflict waning, to be replaced by new disputes between 'the West' and 'the Rest'. In this view, tension shifts from the political to the cultural realm and takes on different dimensions. This thesis has attracted its share of criticism within the West as well as in Asia, but it has also complemented attempts by some Asian political leaders to insulate their regimes from a variety of criticisms including charges of human rights abuses and to justify authoritarian rule. The notion that there is something culturally different or even mysterious about Asians has led some to argue that the West should get used to the idea that 'they' will never be like 'us' and that, in the words of Rawdon Dalrymple, former Australian Ambassador to Indonesia, 'Confucian-style authoritarianism' will prevail over liberal–democratic values, including human rights.[2] While this scenario may unfold, the question is whether it is culture or a contest of power that underlies it.

The East–West dichotomy of the 'clash of civilisations' thesis has assisted Asian political leaders to posit a general Asian cultural aversion to some 'Western' concepts. With the global economic centre of gravity apparently shifting toward Asia, these leaders exhibit a stridency both in their rejection of criticism, from both domestic and external sources, and in the delineation of supposed fundamental Asian cultural values. What are depicted as 'Western values' are especially challenging now because local opposition groups (no longer simply labelled and rejected as 'communists') are calling for 'human rights', extended democratic rights and the like. By labelling these calls 'alien', domestic challenges are blunted or made to seem less than legitimate. To do this, an alternative 'Asian' set of 'values' is constructed.

What is particularly interesting in this is that the account of 'Asian values' provided by a select group of authoritarian political and community leaders in Asia is not without its adherents in the West. This fact carries with it significant foreign policy implications, and is especially important for the attempt by Australian policymakers to effect more extensive ties with countries in the region.

The argument in this chapter is that the notion of a clash of cultures is grossly misplaced. In our view, the more interesting and profound development embodied in the changing position of Asia in the global political economy, and the attendant assertion of 'Asian-ness', is the apparent development of comparable configurations of political ideologies in the 'West' and 'Asia'; a fact that is obscured by the proclaimed cultural dichotomy. Indeed, with nearly every attempt by self-proclaimed Asian leaders to specify a particular variety of 'Asian' cultural values distinct from those of the West, it becomes clearer that it is predominantly conservative political philosophy that they are championing. Their criticisms of Western society are invariably ethnocentric and stereotyped attacks on liberalism and, in many respects, mirror long-standing critiques of liberalism by Western conservatives.

This is not to suggest such positions are simply derived from earlier 'Western' thought, nor to contend that the broader political and ideological positions of different authoritarian leaders in Asia can be understood solely in these terms. Rather, recourse to conservative rhetoric by certain Asian leaders reflects long-standing concerns, which now combine with a recognition of the changing political challenges confronting them. The ideology of many anti-colonial movements and some of the first post-colonial governments drew heavily on anti-liberalism sentiment. The Asian socialist movement, strong in the South Asian countries, Burma, Malaya and Singapore, was built on anti-communism *and* anti-liberalism.[3] For example, once a self-styled socialist, Singapore's Lee Kuan Yew was an outspoken critic of both ideologies, but was not yet the critic of the West he was later to become. While many of these anti-communist socialists fell by the political wayside, anti-liberal sentiment remained an element of anti-colonialism and nation-building.

Having presided over major social, economic and political transformations, it is now the preservation of the order they have established that is perceived as the task at hand. We suggest that one of the consequences of this is that the preconditions for new political alliances spanning East and West are emerging and are potentially more significant than the forecast clash of cultures. As this chapter attempts to demonstrate, opponents of liberalism and social democracy, both inside and outside 'Asia', are drawing on each others' arguments and views with a growing synergy.[4]

In attempting to advance the above-stated thesis, we concentrate on the resonances between conservatism across 'East' and 'West'. If space permitted we could detail the serious divisions *within* the 'East' over the positions enunciated by the self-appointed articulators and custodians of 'Asian values'. Such challenges further expose the superficiality and conceptual obfuscation of the supposed 'East–West' divide. The implications of this analysis for policymakers and others in Australia seeking to accelerate and deepen economic, social and political engagement with the region are by no means negative. Certainly the analysis does not suggest such an objective is impossible or undesirable. Rather, it suggests that such engagement is best conducted on the basis of a full appreciation of the complex and diverse social and political realities of the region, and not on the basis of paradigms that conceal these realities. Furthermore, it emphasises that engagement involves political and ideological alliances with forces in the region. The choice of allies should be publicly debated and not concealed behind the veil of culturalist arguments. Finally, these are more than choices about how to 'engage' with 'Asia'. They are also choices about what sort of society Australia should be, since different domestic interests are bolstered or weakened by both the particular forms of economic, social or political relationships with the region and the sort of values selectively identified with.

The 'clash of cultures'

According to the conservative American political scientist Samuel Huntington[5], world politics is entering a new phase in which the fundamental source of conflict will be cultural rather than ideological or economic. The end of the Cold War has coincided with the increased economic and military power of non-Western civilisations who 'no longer remain objects of history as targets of Western colonialism but join the West as movers and shapers of history.'[6] Huntington expects that there will be increasingly active conflict over the issue of Western cultural dominance and a heightening of inter-cultural friction around the globe. This friction, argues Huntington,[7] derives from the fact that people of different civilisations have different views on the relations between God and man, the individual and the group, the citizen and the state, parents and children, husband and wife, as well as differing views of the relative importance of rights and responsibilities, liberty and authority, equality and hierarchy. These differences are the product of centuries. They will not soon disappear.

The consequence of this will be clashes at the local level, where territorial struggles take place between 'adjacent groups along the fault lines between civilizations', and at the macro-level where states belonging to differing civilisations compete for military and economic power, and over the 'control of international institutions and third parties, and competitively promote their particular political and religious values'.[8]

Although Huntington believes that global political dynamics will be increasingly shaped by interactions between seven or eight major civilisations, he essentially sees the division between the 'West and the Rest' as the major source of conflict. Here, there is a stark cultural divide:

> Western concepts differ fundamentally from those prevalent in other civilisations. Western ideas of individualism, liberalism, constitutionalism, human rights, equality, liberty, the rule of law, democracy, free markets, the separation of church and state, often have little resonance in Islamic, Confucian, Japanese, Hindu, Buddhist or Orthodox cultures.[9]

Here, Huntington is drawing attention to elements of liberal thought, and proceeds to draw attention to a 'de-Westernization and indigenization of elites' in the non-Western world that portends a preparedness to confront these differences with a confidence and self-assuredness that has not existed in the past. To be sure, serious conflict will continue between states and groups within the same civilisations, but they will not be of the same intensity as inter-civilisation conflict in general or 'West versus the Rest' conflict in particular.

Huntington also makes observations[10] about regional economic cooperation that have implications for the aspirations of Australian policymakers. Economic regionalism, he argues, stands the best chance of success when it is 'rooted in a common civilization'. For this reason, he sees difficulty in a broad East Asian grouping rivalling the achievements of the European Community. Japan is so different culturally from its neighbours, argues Huntington, that it is the rapid extension of economic relations between China and countries with substantial overseas Chinese communities—particularly Hong Kong, Taiwan, Singapore—that is likely to shape the primary economic bloc unfolding in the region.[11] On this basis, Huntington points approvingly to Owen Harries' reservations about Prime Minister Paul Keating's notion of Australia as an 'Asian country'. Harries[12] cautions against Australia creating an historic first as a 'reverse torn country: a fully Western country in which a significant section of the elite now advocates a move to membership of another, non-Western civilisation'.

While Huntington predicts a shift towards conflict of a more fundamental nature, it does not logically follow that global politics is headed for intractable difficulties, but it is clear that only the West's resignation to a declining ability to have its essential values and its interests institutionalised as universally valid will serious conflict be avoided. It is incumbent on the West to 'develop a more profound understanding of the basic religious and philosophical assumptions underlying other civilizations and the ways in which people in those civilizations see their interests'.[13] For the first time, it is argued, the West faces the challenge of cultural coexistence, and Huntington stresses the need for the West to maintain the economic and military strength appropriate to the defence of its interests.

A comprehensive critical discussion of Huntington's notion of a 'clash of civilisations' is not the purpose of this essay.[14] Rather, we focus on the claim that it is culture, as distinct from ideology, that underlies recent friction between the so-called East and West over such issues as human rights, labour standards and law and order policies, and portends further 'clashes'. We agree that important global shifts in economic and political power favour heightened contestation over these and other issues. Frequent and forceful assertions about 'Asian-ness' from various Southeast Asian leaders reflect a recognition of this changing balance. There is also a discernible measure of concern in some circles in the West about its relative economic decline, although Mahbubani's[15] recent reference to a developing 'siege mentality' is overstating the case.[16]

In this chapter we argue that any friction or tension between 'the West and the Rest' is unlikely to be a manifestation of cultural differences alone, or that such factors are supplanting political and ideological struggle. Rather we argue that the various attempts to portray 'cultural conflict' or a 'clash of civilisations' represent the harnessing of cultural arguments to ideological and political ends; an exercise to which Huntington's thesis lends some intellectual credibility precisely because he operates largely within the same ideological perspective as those who are taking up the cultural cudgels with such alacrity—conservatism. We will attempt to show how protestations about a distinctive Asian culture often mask this more universal political philosophy,[17] sung in two-part harmony. Interestingly, this cross-cultural ideological harmony is challenged by domestic groups in Asian nations who reject assertions that human rights are 'Western' values and associated views derived from culturalist dichotomies expounded by a small but influential group of self-appointed articulators and custodians of 'Asian values'.[18]

The 'clash' and its harmonies

Ironically, while Huntington's thesis has merit in its provocative attempt to capture the dynamics of momentous historical change, it ultimately rests on a rather ahistorical conception of culture. As O'Hagen[19] notes, although Huntington defines civilisations as dynamic entities, his depiction of them is largely as immutable belief systems. Cultures are thus on an unwavering trajectory of distinctiveness. The utility of this understanding to the custodians of authoritarian rule is obvious: deep-seated cultural traditions cannot be expected to change overnight, even if that were considered desirable. The effect of this is to divert attention from the dynamics of social, political and economic life. Yet it is precisely the tremendous change internal to Asian societies that has precipitated both the broader shifts in global economic and political power and the concern shown by some Asian elites with 'traditional Asian values'.

The dramatic social transformations that have accompanied economic development in Asian countries not only ushered in new centres of economic and political power, but also new divisions and conflicts. Questions of wealth distribution, environmentalism and the position of women are surfacing, for example. None of these appear to have much to do with the current interest of some Asian leaders in what they portray as distinctively 'Asian' values. However, issues such as these have much to do with internal challenges—both real and perceived—to existing regimes. In defining 'Asian values', these leaders present themselves as the true bearers of Asian traditions, enabling them to brand dissenting views as 'unAsian' and 'alien'. And this is the clear intention of those Asian leaders who dismiss domestic and regional agitation over such issues as human rights.

Equally, the tendency to depict the 'West' as some sort of cultural monolith downplays significant disputations over liberalism. Certainly there are important points of intersection that bring various liberals and conservatives together. In particular, a market system not only rewards economic individualism and potentially expands the political space outside the state, both attractive to liberals, but it imposes a discipline on individuals and generates an hierarchical order of winners and losers that appeals to conservatives. Understandably, then, both conservatives and liberals share a deep scepticism about independent trade union power which is perceived as a threat to the prerogatives of capital and order more generally. Nevertheless, friction between these camps is not only real, but a central dynamic in the politics of most contemporary liberal democratic societies. The liberals' more optimistic view of human nature and associated emphasis on individualism, their relative lack of reverence for tradition in favour of reason and rationality, and their greater tolerance of the incursions of the market economy on social life have, over time, manifested in a range of unresolved disputes with conservatives. The contemporary conservative backlash against a host of liberal social and economic reforms underlines the thematic dilemma of trying to strike a balance between the respective rights and obligations of the individual *vis-à-vis* the state that would accommodate both conservative and liberal views. Even within liberalism there are significant tensions of this sort, notably between the advocates of a more laissez-faire economic individualism, popularly referred to as neo-liberals or 'dries', and the 'wets' who sanction a more interventionist social and economic role for the state. The former's conception of liberty is an acutely class-specific one which privileges and champions the liberties of those enterprising individuals with capital.

Huntington himself contributes to an idealisation of his own 'culture' by minimising the disputations within and between conservatism and liberalism. In a recent interview he asserted that 'one should not underestimate the central strength of American society which is individualism and the emphasis on competition and mobility, people going out and doing things for themselves and not relying upon government'.[20] This is arguably an ideological account in so much as these are 'strengths' for some groups but weaknesses for others in American society. In their attempts to keep the East–West cultural dichotomy alive, various Asian political leaders happily adopt this simplistic caricature of the West as unproblematically liberal.

'Clash of culture' arguments are seductive, not only for those in the 'East' who wish to oppose dissent, but also to various elements within the 'West' who wish to promote conservative domestic political agendas. Neo-liberals, seeking a greater assertion of market relations at the expense of the state, find the content of some so-called Asian values useful in advancing, for example, the case for labour market deregulation and reduced state welfare spending. Lee Kuan Yew's gratuitous advice to Australians in 1994 was music to the ears of both neo-liberals and conservatives: 'to compete in the same race with Asians, Australians must be weaned from a dependency on public welfare and become more self-reliant and competitive'. He elaborated: 'Deep-seated problems of work ethic, productivity, enterprise, bloody-minded unions protecting unproductive work practices, feather-bedding and inflexibility in wages are neither quickly nor easily cured'.[21] These comments are exactly the ideological recipe to bring liberals and conservatives together in opposing common 'enemies'.

The discussion below concentrates on the correspondence between 'Asian values' and the philosophies and agendas of conservatives in the West who seek the restoration of what they identify as traditional values in their own societies. We will pursue this under the following headings, each of which represents a central and universal characteristic of conservatism: stability ahead of rapid change; human nature and the need for discipline; order and authority; traditional values;

obligations ahead of rights. In taking this approach, it is not suggested that the entire perspective of the selected leaders espousing 'Asian values' can be understood solely in terms of conservative theory and philosophy. Nor is it suggested that all of the Australian conservatives mentioned are friends of Asia or Asians. There are few political actors anywhere who do not fuse different, and often contradictory, ideological elements. We will concentrate on those 'values' that unite them ideologically. Major strands of conservative thought are present in the so-called 'Asian values' these leaders express and this suggests important convergences in political agendas common within and across the alleged East–West conceptual divide.

The survey of ideas by Asian leaders is necessarily limited rather than comprehensive, and draws heavily on proclamations by the activist Singaporean leaders and statements of these values by Thailand's King Bhumibol Adulyadej, who has a strong claim to be a 'traditional' Asian leader, even though he has not been an international advocate for Asian conservatism—his comments have usually been to stifle domestic dissent or activism. Singaporeans have certainly played a disproportionately large role in declarations about 'Asian values', especially in the international arena. But if the self-appointed role as regional custodian and articulator of 'Asian values' has irritated neighbours at times, it has less to do with the content of the proclamations than the diplomacy involved. At the same time, it should be emphasised that there are any number of similar examples that may be drawn from, *inter alia*, Indonesia, China, Vietnam, Malaysia and Burma.

Conservative values

Stability ahead of rapid change

The conservative's primary attachment is with the past, an attachment grounded in the notion that those values, beliefs and institutions that have survived and evolved over time must have done so because of their inherent worth. Even so, conservatives have not been opposed to all change, endorsing change where it is seen as functional for the preservation of the traditional values and the hierarchical social order for which they stand.[22] Change is appropriate where it is drawn from the well of tradition, and conservatives emphasise continuity ahead of change, for too much of the latter violates tradition. Hence, Edmund Burke's fear of revolutionary change, which he thought as 'having no charm but for robbers and assassins, and no natural orgin but in the brains of fools and madmen'.[23] However, if traditional values are reproduced and change grows from them, then change is acceptable.[24]

Since most Asian societies have undergone dramatic change in recent decades, it would seem that this conservative predisposition has little relevance to the outlooks of contemporary Asian leaders. After all, people like Soeharto, Lee Kuan Yew, Mahathir and their cohorts have seen remarkable changes—doing much to transform non-capitalist structures. In their earlier years, in particular, their rhetoric was replete with statements asserting the primacy of change at virtually every level of society. Much of this change was meant to strengthen society and state against challenges from the Left. For example, the Thai king has consistently argued for modernisation, but with the preservation of 'Thai values', the latter being a metaphor for anti-communism.[25]

Yet the wheel has turned. So successful have their respective projects been, including the destruction of much of the Left,[26] that the pace and extent of social change now threatens to loosen the grip of these leaderships over social and political life. The aspirations for change are now far more qualified, with a preference for Western technology and 'Asian' values. The Thai king is an excellent example of this, portraying himself as both a traditional leader and defender of traditional values, but as one who is an educated scientist, who can draw on science to support development.[27] Like their conservative counterparts in the West, these leaders believe that for the preservation of traditional values the only way is to maintain social order amidst the dynamism of economic change and fear the consequences if they do not prevail. Huntington[28] made a similar point, albeit in the theoretical garb of revisionist modernisation theory, some twenty years ago.

In his 1994 National Day speech, Singapore Prime Minister Goh Chok Tong acknowledged that change in Singapore was unavoidable, but contrasted change in his country with that in Britain and the United States. In Singapore, change was said to be 'evolutionary, not revolutionary', and he added: 'We do not have to make fundamental changes in direction because our political and economic institutions, and our public policies, are right'. In the same speech Goh left no doubt about what, above all else, must be preserved:

> Our institutions and basic policies are in place to sustain high
> economic growth. But if we lose our traditional values, our family
> strengths and our social cohesion, we will lose our vibrancy and
> decline. This is the intangible factor in the success of the East Asian
> economies.[29]

Whether or not this is the intangible factor, it should be clear that this is a strong call for the retention of the status quo.

The emphasis on traditional values amid flux and dynamism will be discussed below, but the significance to conservatives of this sort

of argument was highlighted by Australian conservative B.A. Santamaria, whose regular column for the *Australian* was given over to what
he described as the wisdom of former Singaporean Ambassador to
Washington, Tommy Koh. In reproducing Koh's *International Herald
Tribune* article, entitled 'The 10 Values that Undergird East Asian
Strength and Success', Santamaria urged that Australians seriously
consider such values.[30]

Human nature and the need for discipline

Conservatives have a fundamentally negative view of human nature,
seeing humans as imperfect and requiring control.[31] Whereas Rousseau
saw humans as inherently free and good, conservatives understand
humans as naturally evil and prone to anarchy and destruction. Hence,
conservative writer Russell Kirk[32] underlines how the force of tradition
acts as a check on the 'anarchic impulse' of human beings. The
imperfect nature of humans necessitates controls, and Peter Viereck[33]
writes about 'self-expression through self-restraint'.

King Bhumibol has consistently taken this position, arguing that
order and discipline are absolutely necessary if social chaos is to be
avoided. He has stated that:

> At present, discipline is viewed by some quarters as being virtually
> meaningless . . . . As a matter of fact . . . discipline . . . is highly
> essential, for it is the major cause why the rules and regulations that
> exist for the orderliness of men, organization, society or country are
> not rendered useless.[34]

The theme of discipline is also strong in the attempts by Asian
leaders to differentiate so-called Asian values from those of Western
societies. In an ironic statement from the former Prime Minister of
possibly the world's most socially engineered society, Lee Kuan Yew
stated in an interview with the editor of the American *Foreign Affairs*
that:

> There is such a thing called evil, and it is not the result of being a
> victim of society. You are just an evil man, prone to do evil things,
> and you have to be stopped from doing them. Westerners have
> abandoned an ethical basis for society, believing all problems are
> solvable by good government, which we in the East never believed
> possible.[35]

Kishore Mahbubani,[36] permanent secretary in Singapore's Ministry of
Foreign Affairs, links 'East Asian discipline' with economic performance, stating 'the evidence is accumulating that socially cohesive and
disciplined societies are developing a competitive edge in today's
world'. Malaysian Prime Minister Mahathir has also recently talked

about the importance for Malaysia of a 'culture of self-discipline and responsibility towards society'.[37] The Thai King had made similar observations in 1961 after one of his overseas trips, stating that the most advanced nations were the most united and well-disciplined. His argument was, however, the reverse of Mahbubani's, noting that the Asian nations were undisciplined and therefore performing badly in economic terms.[38]

In Goh's 1994 National Day speech, he extended this theme, decrying what he regards as the light treatment meted out to criminals in the US and Britain. Echoing the criticisms of conservatives in these countries, he contended that some judges there show more sympathy for the offender than the victim. His intention was to hammer home the point that Singapore's authorities would continue to impose discipline and not shy from this responsibility. The alternative was social chaos and breakdown, as was now manifesting in the West.

This was a timely observation given that Singapore and the United States officials had, in previous months, been exchanging views over the sentence of an American teenager living in Singapore, Michael Fay, who had been convicted by a Singapore court on charges of vandalism. Sentenced to four months' jail, a S$2200 fine and six strokes of the cane, Fay ultimately had his caning reduced to four strokes as a limited gesture to the American government which had actually appealed for a more generous clemency to avoid the caning altogether. President Clinton had referred to the punishment as 'excessive' and charges of barbarism were invariably levelled by human rights spokespersons and individual commentators in the United States and elsewhere. In the United States, a *Christian Science Monitor* editorial maintained, 'It is not going too far to say that the caning of Fay is almost a literal expression of what Samuel Huntington has called an "emerging clash of civilizations" '.[39] Lee Kuan Yew took the opportunity to claim the Fay affair evidenced America's moral decay: 'The [US] dares not restrain or punish individuals, forgiving them for whatever they have done. That's why the whole country is in chaos: drugs, violence, unemployment and homelessness'.[40]

However, the reaction within the West to incidents such as the Fay caning actually demonstrates that the Singapore government's preference for a tough stance on law and order is by no means culturally based. Rather, like-minded conservatives in the West with the same basic mistrust of human nature were among the strongest supporters of the Singapore government's stances.[41] Such attitudes are familiar to any reader of almost any popular Australian (or US or British) newspaper, often flying in the face of crime statistics that do not indicate massive crime waves. Severe discipline is seen as a force for order. In Australia, Queensland National Party Member of Parliament, Vince

Lester, not only applauded the Singapore system but called for the adoption of flogging in Australia. Other sections of the Queensland National Party echoed this view and the Young Nationals went so far as to advocate flogging for minor crimes such as evasion of taxi or bus fares.[42] The conservative Call To Australia Party, led by the Reverend Fred Nile, has demanded that government 're-introduce the tougher penalties [for law-breakers] we used to live by'.[43]

Amid the Fay controversy, Western Australian Premier Richard Court visited Singapore in February and on his return publicly embraced the reintroduction of the death penalty in his state.[44] He spoke admiringly about the achievements of Singapore's authorities: 'They have entrenched a highly disciplined approach to law and order issues where everyone clearly knows the ground rules.' He continued to remark, 'there is no doubt that the discipline at a younger age has helped instil a strong sense of responsibility and pride in their country'.[45] His Attorney-General, Cheryl Edwardes, also visited a Singapore Reformation Working Centre, in her search for a model for discipline-oriented work camps for young offenders.[46] We should also keep in mind that the notion of crime as a fundamentally behavioural, rather than social, phenomenon informs much of the push in the United States for expanded expenditure on prisons. Clearly the punitive and disciplinarian approach to law and order in Singapore evokes significant support and respect in the 'West', with key public figures believing at least some elements worthy of recommendation. Interestingly, even Singaporeans are beginning to feel the criticism of this kind of approach from other Asian commentators, including from those who feel that crime is not a reflection of the inherent evil of people.[47]

Order and authority

The conservative emphasis on historical continuity ahead of abrupt social change and upheavals is linked to a conception of society as an organic whole. Society is seen as a natural, organic product of slow historical growth and it is tradition, morality and the force of habit that hold society together. It is enormously complex: embodying far more than the sum of its parts or the mass of its relationships. This living organism constantly renews itself. The importance of order is paramount in this view, and what is functional for order is morally defensible. Given the organic model, conservatives understandably view conflict as dysfunctional and threatening to unity and stability. According to Burke, the customary, unthinking parts of life form a major part of social existence and the life of this organism.[48] Here the centrality of shared values in the maintenance and reproduction of order is underlined. The role of these values in underscoring social order cannot be overemphasised.

The primacy of order marks conservatives off from liberals, who champion individual freedom, and socialists and social democrats who are inspired by notions of social justice. Conservatives believe that without order and stability there can be no liberty or civilisation. Instead, to quote Hobbes,[49] life would be 'solitary, poor, nasty, brutish and short'. Lee Kuan Yew's observations on contemporary American social life reflect this view:

> I find parts of it totally unacceptable: guns, drugs, violent crime, vagrancy, unbecoming behaviour in public—in sum the breakdown of civil society. The expansion of the right of the individual to behave or misbehave as he pleases has come at the expense of orderly society. In the East the main object is to have a well-ordered society so that everybody can have maximum enjoyment of his freedoms. This can only exist in an ordered state and not in a natural state of contention and anarchy.[50]

This quote was also reproduced approvingly by Australian conservative columnist B.A. Santamaria in an article entitled 'US decadence in a festering time'.[51]

Given their negative view of human nature, it is no wonder conservatives should place great store in order and fear imminent disaster in the event that it should break down. This surfaces in many of the Thai King's speeches, where he emphasises unity as a key factor in society, believing, for example, that political conflict will lead to the 'utter destruction of Thailand. It will mean that the Thai Nation which the Thai People have built up for so long will turn into an insignificant country . . .'[52] He has argued that unity could only be maintained through compromise, and urged that 'everybody must 'know how to treasure Unity'.[53] The King's view is that unity prevents trouble, and where unity does not exist, subversion and crime result.[54]

This theme also emerges in Mahbubani's complementary reservations about the direction of American society. He argues that:

> American society, by permitting all forms of lifestyle to emerge—without any social pressures to conform to certain standards—may have wrecked the moral and social fabric that is needed to keep a society calm and well ordered. A well-ordered society needs to plant clear constraints on behaviour in the minds of its citizens. In the United States it is clear that many such fundamental psychological constraints have collapsed, with the acceptance of all forms of lifestyle as legitimate.[55]

Here Mahbubani is not only expressing concern about the collapse of order, but attributing it to the absence of a clear and unambiguous moral stance in defence of a particular order. Despite the general reverence for order by its advocates, it is not a case of any order will do. Rather, an hierarchical order with clear lines of dominance and subordination and undisputed authority is mutually attractive to Western conservatives and Asian leaders championing the East Asian way. Thus, conservatives have historically looked to the institutions of family, church and nation rather than representative political institutions.

Interestingly, Malaysian Deputy Prime Minister, Anwar Ibrahim, whose active promotion of an 'Asian renaissance' has included some notion of 'political liberality' and a rejection of the idea that this is inimical to economic development in Asia, is also strongly wedded to the primacy of order: 'In facing the manifold challenges to civil society, we must remain focused on its basic needs. Foremost of these is the creation and preservation of social order, without which there would be chaos'. Significantly, Anwar's greater declared tolerance of dissent is related to his view that 'Properly instituted, democracy will ensure order and stability'.[56]

Traditional values

Both in the emphasis on traditional values and in the supposed content of East Asian values, we again see a strong resonance with conservatism, where one of the major philosophical elements is the opposition to the idea of radical change and a preference for *conservation* of values and traditions considered essential to society.[57] For others, there is a desire to conserve particular social and political institutions.[58] While the discipline of market relations is attractive to conservatives, they have always had reservations about capitalism, insisting that there be a moral basis to the social and political order that transcends mere market logic. Irving Kristol's *Two Cheers for Capitalism*[59] is but the most striking contemporary reminder of this. As is observable in Australia and other advanced industrialised countries, this creates some tensions on the right of politics, distinguishing conservatives from liberals. Issues such as sexuality and civil liberties separate conservatives and liberals.

Asian conservatives have also stressed the importance of non-economic factors and the alleged centrality of traditional Asian values. Like Thailand's King Bhumibol,[60] who has always opposed change for its own sake, believing that there is much 'good in the old-fashioned things', Singapore's Prime Minister Goh argues that a sense of community and nationhood, a disciplined and hardworking people, strong moral values, and family ties are the critical Asian values: 'These values are tried and tested, have held us together, propelled us forward.

We must keep them as the bedrock of our society for the next century.' He continued: 'It is not simply materialism and pursuit of individual rewards which drive Singapore forward, but more important is the sense of idealism and service, born out of a feeling of social solidarity and national identification'.[61] This call for an emphasis on Asian values is based on a fear that they 'are giving way to a more Westernised, individualistic, and self-centred outlook on life'.[62]

As is so often the case with Western conservative critiques of their own societies, Goh emphasises the centrality of traditional family structures and values. When conservatives extol the virtues of the family, it is the patriarchal family they have in mind.[63] This institution has a number of attractions for them. First, it embodies a clear power structure which is hierarchical and based on authority. The sexual division of labour and relations between parents and children are not based on egalitarian principles but tradition and the utility of those relations to order—both within the family and the society more generally. Second, it is a pivotal institution for socialisation—hence the common notion that the family is the building block of society.[64] In particular, it engenders a sense of obligation and commitment to a broader community. This is one of the reasons that conservatives are often hostile to state-provided social welfare—it undermines the authority of family and community.[65] Lee Kuan Yew is certainly in agreement with this, although he seems to claim it as a distinctively Asian view:

> Eastern societies believe that the individual exists in the context of his family. He is not pristine and separate. The family is part of the extended family, and then friends and the wider society. The ruler or the government does not try to provide for a person what the family best provides.[66]

Such views of the family allow for attacks on supposedly negative trends in society, pointing to the erosion of parental authority and discipline over children and the lack of respect for elders. Such statements are as common in the West as they are in the East, with Goh recently expressing concern that divorce rates are rising in Singapore and that there are indeed some single parents and juvenile delinquency in the island state.[67] This perspective resulted in a recent policy announcement that unmarried mothers would be barred from buying homes from the Housing Development Board (HDB), rectifying a loophole that had seen 1000 unmarried mothers purchase HDB homes.[68] Goh also reaffirmed government policy not to allow women civil servants the same medical benefits as men, on the basis that it was the government's underlying philosophy to 'channel rights, benefits and privileges through the head of the family so that he can enforce the obligations and responsibilities of family members'.

The Singapore government has also established a Family Values Promotion Committee involving people from the public and private sectors, which has identified five family values to uphold: love; care and concern; mutual respect; filial responsibility; commitment and communication in their roles as parents, spouses, sons and daughters.[69] Consistent with this, the government has supported the Maintenance of Parents Bill, which will legally enforce financial support for parents in old age,[70] and has pressed for a new clause in the Advertising Standards Authority of Singapore's code stating that advertisers should consider society's mores as well as the five core family values.[71]

The Singapore government's policies on the family are not without their contradictions. One of the measures Prime Minister Goh used of Singapore's progress in an address to party cadres in early 1995 was the growth in foreign maids. This rose dramatically from 56 000 to 89 000 between 1990 and 1994.[72] These maids not only undertake domestic duties but are the primary carers of children. Traditional child-rearing responsibilities within the family are thus being transformed, and presented as a measure of social advancement.

Nevertheless, Goh's general concerns were echoed and extended by Malaysian Prime Minister Mahathir in his claim that the Western concept of a family is a clear indication of its moral decline. He condemned the West for recognition of a gay or lesbian couple as a family if it adopted children, and for recognition of de facto relationships as family units. 'It will only produce illegitimate children who may, in turn, have incestuous marriages with their siblings'.[73]

There is much support for these family values. Goh declared that he had even received positive feedback from housewives in the United Kingdom.[74] Coincidentally, at about the same time, the Governor of Western Australia, Major-General Michael Jeffrey, delivered a speech in Perth that expressed similar concerns about divorce rates and the growth of single-parent families. Governor Jeffrey claimed that a 'British study found a direct statistical link between single parenthood and virtually every major type of crime'.[75] Like many conservatives before him, he was expressing a clear preference for the traditional family structure which he saw as 'in some trouble'.[76] The Call to Australia Party also emphasises the need to restore family values to prevent declining moral standards and to again make Australia great.[77] Hence, the Australian Broadcasting Commission's televising of Sydney's Gay and Lesbian Mardi Gras in 1994 brought a variety of group and individual protests, calling for the promotion of the 'traditional' family, while the Lyons Forum, a group within the Federal Liberal Party, maintained that only traditional families bonded by 'God-ordained' principles could bring up children properly.[78] Conservative United States House Speaker Newt Gingrich could also identify with these perspectives, and has no trouble citing the problem and enemy—liberalism.[79]

Having emphasised 'traditionalism', it is not our intention to suggest that this is becoming the exclusive rationale for the contemporary social, political and economic order, but an increasingly central one. The new order is also, to differing extents, justified in functional terms tied to developmental imperatives. This is most conspicuous in Singapore, where an elaborate elitist ideology also exists which insists that a genuine meritocracy now prevails. Hierarchy and merit are thus seen to coexist and the challenge is to reproduce such an order.

Obligations ahead of rights

As we have discussed, according to conservatives, human nature is such that we should be very cautious about individual freedom. Social institutions such as the family, army and organised religion that suppress individual drives and aspirations thus play a critical role in generating order and continuity and are valued accordingly. But the importance attached to order and the overall interest of 'society' as a living entity also logically leads conservatives to attribute moral superiority to the 'community' over the 'individual'. Hence, it is obligations to community, society, nation, family and other established social institutions that conservatives stress, over the rights of individuals. As British conservative writer Roger Scruton puts it:

> In politics, the conservative attitude seeks above all for government, and regards no citizen as possessed of a natural right that transcends his obligation to be ruled. Even democracy—which corresponds neither to the natural nor the supernatural yearnings of the normal citizen—can be discarded without detriment to the civil well-being as the conservative conceives it.[80]

Thailand's King has expressed the essence of this perspective, by placing emphasis on duties rather than rights. In summarising his perspective, he encapsulates the conservative world-view:

> A nation is made up of various institutions in the same way as all the organs which make up a live body. Life in a body can endure, because the organs, large or small, function normally. Likewise, a nation can endure, because its various institutions are firm and are fully discharging their respective duties. You must all realize that the nation is the life, the blood and the property of everyone . . . . To uphold and safeguard the nation is the duty . . . of every party. Each and everyone must work together . . . , sharing common aims and

objectives. Should any group fail in its duty . . . the entire nation may collapse and be destroyed.[81]

When individuals assert political, social or economic rights, conservatives view these as having no basis in history nor proven utility to society. This is another reason for the conservative antagonism to social welfare, which tends to institutionalise dubious 'rights'. Conservatives despise the so-called 'new class' for its part in fostering such claims.[82] It is Goh's fear of this that underscores his recent attack on welfare as 'misguided compassion' which 'has led to disastrous results'.[83]

The conservative understanding of inequality as natural also contributes to a mistrust of and hostility to democracy and calls for equality and rights. Such notions are wrong and dangerous, and pose a threat to order and stability. People do have differential abilities and capacities, not the least in the area of political leadership, and the real task is to ensure that the gifted are ensured their rightful place for the overall good of society. Inequality is thus both natural and functional and it is folly to attempt to disturb this truth. Obviously this reasoning provides a perfect rationale for hierarchical structures and elitist ideologies. Lee Kuan Yew has, of course, never been in any doubt about this in the construction of Singapore's 'meritocracy'.[84]

When we turn to the numerous efforts by the various leaders to specify distinctive Asian cultural values, none is more thematic or important than the insistence on society or community ahead of the individual. Articulations of this difference are heavily weighted towards explicit attacks on 'Western liberalism': individualism and liberal democracy. What becomes clear is the depth of anti-liberalism rather than any detailed self-awareness of traditional Asian values. It is this position that forms the basis of a spirited rejection of human rights as either an alien or culturally loaded concept from the West as well as the more general defence of authoritarian rule.

The dispute between the American and Singapore governments over the Fay sentence was contested around notions of human rights. Leading Singaporean business figure Ho Kwon Ping added weight to the notion of a 'clash of civilisations' by portraying it in terms of contrasting attitudes in East and West over the rights of individuals versus those of the community. In an address to lawyers on the day Fay was caned, he observed:

> The Western cliché that it would be better for a guilty person to go
> free than to convict an innocent person is testimony to the importance
> of the individual. But an Asian perspective may well be that it is
> better that an innocent person be convicted if the common welfare is
> protected than for a guilty person to be free to inflict further harm on
> the community.[85]

The common depiction of the West as characterised by rampant individualism—and at considerable social cost—is lucidly summarised by Mahbubani:

> In working so hard to increase their scope of individual freedom within their society, Americans have progressively cut down the thick web of human relations and obligations that have produced social harmony in traditional societies. Effectively in tearing down such social constraints, upon individuals, American society has carried out slash and burn tactics that have, as in natural forests, left sections of their society denuded of social obligations.[86]

Here we again clearly see the assumption of a natural proclivity for evil on the part of individuals and the moral superiority of community.

Asian leaders have advanced a variety of reasons to explain why they believe liberal democracy is unsuitable in the Asian context, but disputation over human rights has generated a conception that Asian systems should be judged not on human rights but in terms of economic development by 'good government'. For Mahbubani[87] and Koh,[88] the common characteristics of East Asian regimes define good government: political stability; wise leadership; sound bureaucracies based on meritocracy; economic growth with equity, but rewarding enterprise and achievement; fiscal prudence; social policies in such fields as housing, education and health care that make every citizen feel a stakeholder; national teamwork and partnership between government, business and labour; acceptance of the rule of law and an independent judiciary; and relative lack of corruption. According to Mahbubani,[89] 'to have good government, you often need less, not more, democracy'. Koh, however, sees a role for government in developing civil society.

The attempt to portray the concept of human rights as 'alien' may reflect concern about internal pressures in that direction no less than the international—or at least a concern that the latter may fuel the former. While human rights NGOs are still in their infancy or non-existent in China, Vietnam, Laos, North Korea, Burma and Singapore, there is a developing Southeast Asian Human Rights Network, which met in Bangkok in July 1994. Furthermore, of the 1800 non-government organisations that sent representatives to the United Nations World Conference on Human Rights in Vienna in 1993, some 250 were from the Asia-Pacific region.[90] Australian Prime Minister Keating's reference in July 1994 to Indonesia as a nation of 'great tolerance' came in for criticism from human rights activists in Indonesia and the region. During a later visit to Australia, Indonesian human rights lawyer, Buyung Nasution, underlined his disappointment at this remark:

If you were in our position, people who were oppressed, harassed, some of us were arrested unlawfully, even tortured . . . of course we could not expect too much—that foreign countries will jump in and help us or get us relief but that at least we would expect that foreign governments would not praise oppressive measures.[91]

Recent attempts to link labour conditions to human rights and to tie trade concessions to progress on human rights has also elicited illuminating responses in Asia and the West. A US government sub-committee suggested linking privileges under the generalised scheme of preferences to improvements in these areas,[92] a position US Trade Representative Mickey Kantor threatened the Indonesian Government with. Asian leaders dubbed the push a blatant attempt at disguised protectionism.[93] Malaysia's Mahathir contended that the West was hell-bent on sabotage and would prefer Asia to experience the chaos: 'This is what the West wants—not democracy, not free trade and not human rights'.[94] He added: 'Actually, they want us to practice the democracy which brings about instability, economic decline and poverty. With such a situation they can threaten and control us'.[95]

However, the threatened withdrawal by the United States government of Most Favoured Nation (MFN) status for China gave expression to significant US-based interests associated with China's regime. The Clinton administration was subject to intense lobbying on behalf of US companies to sever the link between trade and human rights, to safeguard access to both the huge market and access to cheap labour. As the *Far Eastern Economic Review*[96] reported, opponents:

> argued that revocation of China's MFN status would mean the loss of American jobs; that trade would enhance social and political evolution in China, thus improving human rights; and that good US–China relations were essential for the security of the Asia–Pacific region.

These views seem to have prevailed, demonstrating that the liberal human rights push in the West has to confront powerful domestic interests that either rationalise or endorse the conditions and practices that are the subject of controversy.

Implications

The aim of this chapter has been to suggest a rather straightforward yet generally neglected point. That point is that the rhetoric about 'Asian values' and a potential for a clash of cultures, especially between the 'West' and 'Asia', masks convergences of political ideologies across nations. Although we chose to concentrate on the conservative elements of this rhetoric, we have not sought to depict the Asian leaders involved as conservatives per se. Their political and ideological positions are more complex than this. It would be possible to isolate other ideological elements in their broader political rhetoric, such as economic individualism and developmentalism, which also find sympathetic audiences in the 'West'. Even so, it is significant that the discussion of 'Asian values' has concentrated on essentially conservative values.

The nonsense that 'Asian values' are culturally defined has recently been demonstrated by a strong proponent of this perspective, Dr Mahathir, who joined with the conservative Japanese politician and author Shintaro Ishihara to write the Japanese-language book, *The Asia That Can Say No: A Policy to Combat Europe and America*. In the following publicity blitz, Mahathir, frustrated with the Japanese Government's support of the US, Australia and New Zealand position on his proposed East Asian Economic Caucus, accused the Japanese of not being 'East Asian'.[97]

A nonsense indeed, but the 'Asian values' line has a strong appeal in Australia and elsewhere—and not just among conservatives. In Australia this perspective has been accepted unproblematically by a host of policymakers, journalists, educationalists, public commentators and business people. This not only reflects the fact that various political and social ideologies have some points of intersection, it also reflects changes within Australia that render conservative and anti-liberal rhetoric by Asian leaders useful for domestic political projects. The changing global political economy, involving a new status and importance for Asian economies and societies appreciates the currency of this rhetoric; after all, such economic development is seen to demonstrate that 'Asian values' actually 'work'. This process might be understood, as suggested by Robison in the introduction to this volume, as the 'internationalisation' of political and ideological contestations.

Not surprisingly, then, conservatives hoping to overturn social reforms of previous decades and neo-liberals intent on an agenda that would bolster economic individualism will select those elements of the 'Asian values' rhetoric that suit their particular cause. While the former may admire the attempt to retain patriarchal family structures, deference to authority and harsh penalties for crime, the latter see merit in emulating the relatively unencumbered business environment in its call for greater 'labour market flexibility' in Australia.

While it is easy to see that the cultural relativist positions of these self-proclaimed Asian leaders will have a particular appeal to those conservatives who believe that society is ultimately held together by traditional values, it is ironic that they also have an appeal for some liberals and radicals who believe their cases against ethnocentrism, racism or Western imperialism are bolstered by such rhetoric.[98]

Non-governmental development organisations have been particularly prone to feel that there is some truth in the 'Asian values' argument, even if they are uncomfortable with the politics of some of these Asian leaders who espouse them. Part of the reason for this is that some of the development groups they support in Asia adopt culturalist perspectives themselves.[99]

Independent of the increasingly conservative rhetoric by some Asian leaders, the influence of economic rationalism in policy circles over the last decade in Australia, and indeed, to differing extents, many other liberal democratic societies, has led to the institutionalisation of instrumentalist and functionalist values in the public sector.[100] A not unrelated trend towards managerialist and pseudo-corporatist structures has accompanied this development.[101] This is especially evident in education, where the usefulness of activities in this enterprise are assessed by ever-narrowing criteria relating to the interests of business and government. Technocratic problem-solving seems to have been successfully projected as the chief business of public policy. Such a direction opens up the possibility of stronger ideological convergences between bureaucratic elites across 'East' and 'West' than has hitherto been the case. This is not without application to bureaucratic elites in trade unions. Michael Easson,[102] for example, has expressed a qualified defence of Lee Kuan Yew's philosophy on trade unions in Singapore. Easson, a recent Secretary of the Labor Council of New South Wales and Vice-President of the Australian Council of Trade Unions (ACTU), appears to find some attraction in instrumental and corporatist aspects of unionism in Singapore without endorsing the overall model.[103]

The implication is that, far from there being some imminent 'clash of cultures', we have unfolding preconditions for stronger political and ideological convergences across 'East' and 'West'. The facade of 'Asian values' conceals this crucially important development, effectively defining out of existence all opposition to the content of these values within Asia as 'Western' and/or 'alien'. For pragmatically minded governments and business people, desperately seeking to make a success of greater economic involvement with the region, the notion that 'Asians' are different provides a seductive rationale for double standards on human rights, freedom of expression and other universally meaningful issues. The most worrying scenario is that far from the internationalisation of political and ideological contestation offering new hope for the oppressed in Asia, it will not only dash such hope but also serve as a new offensive against liberal and social democratic ideas in the so-called 'West'.

Notes

1 Our thanks goes to Amanda Miller for her able research assistance on this project and Richard Robison for his constructive criticisms on an earlier draft.

2 Cited in *Weekend Australian* 29–30 October 1994, p. 2.

3 Josey, Alex, *Socialism in Asia*, Donald Moore, Singapore, 1957.

4 Of course, even the notion of 'Asia' as a cultural or even political entity is a fiction, but we do not propose to take this up here.

5 Huntington, Samuel P., 'The Clash of Civilizations?', *Foreign Affairs*, vol. 72, no. 3, 1993, pp. 22–49.

6 ibid., p. 23.

7 ibid., p. 25.

8 ibid., p. 29.

9 ibid., p. 40.

10 ibid., p. 27.

11 Muzaffar, for example, has observed that ASEAN is a regional grouping encompassing four civilisations that has operated quite effectively, in spite of cultural differences between member states; see O'Hagen, Jacinta, '*Inter-Civilizational Conflict: A Critique of the Huntington Thesis*', Working Paper 1, Department of International Relations, The Research School of Pacific and Asian Studies, Australian National University, 1994, p. 9.

12 Harries, Owen,'Clash of Civilisations', *Weekend Australian*, 3–4 April 1993, p. 19.

13 Huntington, op. cit., p. 49.

14 For discussions and critiques of Huntington's thesis, see O'Hagen, op. cit., *Foreign Affairs*, vol. 72, no. 4, 1993 and *Asian Studies Review*, vol. 18, no. 1, 1994.

15 Mahbubani, Kishore, 'The Dangers of Decadence', *Foreign Affairs*, vol. 72, no. 4, 1993, pp. 10–14.

16 The Singaporean Minister of Information and the Arts and Second Minister of Foreign Affairs, George Yeo, drew attention to what he saw as anti-Asian sentiments rising in the West in response to the emerging economic might of Asia. See 'East Asia must not fuel insecurity in the West', *Straits Times*, 8 Dec. 1993, p. 27.

17 This chapter does not propose to test the accuracy of the historical and social observations made by some Asian leaders. Some other forum is required to debunk the myths they purvey.

18 Aung San Suu Kyi, 'Empowerment for a Culture of Peace and Development', address to a meeting of the World Commission on Culture and Development, 21 November 1994, (presented on behalf of the author by Corizon Aquino); Kim Dae Jung, 'Is Culture Destiny? The Myth of Asia's Anti-Democratic Values', *Foreign Affairs*, vol. 73, no. 6, 1994, pp. 189–94; Lung Ying-tai, 'Stereotyping of Asians and Westerners is Unproductive', *The Straits Times*, 27 October 1994, p. 29; *Far Eastern Economic Review*, 10 Dec. 1992, p. 29; Vitat Muntarbhorn, *Human Rights in Southeast Asia. A Challenge for the 21st Century*, Chaiyong

52 *Pathways to Asia*

Limthongkul Foundation, Bangkok, 1993; Wain, Barry, 'Press Freedom is an Asian Value', *Asian Wall Street Journal*, 9–10 December 1994, p. 8; Kohut, John, 'Asian Equations for Human Rights', *South China Morning Post*, 17 February 1995, p. 19; Shenon, Philip,'The World: Models for China', *New York Times*, 5 February 1995, p. 1.

19 O'Hagen, op. cit. p. 18

20 Huntington, quoted in *Asiaweek*, 6 April 1994, p. 36.

21 Quoted in *Australian*, 19 April 1994, p. 1. One of the rebuffs to this view came from a senior Hong Kong bureaucrat who happened to be in Australia at the time. Michael Sze, Hong Kong's civil service secretary and former director of foreign trade described Lee's view as outdated. Sze said he was 'most impressed with Australia's service sector and the massive reforms in the public service' (quoted in *West Australian* 27 April 1994, p. 4).

22 Kirk, Russell, *The Conservative Mind: From Burke to Eliot*, Gateway, South Bend, Indiana, 6th rev. edn, 1978.

23 Quoted in O'Sullivan, Noël, *Conservatism*, Dent, London, 1976, p. 84.

24 O'Gorman, Frank, 'Introduction', *British Conservatism: Conservative Thought from Burke to Thatcher*, ed. F. O'Gorman, Longman, London, 1986, pp. 1–65; see also O'Sullivan, op. cit.; Viereck, Peter, *Conservatism: from John Adams to Churchill*, Greenwood Press, Westport, 1978 and *Conservatism Revisited*, Free Press, New York, 1962.

25 King Bhumibol Adulyadej, *Collection of Royal Addresses and Speeches During the State and Official Visits of Their Majesties the King and Queen to Foreign Countries 1959–1967 (B.E. 2502–2510)*, Bangkok, 1974, p. 60.

26 See Hewison, Kevin & Rodan, Garry, 'The Decline of the Left in Southeast Asia', *The Socialist Register 1994*, eds L. Panitch & R. Miliband, The Merlin Press, London, pp. 235–62.

27 See Hewison, Kevin, 'The Monarchy and the Future of Democracy in Thailand', *'Locating Power: Democracy, Opposition and Participation in Thailand'*, paper presented to the Asia Research Centre Workshop, 6–7 October 1994, Murdoch University, Perth.

28 Huntington, Samuel P., *Political Order in Changing Societies*, Yale University Press, New Haven, Connecticut, 1968.

29 Quoted in *STWE*, 3 September 1994, p. 24.

30 *Australian*, 1–2 Jan. 1994, p. 14.

31 O'Sullivan, op. cit., pp. 14–15.

32 Kirk, op. cit., p. 8.

33 Viereck, op. cit., p. 32.

34 King Bhumibol, op. cit., p. 88.

35 Quoted in Zakaria, Fareed, 'Culture Is Destiny. A Conversation with Lee Kuan Yew', *Foreign Affairs*, vol. 73, no. 2, 1994, pp. 109–26.

36 Mahbubani, Kishore, 'The United States: "Go East, Young Man" ', *Washington Quarterly*, vol. 17, no. 2, 1994, pp. 5–23.

37 *Straits Times Weekly Edition (STWE)*, 3 Sept. 1994, p. 10.

38 King Bhumibol, op. cit., p. 8.

39 Quoted in *STWE* 23 April 1994, p. 13.

40 Quoted in *Asiaweek* 25 May 1994, p. 38.
41 *STWE*, 23 April 1994, p. 13; Lal, Vinay, 'The Flogging of Michael Fay. Culture of Authoritarianism', *Economic and Political Weekly*, vol. xxix, no. 23, 1994, pp. 1386–88.
42 *Courier Mail*, 5 July 1994, p. 3
43 Coleman, Bruce, Call To Australia Party, pamphlet for the New South Wales State Election, 25 March 1995.
44 *West Australian*, 18 March 1994, p. 9.
45 ibid.
46 *Sunday Times* (Perth), 31 July 1994, p. 23.
47 Tan Sai Siong, 'Singapore-bashing takes another turn with Lingle issue', SIF Diary on the Technet Gopher in Singapore, no. 77, 28 October 1994.
48 O'Gorman, Frank, *Edmund Burke. His Political Philosophy*, George Allen & Unwin, London, 1973, pp. 114–17.
49 In Scruton, Roger, 'Authority and Allegiance', *Politics and Ideology*, eds J. Donald & S. Hall, Open University Press, Milton Keynes, 1986, pp. 73, 105–109.
50 Quoted in Zakaria, op. cit., p. 111.
51 *Weekend Australian*, 23–24 April 1994, p. 24.
52 King Bhumibol Adulyadej, *Royal Advice by His Majesty the King, 20 May 1992/2535 at 21.30*, Bangkok: Office of His Majesty's Principal Private Secretary, 1992, para. 2.
53 King Bhumibol Adulyadej, *Royal Speech Given to the Audience of Well-Wishers on the Occasion of the Royal Birthday Anniversary*, Wednesday, 4 December 1992, pp. 1, 12, no publication details.
54 King Bhumibol, op. cit., 1974, pp. 64–5, 91. King Bhumibol, op. cit., 1992, pp. 28–30.
55 Mahbubani, op. cit., p. 11.
56 Anwar Ibrahim, 'The Pacific Century', *Far Eastern Economic Review*, 2 June 1994, p. 34.
57 O'Sullivan, op. cit., p. 9; Viereck, 1962, p. 36.
58 O'Gorman, op. cit., p. 2.
59 Kristol, Irving, *Two Cheers for Capitalism*, Basic Books, New York, 1978.
60 King Bhumibol, op. cit., 1974, p. 60.
61 Quoted in *STWE*, 27 Aug. 1994, p. 1.
62 Quoted in *Shared Values*, Presented to Parliament by Command of The President of the Republic of Singapore, 2 January 1991, p. 1.
63 Stavropoulous, Pam, 'Conservative Intellectuals and Feminism: the Australian Case', *Australian Journal of Political Science*, vol. 25, no. 2, 1990, pp. 218–27; Chipman, Lachlan, 'Abortion: Time to Turn Back the Clock', *Quadrant*, April, 1986, pp. 30-3.
64 The family as the basic building block of society is one of the four identified in the *Shared Values* document produced by the Singapore Government in 1991. See also Nisbet, Robert, *Conservatism: Dream and Reality*, Open University Press, Milton Keynes, 1986, p. 37; Heywood, Andrew, *Political Ideologies. An Introduction*, Macmillan, London, 1992, pp. 62–3.

65 Nisbet, op. cit., pp. 58–9; Scruton, Roger, 'Introduction: What is Conservatism?', *Conservative Texts,* ed. R. Scruton, Macmillan, London, 1991, pp. 1–28.
66 Cited in Zakaria, op. cit., p. 113.
67 *Australian,* 23 Aug. 1994, p. 12.
68 *Australian,* 23 Aug. 1994, p. 10. This policy was later expanded to include the fathers of 'illegitimate' children, if the mother was prepared to identify the father. The president of Singapore's Association of Women for Action and Research pointed out, there has been no increase in the number of unmarried mothers in the last five years (*STWE,* 3 Sept. 1994, p. 2).
69 *STWE,* 23 July 1994, p. 5; 20 Aug. 1994, p. 6.
70 *STWE,* 30 July 1994, p. 24; Seven PAP MPs voted against it. It has aroused considerable protest. Like most other Asian societies, Singapore is facing the problem of providing for an ageing population (*Asiaweek,* 17 Aug. 1994, pp. 19–22). In its case, is determined to avoid the state welfare route.
71 *Straits Times* (*ST*), 13 Sept. 1994
72 Goh Chok Tong, 'Have You Done Your Part ?' *Petir,* January/February 1995, p. 9.
73 *West Australian,* 16 Aug. 1994, p. 20. Goh's aggressive promotion of what 'family values' are, has prompted strong local reaction, most particularly from a women's group, the Association of Women for Action and Research (AWARE). Local writer Mary Lee's comment at a public forum possibly encapsulated the views of many of the dissaffected when she contended that the government's Asian values paradigm 'seems to be the basis of its anti-women policies' (as quoted in *Asiaweek,* 21 Sept. 1994, p. 25). NMP Kanwaljit Soin also protested that Goh's speech was unfair to women and interpreted it as an apparent hardening of the government's position on the roles of men and women (*STWE,* 10 Sept. 1994, p. 1).
74 *STWE,* 10 Sept. 1974, p. 1.
75 Quoted in *West Australian,* 19 Aug. 1994, p. 31.
76 Jeffrey, Major-General Michael, Opening Address to The Western Australian Country Women's Association Annual State Conference, 8 Aug. 1994, unpublished mimeograph. Australian Bureau of Statistics data show that nine out of ten Australian families still live in a 'conventional' family setting. See *Australian* 7 December 1993, p. 1.
77 Coleman, op. cit.
78 *Canberra Times,* 4 March 1994, p. 1.
79 *Weekend Australian,* 5–6 March 1995, p. 3.
80 Scruton, Roger, *The Meaning of Conservatism,* Macmillan, London, 1984, p. 16.
81 King Bhumibol, op. cit., 1974, p. 49.
82 Kristol, op. cit.
83 *Australian,* 12 Sept. 1994, p. 12.
84 George, T.J.S., *Lee Kuan Yew's Singapore,* Andre Deutsch, London, 1973; Minchin, James, *No Man is an Island: A Portrait of Singapore's Lee Kuan Yew,* Allen & Unwin, Sydney, 2nd edn, 1990.

85 Quoted in *Asiaweek*, 25 May 1994, p. 38.
86 Mahbubani, op. cit., 1994, p. 7.
87 Mahbubani, Kishore, 'The West and the Rest', *National Interest*, no. 19, Spring, 1992, p. 9.
88 Koh, op. cit., p. 6.
89 Mahbubani, op. cit. 1994, p. 17.
90 *FEER*, 8 July 1993, p. 15.
91 Quoted in *Australian*, 13 Sept. 1994, p. 6.
92 *ST*, 11 May 1993, p. 12.
93 STWE, 23 April 1994, p. 4.
94 Quoted in *FEER*, 17 June 1993, p. 20.
95 Quoted in *STWE*, 4 Sept. 1993, p. 10.
96 2 June 1994, p. 25.
97 *Weekend Australian*, 12–13 Nov. 1994, p. 16.
98 Robison, Richard, 'Mahathir Paints False Picture of Asian Region', *Australian*, 14 Dec. 1993, p. 9.
99 Hewison, Kevin, 'Nongovernmental Organizations and the Cultural Development Perspective: A Comment on Rigg', *World Development*, vol. 21, no. 10, 1993, pp. 1699–1708.
100 Pusey, Michael, *Economic Rationalism in Canberra: A Nation Building State Changes its Mind,* Allen & Unwin, Sydney, 1991; Gruen, Fred & Grattan, Michelle, *Managing Government: Labor's Achievements and Failures,* Longman Cheshire, Melbourne, 1993, pp. 40–57.
101 Hughes, Owen, *Public Management and Administration: An Introduction*, Macmillan, London, 1994.
102 Easson, Michael, 'The Bud That Will Never Flower? East Asian Trade Unions', *Living with Dragons: Australia Confronts its Asian Destiny*, ed. G. Sheridan, Allen & Unwin, Sydney, 1995, p. 194–216.
103 It is also noteworthy that the ACTU has supported the state-controlled SPSI in Indonesia through a workers' education program. Money for this program was provided by the Australian government and channelled through the International Labour Organisation. Although various members of the ACTU challenged this support ahead of advancing the position of independent unions in Indonesia, the close relationship between the ACTU hierarchy and the Federal Labor Government worked in favour of support for the government's position—as has been the case in a range of policy areas. The ACTU also came in for criticism from independent labour organisations in Indonesia. See Michael Casey, 'ACTU pair betrayed us: union', *West Australian*, 15 Dec. 1994, p. 14.

Further References

Goh Chok Tong, 'Three Lessons for Singapore', *Straits Times Weekly Edition,* 27 August 1994, p. 4.
King Bhumibol Adulyadej, *Royal Speech Given to the Audience of Well-Wishers on the Occasion of the Royal Birthday*, Dusidalai Hall, Chitralada Villa, Dusit Palace, 4 December 1990, no publication details.

3

Recalcitrant or *Realpolitik?* The politics of culture in Australia's relations with Malaysia

Peter Searle

Introduction

Recent crises in Australia's relations with Malaysia raise questions about Australia's capacity to 'enmesh' with the countries of the Asian region. During 1991 and 1993 the tensions in that relationship generated by the so-called *Embassy* and *Recalcitrant* affairs presented illuminating case studies of the difficulties faced by Australia when our neighbours play the 'cultural card'. That is when Australia is branded a cultural outsider, insensitive to 'Asian' values and concerns, and by extension unqualified to gain acceptance in the region as something like a charter member of their club. Malaysian claims of Australian cultural insensitivity were played at a policy and ideological level on the one hand, and at an institutional and operational level on the other. At both levels Australia was caught off balance as the stimulation of a variety of agendas and interest groups, domestic as well as regional, made a coherent and cohesive response difficult. It is suggested however that if we learn from past experience such difficulties may be contained in future as Australia, or at least Australian policymakers, become more adept in their responses to 'plays of the cultural card'. Furthermore the sharp shocks in our relationship with Malaysia may also provide valuable long-term lessons for our relations with the Asian region in general.

Australia–Malaysia relations: an overview

'Alone among all the nations of Southeast Asia, or any other part of Asia for that matter, the Federation of Malaya . . . can lay claim to a common colonial heritage with Australia, and to manifold culture contacts and collaboration in peace and war; precursors perhaps to an ultimate Australian reconciliation with her Asian environment'[1]. Boyce's guarded optimism over 30 years ago as to the possibilities of Australia's relations with Malaysia reflected the relatively easy and intimate nature of that relationship in the early 1960s. The rather artificial intimacy of those years when Australia's relations with Malaysia were more narrowly based, largely on defence ties and development assistance, was replaced in the 1970s and 1980s by a more complex and broadly based relationship reflecting important political, social and economic changes in both countries.

Generally, however, perceptions by Australians of contemporary Malaysian realities, and vice versa, did not keep pace with the changes taking place, but remained locked in old images more in accord with social and economic profiles associated with the 1960s. As Malaysia rapidly advanced towards Newly Industrialising Economy (NIE) status, and saw itself as an integral part of East Asian 'economic success', Australia came to represent the opposite, a part of the Western world that was not only falling behind in economic terms but was socially self-indulgent, arrogant and patronising as well. Many Australians, some in the media, in Parliament and the wider community, were either little aware of or concerned to address the complex processes of social, economic and political change in Malaysia and fell back on old or outmoded cultural stereotypes when pronouncing on Malaysian affairs.

For instance at a political level, when Australian parliamentarians condemned Malaysia's 'blatant violations of human rights' after the arrest and detention in October 1987 of 105 people under the Internal Security Act (ISA), no attempt was made to at least couple that condemnation with a recognition that, at least in that instance, the ISA was employed to contain an imminent threat of ethnic violence. Put bluntly, detention and the temporary curtailment of political freedom was, in the view of most Malaysians, a lesser evil than the alternative—the real prospect of a devastating racial riot. At a social and cultural level Australian television documentaries also frequently fell back on old ethnic and religious stereotypes. In an attempt to vividly portray the racial divide in Malaysian society, one documentary juxtaposed the 'energetic and enterprising' Chinese in Kuala Lumpur with the 'lazy' Malays portrayed in a rural setting waiting for their trained monkeys to gather coconuts for them. (By the mid-1980s a young Malay businessman attentively following the prices on the Kuala Lumpur Stock Exchange would have better captured contemporary social realities.) Similarly programs dealing with Islam in Malaysia showed little appreciation either of the generally tolerant approach

taken by the Malaysian government to other religions or its determination to block measures advocated by the Pan Malaysian Islamic Party
(PAS) for the introduction of Muslim law. Rather, as in the case of
'Five Faces of God', part of a series produced for the ABC under the
title 'Slow Boat to Surabaya', fundamentalist Islam was constantly
referred to as the 'Malaysian disease'. Indeed the presenter of the
program, Jack Pizzey, seemed to almost salivate at the prospect of such
Islamic punishments as amputation and death by stoning, despite the
fact that such punishments have never been a feature of Islamic practice
in Malaysia or are ever likely to be.

This is not to argue that growing difficulties in the relationship in
the 1970s and 1980s were only a problem of outmoded stereotypes.
They were but one aspect of a relationship that had become more
complex and involved conflict at many points, particularly as more
difficult economic issues loomed large in the relationship. In the
decades of the 1970s and 1980s a cluster of economic and foreign
policy issues provoked severe strain and on several occasions threatened to rupture relations. Such issues included Australian tariffs, the
bilateral trade imbalance, international civil aviation policy (ICAP),
sugar contracts, student fees, refugees, and differences of policy on
Kampuchea, Antarctica and, more recently, over the Australian-spon-
sored Asia Pacific Economic Cooperation (APEC) initiative and the
Malaysian-sponsored East Asian Economic Caucus (EAEC).

As indicated earlier economic and trade issues provoked the greatest
tension in the bilateral relationship and it was as a result of such issues,
notably the level of Australian tariffs and Australia's 'trade imbalance'
with Malaysia, that even in the late 1970s there were Malaysian threats
of a 'buy Australia last' campaign. At the time Dr Mahathir, then
Deputy Prime Minister and Minister of Trade and Industry, observed
that 'relations (with Australia) were deteriorating like a house on fire'.[1]
Tensions arising from important differences over economic and trade
issues were 'overlain' from time to time by so-called 'cultural irritants',
that is the role of the Australian media in its portrayal of Malaysian
leaders and that country's record on such matters as the environment
and human rights. There was also a 'personal' dimension to these
'cultural' irritants. Whereas on the Australian side the political and
bureaucratic personalities dealing with the considerable cluster of
contentious issues in the relationship constantly changed, on the
Malaysian side such issues were invariably dealt with by the same
members of Malaysia's political and bureaucratic elite. As a result, a
number of key figures in that elite, including most notably Dr Mahathir
himself, developed what may be called a fairly severe case of bilateral
repetitive strain injury or 'bilateral RSI' where the relationship with
Australia was concerned.

While both substantive and cultural issues have disturbed Australia's relations with Malaysia, it has been the latter that have invariably drawn the most ire from the Malaysian side. So while there have been real policy tensions in the relationship, Malaysian sensitivity, and in the Australian view, over-reaction to perceived insults would appear to have deeper origins—that is in Australia's position as a white Western nation and that of Malaysia as an increasingly confident and self-assertive Asian nation. In that regard Malaysian leaders, and Dr Mahathir in particular, have frequently complained that Australians have not yet fully rid themselves of a 'colonial mentality' or a 'superiority complex' where their pronouncements and dealings with Malaysia are concerned. Such sentiments and concerns about perceived slights from 'the West' are genuine and arise in large part from the colonial experience that Dr Mahathir and many of his generation had. As Crouch[3] has pointed out, 'while many of the first generation of Malay leaders were drawn from the upper reaches of Malay society which had greatly benefited from British rule, the social origins of later generations were more humble and many among them, including Dr Mahathir, were more resentful of patronising Europeans and racial discrimination'. For many of that generation of Malays who reached adulthood in the 1950s and 1960s the 'white/Western' attitudes of Australians they encountered in that era, whether at home or as overseas students, were often little different from, if not synonymous with, those of their British colonial rulers.

Thus Australia's often troubled relationship with Malaysia in the 1980s and 1990s has had a West versus Asian aspect to it. Indeed the *Embassy* and *Recalcitrant* affairs of 1991 and 1993 can in large measure be explained by a series of incidents and pronouncements that, in the view of the Malaysian leadership, seemed to indicate that paternalistic attitudes remained a feature of much Australian comment on Malaysian affairs. It does not follow from this however that Australia, by somehow becoming more 'Asian', will resolve its bilateral difficulties with Malaysia. More pertinent in that regard are the dynamics of social and economic change in both countries and the coming to power of a new generation of Malay leaders (best epitomised by the Deputy Prime Minister, Anwar Ibrahim) who are unencumbered by prejudices regarding 'the West' and the colonialist experience of a bygone era. However while the saliency of such categories as West/white/Asian will lose much of their potency, members of the new generation of Malay leaders will be no less resentful, as the crises of 1991 and 1993 showed, to what they regard as patronising attitudes or ill-informed comment from foreigners as to how best they should manage their own affairs.

The crises of 1991 and 1993

For the Malaysians the 'scar tissue' from many earlier conflicts was rather thin when, in the 1980s, other issues and incidents arose that strained the relationship. In 1986 Malaysian leaders were enraged when Prime Minister Bob Hawke described the hanging of two Australian drug smugglers as 'barbaric', a comment they were later to recall and interpret as saying Malaysians were barbarians. As noted earlier, the protest by Australian parliamentarians against the arrest of Malaysian activists in October 1987 and demonstrations by some Australians against rainforest logging in Sarawak also irritated the Malaysian leadership. Coverage by the Australian media of Malaysian affairs became another source of contention. Pertinent in that regard was the promotion of an SBS documentary on Malaysia which was accompanied by a large photograph of Dr Mahathir and posed the question, 'Is this man running a police state on our doorstep?', as well as the depiction of Malays as backward and inclined to religious fundamentalism in the ABC documentary 'Five Faces of God'.

As Foreign Minister Gareth Evans was later to observe, 'these things have a cumulative impact'. A TV drama series, *Embassy*,[3] was as much the straw that broke the camel's back as a *cause célèbre* in itself. But it was in response to *Embassy,* which the Malaysians regarded as an offensive caricature of Malaysian society, that the Malaysian Government first cancelled a number of official Australian visits to Malaysia, and then in March 1991, suspended 'all non-essential cooperative projects with Australia'.[5]

As tensions over the *Embassy* affair escalated and fears grew that Malaysia had put in train a de facto 'buy Australia last' campaign, the Foreign Minister, Senator Evans, went to Kuala Lumpur in July 1991 carrying with him a private letter from Mr Hawke to Dr Mahathir. In the letter, it seems, Hawke acknowledged that Australia was at fault. Later, in October when Hawke met Mahathir at the Commonwealth Heads of Government meeting in Harare, a novel agreement was worked out whereby the two governments agreed to disassociate themselves from 'inaccurate' news reports about each others affairs.[6] After that meeting the rift was officially declared over.[7]

Was the *Embassy* affair largely a matter of Australian insensitivity to Asian/Malaysian values as Dr Mahathir claimed or were there other dynamics at work? A key element in the *Embassy* dispute was the fact that the series clearly poked fun at Dr Mahathir by replicating an incident that involved comments made by him as Deputy Prime Minister in 1978.[8] It seems unlikely that the *Embassy* rift would have assumed the proportions it did without the personal reference to Dr Mahathir as well as the series of incidents that preceded it, that is

Senator Evans' 'cumulative impact' diagnosis. This is not to deny that once the rift was underway other agendas also came into play. The *Embassy* rift did put Australia on the backfoot somewhat both in its efforts to promote the process of Asia Pacific Economic Cooperation (APEC) *vis-à-vis* the Malaysian-initiated East Asian Economic Caucus (EAEC); it sowed discord and undermined confidence regarding Australia's capacity to 'enmesh with Asia'; while *Embassy*/Australia also provided a convenient foreign 'whipping boy' for Dr Mahathir to rally domestic support across Malaysia's political/ethnic spectrum. But after the Hawke–Mahathir meeting in Harare in October 1991 peace and normalcy appeared to have been restored to the relationship.

Suddenly however in November 1993 the acrimony and tensions associated with the *Embassy* saga resurfaced. Whereas the ructions of the *Embassy* affair had been a culmination of perceived slights or offensive portrayals of Malaysia, the tensions of November 1993 arose from a combination of significant differences over policy on the one hand and, on the other, a feeling on the Malaysian side that off-the-cuff remarks by Prime Minister Keating were dismissive both of Dr Mahathir and of Malaysia's role in the region.[8] Since 1989 Malaysian views as to the purpose and evolution of APEC contrasted sharply with those of Australia and the United States. Those policy differences and their implications will be explored later; suffice to note here that it was as a result of such differences that Dr Mahathir boycotted the first APEC heads-of-government meeting in Seattle in November 1993, an action for which he was called 'recalcitrant' by Mr Keating. Mr Keating's use of what became the 'infamous R word' should however be placed in context. Mr Keating had been subject to persistent questioning by journalists concerning Dr Mahathir's refusal to attend the APEC summit; they had also continued to draw his attention to Dr Mahathir's comment at the time of the meeting that, 'Perhaps you have to thumb your nose at people before they notice you'. Finally, it seems, Keating lost patience and said: 'Please don't ask me any more questions about Dr Mahathir. I couldn't care less, frankly, whether he comes or not next year. APEC is bigger than all of us—Australia, the United States, Malaysia, Dr Mahathir and any other recalcitrants'.[10]

The nature of the Malaysian response to the 'recalcitrant' jibe was in many ways a repeat of the earlier *Embassy* episode and involved much the same cast of characters, though its rapid escalation into a full-blown crisis owed much to the media and some 'hard comment' on both sides. It was in reaction to some of the 'hard comments' about Australia, that Keating's reference in the course of the three-week affair to 'feigned indignation' on the Malaysian side may have further exacerbated the real indignation that was certainly felt by some Malaysians. Nevertheless in an effort to defuse the crisis Mr Keating sent a

letter to the Malaysian Prime Minister on 2 December—that is after
the affair had gone on for about ten days—which apparently informed
him that his (Keating's) remarks in Seattle 'were not calculated to give
offence to Dr Mahathir'. Rather they were made to make it clear that
'it was a decision for Malaysia and Dr Mahathir if Malaysia wished
to absent itself from the APEC meeting' . . . Unfortunately Keating
could not resist putting a sting in the tail of the letter when he added
that, 'Australia had clear interests in the architecture of APEC, interests
it would defend vigorously'.[11] Mahathir's response to the letter was
that 'I don't expect an apology . . . but I cannot define this letter as
being conciliatory'. The relationship appeared set to deteriorate further
when in response to mounting pressure from business and public
opinion Keating in the course of the inaugural Sir Edward 'Weary'
Dunlop Asialink lecture said his description of Dr Mahathir 'was not
intended to cause offence and I regret that offence has been taken'.[12]
Meanwhile pressure was also building on Malaysia from local businessmen and foreign investors as well as (albeit indirectly) fellow
members of ASEAN to end the rift. In the third week of the crisis Dr
Mahathir suddenly signalled an end to the anti-Australia campaign and
on 11 December the Malaysian cabinet decided that Keating's expression of regret was sufficient and announced that it 'does not wish to
prolong this issue and will take no further action'.

Should Australia have apologised or indicated 'regret' in the
Embassy and *Recalcitrant* affairs? There are two questions here, one
of diplomatic strategy and one as to whether Dr Mahathir's explanation, that Australia was insensitive to Asian values, was correct. As to
the former, comments by Senator Evans indicated that while Australia
conceded that there were grounds to the Malaysian case on both
occasions, and that an expression of regret was called for, that decision
was largely one of diplomatic strategy, that is to contain the rift with
Malaysia from affecting broader Australian interests in the region. At
the same time the scale those crises assumed (particularly the latter)
were out of all proportion to the offence. So equally pertinent was the
extent to which Dr Mahathir exploited the 'cultural' aspect of the
Embassy and *Recalcitrant* affairs for purposes of *Realpolitik,* that is
to enfeeble and isolate a rival who was promoting an alternative design
for the region. How this was done and the Australian response provides
valuable lessons as to the 'dynamics of engagement' and so it is to
this more important aspect that we now turn.

Culture or Realpolitik: *restraints and opportunities in Australia's
relations with Malaysia*

In both the *Embassy* and *Recalcitrant* crises of 1991 and 1993, Australian policymakers were caught off balance at two levels. At one level

Malaysia's indirect diplomatic style and capacity to exploit a variety of agendas and interest groups in Australia made an effective and coherent response by Canberra difficult. At a second level claims by Malaysia of Australian cultural insensitivity threw doubt on a key domestic and foreign policy goal, that is Australia's capacity to fashion an Asia-related future. At the same time it was also a useful ploy, a piece of *Realpolitik*: it diverted attention from Dr Mahathir's absence from the symbolically important Asia Pacific Economic Cooperation (APEC) leaders' summit in Seattle; it allowed him to bask as the defender of Malaysian pride; and more importantly, for the moment at least, it mobilised the Malaysian elites around his position on regional issues. As the *Embassy* and *Recalcitrant* crises unfolded, matters of policy and style, of *Realpolitik* and 'culture', became inextricably entwined. We shall explore the interweaving of these factors under three headings:

1 'culture' and the conduct of Australian–Malaysian relations;
2 domestic agendas: Malaysian celebration and Australian alienation; and
3 Australia–Malaysia relations and the 'Asia debate'.

'Culture' and the conduct of Australian–Malaysian relations

We have noted earlier the changes that had taken place in the bilateral relationship but what were the implications of those changes for the management of the relationship and how did each side affirm its importance? Both Crouch and Kessler give 'cultural' explanations, some elements of which are not dissimilar. Kessler[12] has argued that from a Malaysian perspective it was felt that 'if the bilateral relationship was as important as Australia claimed then having caused offence, intentionally or not, Australia should offer an apology, issue a statement of regret or at least make the first move to repair the breach'. He adds that 'in the Malaysian view until some such indication of regret, or at least recognition of the problem was received, the future of the entire relationship was in question'. From the Australian side the 'cultural logic' was different. 'If the Malaysians valued the relationship then whatever problems there were should be amenable to resolution within it'.

Crouch[14] also draws on Malay cultural values in his explanation of Dr Mahathir's approach to the rifts of 1991 and 1993. He argues that Dr Mahathir's behaviour can be explained in terms of *merajuk,* a Malay term usually translated as 'sulk' but which has special connotations in Malay culture wherein to *merajuk* is an acceptable means of indicating displeasure. ('An offended Malay sultan, for example will not explain what has offended him but will simply refuse to have anything to do with the person who has given offence. It is up to the offender to realise what he has done wrong and to apologise.') However as Crouch points out, 'problems arise when outsiders are involved because they may not realise what it is that has caused offence in the first place, and the sulking sultan is not going to tell them'. So the question arises, in the conduct of the relationship was the problem a matter of cultural misunderstanding or was the indirect style of Malaysian diplomacy employed for hardnose political reasons to keep Australia off balance? The development of both crises indicates that it was a mixture of both.

Clearly the attempt by the Australian Government in both the *Embassy* and *Recalcitrant* episodes to deny that trade and diplomatic ties with Malaysia were under threat because no 'formal advice' had been received from the Malaysians only exacerbated the problem and left the initiative with Dr Mahathir. According to the 'cultural' interpretations outlined earlier, such a response, that is an unwillingness to acknowledge the problem/hurt, indicates a lack of regret and a devaluing of the relationship itself. This was certainly an element in the Malaysian response. The obstreperous Australians refused to recognise the problem so after four months into the *Embassy* affair the Malaysians upped the ante when on 14 March 1991 the Malaysian cabinet decided to suspend 'all non-essential cooperative projects with Australia'.[14] In the *Recalcitrant* affair the Australian Prime Minister Mr Keating compounded the problem by insisting for days on end there wasn't one. Mr Keating and his office portrayed the controversy as a 'media beat-up' and one where there was lots of 'background static' but nothing concrete from the main player concerned, Dr Mahathir. Alluding to the problem of different cultural or diplomatic styles Senator Evans was later to concede that 'we misread the signals about the intensity of the protest being registered by Malaysia'.[16]

It would be misleading, however, to ascribe Australia's apparent clumsy response to the Malaysian crises as being all due to 'cultural ignorance' or 'misreading the signals'. Here it is pertinent to note that of all Southeast Asia's elites few are more familiar with 'Western' manners and mores than Dr Mahathir and his cabinet colleagues, most of whom are English-educated. It should also be recalled that in May 1992 when Mr Hawke attempted to arrange a telephone call to speak with Dr Mahathir directly, Dr Mahathir was 'unavailable'.[17] (At a delicate stage in Malaysia/US relations a year earlier when President Bush attempted to phone Dr Mahathir the line in KL was again dead.) Moreover at a very early stage in the *Recalcitrant* crisis the Foreign

Minister Senator Evans moved quickly to place Mr Keating's *'Recalcitrant'* gaffe in context but the Malaysians chose to ignore it. Nevertheless in both crises Australia made two assumptions of 'cultural logic', neither of which were correct. They were first, if strains in the bilateral relationship were downplayed it was possible, as Senator Evans said, to 'work quietly and patiently' through the problem. Second, Australia assumed that tensions arising in one area of the relationship could be 'quarantined' from others, and that whatever difficulties we had with Malaysia could be 'quarantined' from other relationships in the region.

The first assumption, that tensions arising in one area of the relationship could be isolated from others, assumed that Australia's relationship with some countries of the Asian region were little different from those Australia has with the United States or the countries of Europe, where vigorous disputes in one area of a relationship does not disrupt other elements of it. However as the rocky period in Australia's relations with Indonesia from the mid-1970s to the mid-1980s showed, relationships with our neighbours are more 'porous'. This soon became apparent in the *Embassy* and *Recalcitrant* affairs as the Malaysian leadership, through third parties, quickly moved to increase the pressure on the Australian Government as first media contacts, then educational links, trade (threats of 'buy Australia last' campaigns) and finally defence ties under the Five Power Defence Arrangements (FPDA) were threatened. Indeed as Senator Evans later observed it was because 'the stain was spreading' (to all areas of the relationship) that it became imperative he undertake his 'high risk' visit to Kuala Lumpur in July 1991.

In both crises Malaysia's preparedness for 'the stain to spread' to a point where the relationship itself was put into question also highlighted its lack of symmetry. Australia's attempt to quarantine or contain the problem meant that Canberra was constantly on the backfoot and the burden of making the relationship work, or repairing it, fell entirely to us. In the course of the *Recalcitrant* saga Australia recognised the problem and changed its approach. After Keating's letter to Mahathir had been judged by the Malaysians as not sufficiently 'conciliatory', and his expression of 'regret' to Dr Mahathir on Channel 9's 'Sunday Program' was ignored, Keating made it clear he would not attempt to contact Dr Mahathir again. Keating also addressed the asymmetry in the relationship when he said he would like a good relationship with Dr Mahathir, 'But he's got to want it too'. Adding that, 'any relationship of substance and value requires commitment from both sides. For our part we are committed. We are willing to put in the effort necessary to keep the channels of communication open'.[18] More importantly Keating stressed that the issue had been 'blown out of proportion', and that both governments should 'act in a way which clearly draws a line under what has happened and avoid any further deterioration in the relationship or any slide into tit for tat retaliation'. 'Those last words were a clear warning that Australia would respond if further provoked'.[19] At the same time Senator Evans indicated that the Malaysians risked losing Australian investment and technology transfer and warned Malaysia against sending risky messages to regional investors. The Australian Government was also reported to be considering a range of options if Malaysia continued to escalate the crisis, including downgrading defence cooperation under the Five Power Defence Arrangement.[20] In short, Australia indicated that it would now play by the same rules as Malaysia and if Malaysia pursued a course of escalation, Australia's hitherto approach of 'containment' would no longer apply and the entire relationship would indeed be placed in question. At that point a number of Malaysian ministers counselled caution and it was reported that a group of influential businessmen from Australia, Malaysia and Singapore were also lobbying regional diplomats and their political contacts in a bid to break the diplomatic impasse.[21]

That ultimately Malaysia's approach would not be cost free[22] also had a regional dimension of which both Australia and Malaysia had to take account. Australia found that tensions with Malaysia could not be 'quarantined' from other relationships in Southeast Asia including, more importantly, the Government's broad objective of a greater interlocking with Asia across a broad band of policy interests. More specifically it threatened to impede progress in support of the Australian-initiated process of Asia Pacific Economic Cooperation (APEC) among the ASEAN states. A key element of Keating's drive into Asia was the cordial relationship he had forged with Indonesia's President Soeharto and the importance that relationship assumed with Indonesia as host of the next APEC forum. At that forum, and in the lead-up to it, Soeharto would be a key figure in supporting progress on APEC in the face of Dr Mahathir's resistance and determination to push his alternative concept of an East Asian Economic Caucus (EAEC). A complicating factor in that regard, however, was the difficult relationship between Soeharto and Mahathir; nevertheless in the spirit of ASEAN consensus Soeharto would have to accommodate Mahathir, to some degree at least. And in that regard the rift in Australia's relations with Malaysia only served to 'put more lead in Soeharto's saddle-bags' where Indonesian support for a more integrated APEC was concerned.[23]

Bilateral relations aside, Australia had, therefore, to consider wider implications for its interests in the region. Simply 'bringing down the shutters' or attempting to 'sit it out', as the British and Americans had done during various times when their relations with Malaysia had soured, were not options open to Australia. Senator Evans consulted widely in the region and was told it was in everyone's best interests that 'the problem' be fixed quickly. In the wake of the *Embassy* affair Evans revealed that 'our strategy in handling the Malaysian problem was premised all along on how it was playing in the region. If we had acted with wounded indignation it would have won us no points at all'.[24] There was a *quid pro quo*. By taking account of the regional 'vibes' the compliment was returned, in a sense, when at the height of the *Recalcitrant* crisis, barely eighteen months later, President Soeharto at a rather opportune point said he 'expected Dr Mahathir to attend the next APEC forum under the spirit of ASEAN cooperation among members of ASEAN'.[25] It was also apparent that Malaysia's ASEAN partners did not show any enthusiasm in supporting Malaysia's case in the latter episode, a factor which no doubt contributed to Malaysia's decision to end the row.[26]

In summary, while Australia misread some of the 'cultural' signals from Malaysia in the course of the *Embassy* and *Recalcitrant* crises, Malaysia was also not above 'mixing' the diplomatic and cultural signals and, when it suited, simply not playing the game—any game. Those crises also showed the 'porous' nature of Australia's bilateral relations with Malaysia and, by extension, with the region. While such 'porousness' required adjustment and accommodation on Australia's part, it also required adjustment on Malaysia's part, as Kuala Lumpur recognised that when Australia played the same game bilaterally and regionally it could not be isolated or dismissed as the 'odd man out in Asia'.

Domestic agendas: Malaysian celebration and Australian alienation

Culture and politics were also inextricably entwined in the contrasting approaches taken by the media and various interest groups in Australia and Malaysia in the course of the bilateral disputes. In Malaysia the rifts with Australia provided the opportunity for Malaysians irrespective of race or politics to celebrate Malaysian nationalism through common vilification of the foreigner. In describing such a response Senator Evans commented that 'in Malaysia when some real or perceived international slight is reported then—all things being equal— the media and just about all other interest groups tend to reflexively line up in defence of the person or institution being questioned'.[27] (Such a 'reflexive' national solidarity tends in the Australian case to be more limited, that is to criticisms by outsiders of such matters as Australian sporting ability or military prowess.)

So whereas the Malaysian body politic and community generally rallied in solidarity in the disputes with Australia, their Australian counterparts fragmented in acrimony. Gerard Henderson aptly characterised the Australian response in terms of the 'alienation industry' at work. Henderson argued that 'the diplomatic fallout was made much worse by a whole host of self-doubting Australian journalists, politicians and commentators. Some wanted a good story, others political revenge; still others felt the need for a cleansing ideological apology. In effect, all encouraged Dr Mahathir to go in harder—in spite of the fact that any deterioration in relations (would) damage Australia as well as Malaysia'.[28] In a somewhat similar vein Robison noted that 'for the political opposition, whoever it might be, it was an opportunity to score political points. For a broad range of the press, phrasing the question around the issue of apology was simple, dramatic news. Indeed, the Australian press constituted the instrument through which Mahathir played the quarry'.[29] A short survey of the role played by the media and various interest groups in the rifts with Malaysia shows how Malaysian 'celebration' and 'solidarity' contrasted with Australian 'alienation' and 'fragmentation', and how Malaysia was able to exploit the latter.

On the Malaysian side, nationalist solidarity and indignation went hand in hand with a degree of political opportunism. In both the *Embassy* and *Recalcitrant* affairs the UMNO Youth movement (the youth wing of the dominant partner in the ruling coalition) 'spearheaded' the Malaysian cause in calling for action against Australia. The perceived national slights at the hands of Australia provided of course an attractive opportunity for young and ambitious politicians to burnish their nationalist image. Tan Sri Rahim Tamby Chik, the newly elected head of UMNO Youth and Chief Minister of the State of Melaka, accused Australia (over the *Recalcitrant* slight) of 'harbouring evil intentions against Malaysia' and of issuing a 'challenge' to all its citizens.[30] Not to be outdone the deputy UMNO Youth leader Nazri Abdul Aziz said, 'We are giving Mr Keating seven days to apologise for ridiculing our leader, failing which we will strongly lobby the government . . . to adopt a "buy Australia last" campaign'.[31]

Domestic Malaysian politics played a role in other ways as well. This is not to suggest, as a number of Australian commentaries have, that Dr Mahathir needed an external issue to rouse national political feeling to shore up his position in UMNO.[32] Since the party split in 1987 Dr Mahathir had successfully established his clear dominance of the party. Nevertheless the rifts with Australia did provide an opportunity for some UMNO ministers who had been losing ground in the party to demonstrate 'loyalty' to the leader in the hope that such 'demonstrations' might improve their political stocks.[33] Some of the most prominent ministers in the 1993 anti-Australia campaign included Datuk Mohamed Rahmat, the Minister of Information, and Datuk Abu Hassan Omar, the Minister of Domestic Trade and Consumer Affairs. The political fortunes of these individuals in particular had been eroded by the rise of Anwar Ibrahim and his supporters in UMNO. Mohamed Rahmat was one of the first ministers to act when he ordered an immediate suspension of all broadcasting cooperation with Australia (then jeopardising deals being negotiated worth millions of dollars) and threatened 'further action'.[34] Abu Hassan Omar was also 'quick off the mark' and in his capacity as Minister of Domestic Trade and Consumer Affairs urged a boycott of Australian goods.[35]

Malaysian indignation was not confined to UMNO ministers. Other members of component parties of the National Front coalition government, as well as government and opposition leaders at state level, also rallied in support of Dr Mahathir. The president of the Malaysian Chinese Association (MCA), Datuk Ling Liong Sik, said Keating should apologise to Dr Mahathir and so did Samy Vellu, president of the Malaysian Indian Congress (MIC) who, as Minister for Energy, Posts and Telecommunications also instructed his ministry to 'review' trade and commercial ties with Australia.[36] Upping the ante the Premier of the Opposition Pan Malaysia Islamic Party (PAS-led) Kelantan state, Nik Abdul Aziz Nik Mat, asked, 'What do you expect of a leader whose forefathers were ex-convicts and social discards?' Even Karpal Singh, deputy chairman of the Opposition Democratic Action Party (DAP), weighed in and criticised Keatings 'misbehaviour' in the 'humiliation' of Dr Mahathir.[37] (Karpal Singh, a prominent civil rights lawyer was well known to Australians through his defence of the convicted drug offenders, Barlow and Chambers.)

As the *Recalcitrant* affair escalated it also became apparent however that some sections of the Malaysian Government were becoming concerned about the cost, as trade and defence links were imperilled, and counselled caution. Datin Seri Rafidah Aziz, the Minister for Trade and Industry, said the economic relationship should not be jeopardised and expressed concern that Malaysians who had business links with Australia would suffer.[38] The Defence Minister, Datuk Najib Tun Razak said Malaysia would maintain its defence ties with Australia under the Five Power Defence Arrangements,[39] and while some sections of the Malaysian media gave vent to some emotional editorialising,[40] the influential *New Straits Times* advised restraint and reconciliation. The paper's editor-in-chief, Kadir Yasin, a close confidante of Anwar Ibrahim, warned of the effects on trade: 'we must question the wisdom of tit-for-tat action . . . the faster this problem is sorted out the better' he said.[41]

As noted earlier, for Australians the rifts with Malaysia provoked fragmentation and acrimony as individuals and groups in politics, the media and the community sought to score points or advance a variety of agendas. After the experience of the *Embassy* affair the Federal Opposition initially appeared to support Mr Keating with comments that his frustration was 'understandable', and that a 'little blunt talking' about Dr Mahathir's approach to APEC was warranted. Very quickly however *Recalcitrant* was just too good an opportunity to score a few points against the government so Dr Hewson accused Mr Keating of developing an international reputation as the 'ugly Australian'.[42] But as the crisis quickly escalated it was apparent that the Opposition was at least as flummoxed as the Government and could offer no other advice except to 'pick up the phone' and 'not to grovel',[43] advice that took little account of the recent results of such diplomacy with Kuala Lumpur. The state premiers of Victoria and Western Australia also joined in the fray, with the latter even going so far as to write to Dr Mahathir, to distance himself from his own Prime Minister and stress the good relations between his state and Malaysia![44]

While community attitudes in the *Embassy* affair reflected very much the media's obsession as to whether Australia should 'apologise/grovel or not to this man' (Dr Mahathir), during the *Recalcitrant* saga they generally reflected individual views of the Prime Minister. Some at least were not without humour.[45] In both affairs 'business' was a united and influential lobby for the resolution of the rifts. Although Australian investment in Malaysia was small compared to total foreign investment it was growing significantly.[46] More importantly, however, individual companies stood to make huge losses[47] prompting the Australia–Malaysia Business Council and a plethora of individual companies and businessmen to lobby the Foreign Minister and the Prime Minister privately and through the press.

What role did the Australian media play? As suggested earlier it became the principal instrument through which Dr Mahathir was able to orchestrate the *Embassy* and *Recalcitrant* affairs and highlight the division and rancour in the Australian response. With some notable exceptions, an overview of the *Embassy* saga prompts a conclusion broadly in line with Senator Evans', view that there were only two stories, 'One was the row story and the other was the kow tow story'.[48] In his attempt to diffuse the *Embassy* rift Senator Evans delivered a carefully crafted speech in Kuala Lumpur on relations between the Australian Government and the media. In the speech he acknowledged grounds for Malaysian offence but did not resile from principles of Australia's own political and social culture where the independence of government–media relations were concerned.

In the *Recalcitrant* affair the journalists and TV crews that trailed around KL after Dr Mahathir or members of UMNO Youth with leading questions of the 'how righteously angry is Dr Mahathir' variety, encouraged the Malaysians to go in harder.[49] But also, by not lodging an official protest/boycott or by indicating directly the nature of the offence/s or manner of their reconciliation, Dr Mahathir incited 'third parties' in Malaysia as well as the Australian media to set the tone and parameters of the debate. Such a tactic permitted Dr Mahathir to largely retain the initiative in the disputes both in terms of their level and duration; it also allowed him to remain in the background, unscathed and claim somewhat disingenuously that 'It was (all) the people's feelings' and that he had no 'genuine control of that'.[50] At the same time the variety of signals that emerged from KL as a result sowed confusion in Australian ranks and made a coherent Australian response almost impossible. 'From the Malaysian end it worked brilliantly. Australia's Malaysia relationship was suffering a death of a thousand cuts'.[51]

While the Australian media and Australian 'alienation' facilitated Dr Mahathir's capacity to keep the pressure on the Hawke and later Keating Governments, in 1993 these two elements also provided a face-saving way for Malaysia to end the rift quickly when the *Recalcitrant* affair threatened to spin out of control and bring a total rupture of relations. Dr Mahathir said he had decided to end the row because of the 'reactions of Australians in general to the remarks of their Prime Minister'.[52] This was an apparent reference to Australian opinion polls that showed many Australians believed Mr Keating should apologise to Dr Mahathir. As the polls largely reflected the electorate's attitude to Keating rather than the 'Malaysian question' *per se*, was Dr Mahathir's interpretation a case of 'cultural misunderstanding' or just shrewd politics?

In 1991 and 1993 important interests in the Australia–Malaysia relationship were in danger of being outflanked and derailed by the stimulation in both countries of a variety of temporary and peripheral interests, some in the media, some in politics, and some in the community. Clearly there was fault on both sides. It is doubtful for instance whether Mr Keating would have called President Clinton, Prime Minister Major or President Kohl 'recalcitrant'. (By contrast President Clinton, who was after all the host of the Seattle APEC summit meeting, observed a studied silence, and refused to be drawn by Mahathir's jibe that, 'perhaps you have to thumb your nose at people before they notice you'.) At the same time such provocative remarks and Dr Mahathir's 'sulks' and massive retaliation strategies are clearly at variance with the norms of acceptable diplomatic practice. In that regard Australia has by no means been the only target of Mahathir's confrontational style of diplomacy. Japan, Britain, the United States, Indonesia and Singapore, that is countries of both the

'East' and 'West', have all at various times been the targets of
Mahathir's ire and irascible style. However as the *Recalcitrant* affair
showed, investors, both Malaysian and foreign, have become increasingly impatient with the costs of such confrontational behaviour and
an important influence for moderation and restraint where Malaysian
diplomatic excess is concerned.

Australia–Malaysia relations and the 'Asia debate'

In retrospect there was a positive side to the rifts with Malaysia for,
to misquote Dr Johnson, they concentrated Australian minds on our
identity and place in the region 'most wonderfully'. At a conceptual
level those disputes dispelled much of the fog and confusion that
surrounded the so-called 'Asia debate', and at a policy level they
showed some of the complexities and compromises necessarily
involved in our being a regional player. The two of course are closely
connected.

The rifts with Malaysia stimulated the 'myth-makers' and the
'alienators' on both sides of the relationship. In the *Embassy* and
Recalcitrant affairs Dr Mahathir invoked an image of a monolithic
'Asia' and 'Asian values' and sought to perpetuate a false dichotomy
between Australia and the region that permitted only conditional (Australian) membership of it. In his view there 'might' be room for
Australia in the region provided it understood that by being Asian it
had to be 'culturally Asian'.[53] But by implication only he could define
what 'culturally Asian' meant, whether in terms of conduct or policy,
and doubtless the definition could change according to his convenience
or policy objectives. On that note Mr Keating's *Recalcitrant* gaffe,
coming when it did after the Seattle APEC summit where Dr
Mahathir's alternative and exclusively Asian regional association
(EAEC) had for the moment at least been sidelined, played straight
into his hands. 'Australia's claim that it was part of Asia' said Dr
Mahathir was meaningless 'because Australians do not have the values
of respect and manners that Asians do'.[54]

Not surprisingly Dr Mahathir's views of 'Asia', and Australia's
problematic relationship with it, were echoed by some sections of the
Malaysian media and analysts in government-related think tanks. M.G.
Pillai in an article headed 'Is Australia ready to be truly Asian?'[55] said
that 'Australia should fit in consciously with the political and cultural
"presumptions" of the region', though he was less than specific as to
what those 'presumptions' were. In similar vein, Samuel Huntington's
controversial article, 'The Clash of Civilizations?'[56] was given a good
deal of resonance in Malaysia as some of its principal themes gave

comfort to Dr Mahathir's views on 'Asianess' and an East/West divide which, by implication, marginalised Australia in the region.

So Dr Noordin Sopiee, Director of Malaysia's Institute of Strategic and International Studies (ISIS), wrote of the contradiction between the cultural and value systems of the United States and Western Europe and those of East Asia.[57] In an interview with an Australian journalist[58] Noordin invoked the stereotype of Malay culture as consensual and group-oriented as opposed to the materialism, individualism and adversarial ways of the West. 'Malaysians', he said, 'took great heed of the village model—where everything is debated until consensus is reached: We think we shouldn't quarrel like Western people do!' This was an extraordinary assertion which ignored important contemporary Malaysian realities most notably the pervasiveness of materialism ('money politics') in Malay politics and society, a development that contributed to the bitter divisions that split UMNO, the dominant Malay party in the ruling coalition government for much of the 1980s as rival groups struggled for power and the patronage associated with it.[59] However, notwithstanding the weak basis of Noordin's consensus/adversarial–Asia/West dichotomy, the most important factor revealed by the debate was the way in which the issue was mobilised by domestic political groups in Australia for other agendas.

On the Australian side the rifts with Malaysia reactivated the ideologues or 'mythmakers' of left and right, and the 'alienators'. As to the 'mythmakers', Robison has argued that 'conservatives play the culture game because they can use the anti-liberal and anti-democratic arguments in their domestic ideological battles (economic development requires authoritarian rule and so on)'. 'Ironically', he notes, but for quite different reasons, 'the liberal Left is also sympathetic to cultural relativist arguments—they are used to combat orientalist and racist ideas—a dangerous path to tread'.[60] The 'alienators' also find succour in outmoded images of their own society and of 'Asia' as a monolith where immutable cultural differences predispose or freeze societies in absolutist or authoritarian moulds. Professor Blainey, perhaps representative of the 'alienators', took the 'Asia as a monolith' approach to extremes in his query as to whether Mr Keating wanted Australians to 'borrow China's ideas on civil liberties, Indonesia's attitude to democracy or Malaysia's attitude to Islam'.[61] (The latter observation was particularly silly and highlighted Blainey's own ignorance concerning the generally moderate corpus of beliefs and practice associated with Islam in Malaysia and the strong action the Malaysian Government has taken against so-called 'extremist' or 'fundamentalist' sects.) Like Blainey, Owen Harries properly railed loudly against the naivety of airy propositions about 'making Australia part of Asia', but then proceeded to dismiss any notion of a differentiated Asia to which

Australia could relate. Also drawing on the Huntington thesis, Harries argued that 'Australians would have to accept that the only choice they had was a limited one between the two branches—European and North American—of Western civilisation'.[62]

The 'mythmakers' of left and right and the 'alienators' all facilitated Dr Mahathir's capacity to confront and castigate Australia as the 'outsider' that *ipso facto* was culturally insensitive to 'Asia' and which, almost by definition, could not handle complicated Asian relationships. The self-doubt, dissension, and at times clumsiness that marked the Australian response to the Malaysian crises seemed to validate Mahathir's 'proposition' about Australia's 'un-Asian' way of conducting relationships in the region. (Notwithstanding of course his own record of abrasiveness in dealings with regional neighbours.) But again Australia played into his hands when Senator Evans attempted to give a 'cultural explanation' for the severity of the *Recalcitrant* affair by suggesting that the Malay translation of 'recalcitrant' was *kurang ajar*. *Kurang ajar* would indeed have been offensive but the translation was far from accurate.[63] Nevertheless Dr Mahathir's 'cultural challenges' showed the woolliness of much Australian thinking in the so-called 'Asia debate' and the destructive nature of it. In that regard he probably served as a good catalyst for a firm and clear affirmation of Australia's views of itself and its relationship with the region, which became the subject of Paul Keating's Asialink lecture.

In that lecture, in which Mr Keating expressed regret about the *Recalcitrant* gaffe, he also met head-on Dr Mahathir's challenge of Australians not being Asians. He said:

> Claims that the Government is attempting to turn Australia into an
> 'Asian country' are based on a misunderstanding both of my own
> approach and the direction of government policy . . . Put simply,
> Australia is not and never can be an 'Asian nation' any more than we
> can—or want to be—European or North American or African. We can
> only be Australian and can only relate to our friends and neighbours as
> Australians. We go to Asia 'as we are'. Not with the ghost of empire
> about us. Not as a vicar of Europe or as a US deputy . . .[64]

As noted earlier, a key factor behind the bilateral tensions generated by the *Recalcitrant* affair were the sharp differences of view between Australia and Malaysia concerning the character and evolution of APEC and Malaysia's counter-proposal, the East Asian Economic Caucus (EAEC). A considered examination of the origins and development of APEC and EAEC and their implications for the bilateral relationship is beyond the scope of this chapter, but if Australia is to avoid any perception as 'Western vicar' or 'US deputy', statements such as that by the Minister of Trade, Senator Bob McMullan—that 'Australia would not join EAEC, even if asked', and that we objected to it 'in principle'—would not seem helpful. Besides, EAEC cannot be dismissed as totally wrong-headed or as nothing more than the vehicle of Dr Mahathir's regional ambitions. It does reflect important concerns and reservations other countries in East and Southeast Asia have about the evolution of APEC and in particular its domination by the United States and Washington's own economic agenda.[65] Moreover, neither the Japanese nor the Canadians, who also hold deep reservations about EAEC, have felt the need to 'go public' in the region in the same blunt manner that Australia has.

But notions of US deputy aside, the rifts with Malaysia have had another more important lesson for Australia: they have shown the need for Australian policymakers to keep options open and generally be more delphic in cultivating and maintaining relationships at a number of levels with countries in the region. In that regard it is pertinent to recall that at the height of the *Recalcitrant* crisis, when Mahathir was attempting to sideline Australia from the region because we were not 'culturally Asian', the Thai Deputy Prime Minister, Supachai Panichpakdi, proposed that both EAEC and AFTA (the Asian Free Trade Association) be open to Australia. While APEC may well be the best vehicle for the pursuit of Australian interests in the region it would seem prudent not to disregard such invitations or totally discount other options.

Conclusion

In exposing some of the assumptions Australia had about the relationship with Malaysia, and bringing certain Malaysian responses into the open, the *Embassy* and *Recalcitrant* crises might, in retrospect, be seen as providing a long overdue and necessary catharsis for the relationship. In the course of both crises cultural explanations loomed large in divining the reason for Malaysian political behaviour and the Malaysian response. Cultural values and styles were obviously important factors in the generation of bilateral tensions and in the difficulties associated with their resolution. At the same time, however, this chapter has sought to caution against the loose employment of 'culture' or cultural explanations without the user also being aware that 'culture' may be invoked for a variety of other purposes. At some points charges of cultural insensitivity were a useful ploy for Dr Mahathir to keep Australia off balance and marginalised as a player in the region, particularly as he sought to achieve his own vision of Asia's future through the EAEC in which he expected to play a key role. At other points it was apparent that culture and *Realpolitik* were closely, if not inextricably, intertwined. Yet on other occasions cultural explanations, *kurang ajar,* were in danger of being the means to an easy 'cop-out', a 'quick fix' in preference to more sophisticated analysis of the often complex mix of political, social and economic interests driving certain Malaysian policies and responses. Ultimately the *Embassy* and *Recalcitrant* affairs showed that it was time to put the idea of worrying as to whether or not we were part of Asia behind us. We have important cultural and other differences with Malaysia, just as Malaysia has with Thailand, Singapore, Indonesia and others. Malaysia is part of the region and so is Australia.

In the wake of the *Recalcitrant* affair Australia emphasised that while committed to a constructive relationship with Malaysia, that commitment must be reciprocated. At the same time the Australian Government has, in Senator Evans' words, 'sought to put more ballast' in the relationship through the promotion of a complex network of relationships in a wide variety of areas at both government and non-government level. Such ballast, it is hoped, will in future contain and prevent differences whether at a personal or policy level from damaging the relationship as a whole. While in future the bilateral relationship with Malaysia may be subsumed in APEC and other regional networks, it is already apparent that the dynamics of the relationship are being increasingly driven by a hard-headed mutual appreciation of self-interest, especially in the areas of trade, education and defence cooperation. Of particular importance in that regard are the commercial needs of the growing business relationship and the capacity of business in both countries to play a key role in determining the parameters of the relationship while moderating the volatility that has so often destabilised it in the past.

Notes

1 Boyce, Peter, 'Australia and Malaysia: A Preliminary Study in Commonwealth Regional Relations, 1941–1961, PhD Dissertation, Microfilms International, Ann Arbor, Duke University, Michigan, 1962.
2 *Australian*, 16 March 1979.
3 Crouch, Harold, 1996 (forthcoming).
4 *Embassy* was set in an Australian diplomatic mission located in a fictitious Islamic multi-racial country called 'Ragaan'. It is beyond the scope of this chapter to consider *Embassy* as a cultural construct but it is pertinent to recall that it was one incident in particular that provoked Malaysian ire. In the second episode of the series, Australian diplomats were shown laughing about a Ragaani government minister who responded to the influx of Vietnamese boat people on Malaysian shores by saying, 'We will shoot them', but who after an international outcry it was claimed he said, 'We will shoo them'. This replicated an incident in 1978 involving Dr Mahathir when he was Deputy Prime Minister. As

large numbers of refugees continued to land on Malaysian shores, Mahathir, in understandable exasperation at criticism of his action in having boats turned away, apparently said, 'What do you want me to do, shoot them?' a remark intended to provoke the world into shouldering a share of the global responsibility for refugees (*New Straits Times*, 4 July 1991). When only the words, 'shoot them'were quoted and splashed around the world, it was not Dr Mahathir but another minister, Tan Sri Ghazali Shafie, who claimed that Dr Mahathir had said 'shoo' and not 'shoot' (*New Straits Times*, 4 July 1991). Other aspects of *Embassy* also indicated Malaysian connections. In a fuzzy map appearing in the first episode, Ragaan was not only located in Southeast Asia, but in a bulge halfway down the Malay peninsula between Thailand and Malaysia, and among the list of credits as an adviser to the program was Garry Woodard, a recently retired Australian High Commissioner to Malaysia. *Embassy* as 'a social construct' is considered by Kelly (1994); Kessler (1991, pp. 57–73, 125–131,194); Mitchell (1993, pp. 256–76; and Perera (1993, p. 29).

5 *Age*, 15 March 1991.

6 *Age*, 19 Oct. 1991.

7 Shortly thereafter in February 1992 an Australian film, *Turtle Beach*, which was set in Malaysia, was released. A scene in the film showed the massacre of a boatload of Vietnamese refugees by Malay villagers. The incident, for which there was no historical basis, was offensive to the Malaysians. In terms of the Harare agreement, the Australian Government dissociated itself from the film (which had received some government funding) and the relationship with Malaysia was undisturbed.

8 See Note 3 above.

9 Dr Mahathir's already jaundiced view of Australia was not helped by an article in the *Financial Review* on 19 November just before Keating's recalcitrant comment. The article described Mahathir, who is of part-Indian descent, as a mamak which, as Crouch points out, is rather like describing an Australian of part-Italian descent as a 'dago'. See Crouch, H., 'Malaysia 1993', *Asia–Australia Survey 1994*, ed. R. Trood, Macmillan, Sydney, 1994, p. 7.

10 *Financial Review*, 23 Sept. 1993.

11 *Financial Review*, 3 Dec. 1993.

12 *Canberra Times*, 9 Dec. 1993.

13 Kessler, Clive, 'Keating's Blunder: Three Lessons', *Asian Studies Review*, vol. 17, no. 3, 1994, pp. 125–131.

14 *SMH*, 17 April 1991.

15 *Age*, 15 March 1991.

16 *Canberra Times*, 9 Dec. 1994.

17 In early April 1991, staff at the Australian High Commission in Kuala Lumpur tried over two days to arrange the call with Dr Mahathir's office but according to government sources were 'stuffed about' (*Age*, 12 April 1991).

18 *Canberra Times*, 9 Dec. 1993.

19 Sheridan, Greg, 'Relations on Brink of Crisis as Officials Await Malaysia's Answer', *Australian*, 4–5 December 1993.

20 *Australian*, 4 Dec. 1993

21 *Financial Review*, 9 Nov. 1993

22 In December 1993 the Australian Bureau of Statistics released information that may have given the Malaysians pause for thought about a trade ban on Australia. Statistics showed that Malaysian exports to Australia in October topped $100 million for the first time. Moreover in the first four months of the financial year 1993/94, imports from Malaysia rose 17 per cent to $380 million, with biggest increases in imports of TVs and radios, computers and steel (*Age,* 7 Dec. 1993).

23 Mackie, Jamie, 'The Mahathir–Keating Spat', *Canberra Times,* 7 December 1993.

24 *Australian*, 3 April 1991.

25 *Age*, 30 Jan. 1993.

26 In that regard Australian officials revealed that private 'positive' messages had come from ASEAN countries during the row (*Canberra Times,* 9 Dec. 1993).

27 *Australian*, 9 Dec. 1993.

28 *SMH*, Dec. 1993.

29 *Australian*, 14 Dec. 1993.

30 *Australian*, 29 Nov. 1993.

31 *Financial Review*, 25 Jan. 1993.

32 The most blatant example of such misinterpretation was provided by an editorial in the *Financial Review* (3 Dec. 1993) headed 'The Politics of Keating's apology' which claimed that whether or not Dr Mahathir would accept Keating's apology would be a calculation 'heavily influenced by the realities of Malaysian power politics and the pressure now on Dr Mahathir from his deputy and rival, Anwar Ibrahim'.

33 This point is also made by Crouch in his country paper on Malaysia in *Asia-Australia Survey 1994*, Trood, R. (ed.) Macmillan.

34 *Business Times*, 2 Dec. 1993.

35 *SMH*, 6 Dec. 1993.

36 *Financial Review*, 3 Dec. 1993.

37 *Financial Review*, 30 Nov. 1993.

38 *Star*, 11 Dec. 1993.

39 Datuk Najib's position seemed to shift somewhat according to the prevailing political winds. In the second week of the crisis, statements attributed to Najib suggested that the $3 billion bid by the Australian company Transfield to build patrol vessels for the Malaysian navy might be threatened by the row. Keating was reportedly 'incandescent' with rage when he saw the statements and sought 'clarification' (*Australian,* 4–5 Dec. 1993).

40 One of the most strident editorials appeared in the *Business Times*, 26 December 1993, which said that 'Whatever Australia's problems, it should not descend to the level of the gutter, which is not an unfamiliar place for it . . . if we were to dwell on Australia's antecedents, its roots, we will be having a veritable feast, no an orgy . . .'.

41 *SMH*, 6 Dec. 1993.
42 *Canberra Times*, 3 Dec. 1993.
43 *SMH*, 6 Dec. 1993.
44 *Australian*, 29 Nov. 1993.
45 For instance, 'Letters to the Editor' (*SMH*, 29 Nov. 1993) contained this little gem from David Ash of Bondi Beach: 'How dare a senior Malaysian politician suggest that Mr Keating is "ill-mannered" and "uneducated". What a scumbag.'
46 By December 1993 trade between Australia and Malaysia totalled $2.4 billion. Malaysia was Australia's third largest export market in ASEAN, the 11th largest overall and the 14th largest source of imports.
47 Potential losses included a $3 billion contract to supply patrol boats for the Malaysian Navy as well as large contracts for a $400 million power station, a $60 million electricity transmission project and a $100 million port project. See *Australian Financial Review*, 8 December 1993, 'Business pays the price'.
48 The speech (Evans, 1991 'Australia and Malaysia: Doing more together') was largely ignored by much of the Australian media or dismissed as 'Evans in kow tow mode'. See *Age* 26 July 1991. A few headlines give the flavour of much of the media coverage of the Embassy affair: 'Diplomacy not toadying' (*Australian Financial Review*, 24 July 1991); 'Kowtowing to KL' (*West Australian*, 25 July 1991); 'Evans says sorry— for what?' (*Age*, 25 July 1991); 'There there we didn't mean it, no need to sulk' (*Canberra Times*, 26 July 1991).
49 At some points the behaviour of some members of the media touched on the absurd. Henderson gives the example of an excited Philip Williams asking Dr Mahathir when he would be reading Mr Keating's personal letter. He replied: 'Well, when I get the letter'. (*SMH*, 7 Dec. 1993).
50 *SMH*, 9 Dec. 1993.
51 Mills, *Financial Review*, 3 Dec. 1993.
52 *SMH*, 13 Dec. 1993.
53 *Financial Review*, 19 Nov. 1993.
54 *Canberra Times*, 25 Nov. 1993.
55 *Australian*, 4 May 1993.
56 *Foreign Affairs*, vol. 72, no. 3, Summer 1993.
57 Noordin Sopiee, 'The New World Order: Implications for the Asia-Pacific', in Mahmood, Rohana & Sani, Rustam A. (eds), *Confidence Building and Conflict Reduction in the Pacific*, Institute of Strategic and International Studies, Kuala Lumpur, 1993, pp. 3–29.
58 See Bron Sibree, 'A KL view: Asian is as Asia does' (*Canberra Times*, 2 August 1993).
59 The split in UMNO in the late 1980s was in large part a consequence of the rapid social and economic change in Malay society in the 1970s and 1980s and, in particular, the rapid growth of a Malay middle class. That change had implications for the divisiveness of UMNO politics at two levels. On the one hand, traditional Malay notions of respect for hierarchy and authority, associated with the party's former rural/peasant

base, held less sway among members of the new Malay middle class. At a second level, under Malaysia's New Economic Policy (NEP), an affirmative government program to promote Malays in the modern sector of the economy, political power had become synonymous with business opportunities such as contracts, licences and so on. The growing nexus between power and patronage thus also spurred divisions in UMNO as individuals and groups struggled for the rewards of office.

60 *Australian*, 14 Dec. 1993.

61 ibid.

62 *Australian*, 3–4 April, 1993.

63 Senator Evans told the Senate that 'the Malay word for recalcitrant was *kurang ajar*, to call someone *kurang ajar* is in fact extremely insulting, much more than the use of the English word would indicate'. Senator Evans added that the phrase *kurang ajar* meant in Malay that one was ill-educated. 'It reflects seriously on one's background and family, implying that one's parents did not bring one up properly' (*Canberra Times*, 7 December 1993). A closer translation of recalcitrant would be *kepala batu* or *keras kepala* terms that suggest qualities more along the lines of being 'strong-willed'.

64 Keating, Paul, 'The Inaugural Sir Edward "Weary" Dunlop Asialink Lecture', Melbourne, 8 December 1993, mimeograph, p. 10.

65 Both APEC and EAEC have evolved considerably since their formation in 1989 and 1990 respectively. In that regard a number of commentators have noted how Mr Hawke's original APEC proposal, which had excluded the United States, was strikingly similar to Mahathir's later concept (Crouch, 1994, p. 9). As the original character of APEC changed, there was some concern in the ASEAN countries that the development of APEC might supersede ASEAN which had only made slow progress where economic cooperation was concerned. The apprehension expressed by Dr Mahathir about the institutionalisation of APEC, and its domination by the United States and Washington's economic agenda, were shared to a greater or lesser degree by many of his colleagues in the Asian region. Such concerns were not without foundation. Although defeated, a report by the so-called Eminent Persons Group at the Seattle meeting proposed to change the 'C' in APEC from 'cooperation' to 'community'. While the APEC heads-of-government meeting in Seattle opted for APEC remaining as a loose consultative body, the United States, or certainly influential figures in the formulation of US Asia policy, such as C. Fred Bergsten, have continued to see APEC 'operating as a discriminatory trade bloc in a way that directly conflicts with the original concept successfully pressed by Australia' (Wood, *Australian*, 28 June 1994). Australia, in 'pushing at the edges of the APEC envelope' may therefore need to take some care that in doing so it does not appear to be facilitating, albeit indirectly, US interests and thus fit the perception that Mahathir suspects, that of a US deputy.

Further References

Bell, Daniel, *Communitarianism and its Critics,* Oxford University Press, London, 1993.

Bloodworth, Denis, *The Tiger and the Trojan Horse,* Times International Press, Singapore, 1986.

Brown, David, 'The Corporatist Management of Ethnicity in Contemporary Singapore', *Singapore Changes Guard,* ed. G. Rodan, Longman Cheshire, Melbourne, 1993.

Camroux, David, 'Looking East And Defining Inwards: Malaysia as a Self-Conscious Middle Power During The Mahathir Era, 1981–1993' forthcoming monograph for CSAAR Australia–Asia Papers Series, Griffith University, mimeograph, 1993.

Case, William, 'Comparative Malaysian Leadership: Tunku Abdul Rahman and Mahathir Mohamed', *Asian Survey* 31, 5 May 1991, pp. 456–73.

Castells, Manuel, 'The Development City-Sity in an Open World Economy: the Singapore Experience', BRIE Working Paper no. 31, University of California, Berkeley, 1988.

Chan, Heng Chee, *Singapore: The Politics of Survival,* Oxford University Press, Singapore, 1971.

——'Democracy, Human Rights and Social Justice: What Comes First?', *Straits Times,* 22 November 1992.

Chua, Beng Huat, 'Singapore in 1981: Problems in New Beginnings', *Southeast Asian Affairs 1982,* Institute of Southeast Asian Studies, Singapore, 1982.

——'Pragmatism of the PAP Government in Singapore: a Critical Assessment', *Southeast Asian Journal of Social Sciences,* vol. 13, 1986, pp. 29–46.

——'Not Depoliticized but Ideologically Successful: the Public Housing Program in Singapore', *International Journal of Urban and Regional Research,* vol. 15, 1991, pp. 24–41.

——'Australian and Asian Perception of Human Rights', *Australia's Human Rights Diplomacy,* eds I. Russell, P. van Ness & B. H. Chua, Australian National University, Canberra, 1992.

——*Communitarian Ideology and Democracy in Singapore,* Routledge, London, 1995.

Clammer, John, *Singapore: Ideology, Society and Culture,* Chopman Publishers, Singapore, 1985.

Crouch, Harold, 'Mahathir's *Merajuk* Calls for Australian Patience', *Sydney Morning Herald,* 17 April 1991.

——'Malaysia: Neither Authoritarian Nor Democratic', *Southeast Asia in the 1990s: Authoritarianism, Democracy and Capitalism,* eds K. Hewison, R. Robison & G. Rodan, Allen & Unwin, Sydney, 1993, pp. 133–57.

Devan, Janadas, 'Why Singapore Always Looks to Future', *Straits Times,* 12 August 1994.

Drysdale, John, *Singapore: Struggle for Success,* Times Books International, Singapore, 1984.

Evans, Gareth, 'Australia and Malaysia: Doing More Together', Address to Malaysia–Australia Business Council Dinner, Kuala Lumpur, 22 July 1991, mimeograph.

82   *Pathways to Asia*

FitzGerald, Stephen, 'Ethical Dimensions of Australia's Engagement with Asian Countries. Are there any?' The St James Ethic Centre Annual Lecture, 9 November 1993.

Harries, Owen, 'Clash of Civilisations', *Australian,* 3–4 April 1993.

Henderson, Gerard, 'How the Oz media made Mahathir really recalcitrant', *Sydney Morning Herald,* 7 December 1993.

Higgot, Richard, 'The Politics of Australia's International Economic Relations: Adjustment and the Politics of Two-Level Games', *Australian Journal of Political Science,* vol. 26, 1991, pp. 2–28.

——'APEC: A Sceptical View', paper given to the conference on Economic Security and Cooperation in the Asia Pacific: Agenda for the 1990s, Canberra, 28–30 July 1993, mimeograph.

Huntington, Samuel, 'The Clash of Civilizations?' *Foreign Affairs,* vol. 27, no. 3, Summer 1993, pp. 22–49.

Keating, Paul, 'Australia and Asia, Knowing Who We Are', Speech at the Asia Australia Institute, Sydney, 7 April 1993, in P. Keating, *Major Speeches of the First Year,* Australian Labor Party, Canberra, pp. 35–44.

Kelly, Patricia, 'Embassy: Engaging With Difference', unpublished MA dissertation (Literature and Communication), Murdoch University, Western Australia, 1994.

Kemeny, J., *Housing and Social Theory,* Routledge, London, 1992.

Kessler, Clive, 'Negotiating Cultural Difference: on seeking, not always successfully, to share the world with others—or in defence of "Embassy" ', *Asian Studies Review,* vol.15, no. 2, 1991, pp. 57–73.

——'Archaism and Modernity: Contemporary Malay Political Culture', *Fragmented Vision: Culture and Politics in Contemporary Malaysia,* eds J. Kahn & F.K.W. Loh, Allen & Unwin, Sydney, pp. 133–57.

Koh, Tommy T.B., 'The Ten Values that Undergird East Asian Strength and Success', *International Herald Tribune,* 11–12 December 1993.

Kuo, Eddie C.Y., 'Confucianism as Political Discourse in Singapore: the Case of an Incomplete Revitalisation Movement', Working Paper no 113, Department of Sociology, National University of Singapore.

Kuo, Eddie C.Y., Quah, Jon & Tong, Chee Kiong, *Religion and Religious Revivalism in Singapore,* Ministry of Community Development, Singapore, 1988.

Lee, Kuan Yew, *The Battle for Merger,* Ministry of Culture, Singapore, 1962.

Mohamad, Mahathir, 'Future of Regional Groupings', Address at the Foreign Correspondents Club, Hong Kong, 14 October 1992, mimeograph.

——'No Place for Religious Fanatics', translation of a speech to the UMNO General Assembly, Kuala Lumpur, *New Straits Times,* 7 November 1992.

——Statement at the Plenary of the Forty-Eighth Session of the United Nations General Assembly, New York, 1 October 1993.

Milner, Anthony, 'Inventing Politics: The Case of Malaysia', *Past and Present,* no. 132, August 1991, pp. 265–76.

Mitchell, Tony, 'Orientalism in Ragaan: Embassy's Imaginative Geography', *Meanjin,* vol. 52, no. 2, 1993, pp. 265–76.

Murdoch, Lindsay, 'Mahathir Eyes the Olive Branch', *Sydney Morning Herald,* 4 December 1993.

Noordin, Sopiee, 'The New World Order: Implications for the Asia-Pacific', *Confidence Building and Conflict Reduction in the Pacific*, eds R. Mahmood & S. Rustam, Institute of Strategic and International Studies, Kuala Lumpur, 1993, pp. 3–29.

——'Malaysia's Visionary Plan Was "Born of Consensus" ', Interview in *Asian Business Review*, September 1993.

——'Asia Is As Asia Does', Interview with Bron Sibree, *Canberra Times*, 2 August 1993.

Parkinson, Tony, 'Gareth's Malaise', *The Australian*, 3–4 August 1991.

Ram, Kalpana,'Modernist Anthropology's Comparative Project: the Construction of Indian Identity in Tradition', *Modernity and Identity: Asian Illustrations*, ed. A. Gomes, LaTrobe University Press, Melbourne, 1994.

Robison, Richard, 'Mahathir Paints False Picture of Asian Region', *Australian*, 14 December 1993.

Rodan, Garry, 'The Growth of Singapore's Middle Class and its Political Significance', *Singapore Changes Guard*, ed. G. Rodan, Longman Cheshire, Melbourne, 1993.

Said, Edward W., *Orientalism*, Penguin Books, Harmondsworth, 1978.

Seah, Chee Meow, *Trends in Singapore*, Institute of Southeast Asian Studies, Singapore, 1975.

Shamsul, A.B., *Malaysia in 2020—One State Many Nations? Observing Malaysia from Australia*, Seventh James C. Jackson Memorial Lecture, Malaysia Society of the Asian Studies Association of Australia, Universiti Kebangsaan Malaysia, Malaysia, 1992.

——'Australia-Malaysia Relations: "The Negotiation of Cultural Difference": Where Do We Go From Here?', *Asian Studies Review*, vol. 16, no. 3, 1993, pp. 35–45.

Sheridan, Greg, 'Turtle Beach . . . Total Breach? The Next Flashpoint with Malaysia', *Australian*, 26–27 October 1991.

——'One Perfect Whipping Boy for Malaysia', *Australian*, 6 November 1991.

——'Why APEC Will Miss Mahathir', *Australian*, 14 October 1993.

——'Asia Shows There's Life Outside Westminster', *Australian*, 14 April 1993.

——'We're Locking Ourselves Out of Key Asian Body', *Australian*, 4 May 1994.

Stubbs, Richard, 'The Foreign Policy of Malaysia', *The Political Economy of Foreign Policy in Southeast Asia*, eds B. Burton & D. Wurfel, Macmillan, London, 1990, pp. 101–23.

Tu Wei-Ming, 'Confucianism and Human Rights'. Inaugural lecture for the Wu Teh Yao Memorial Lecture Series, 21 March 1995, Singapore.

Vatikiotis, Michael, 'The Mahathir Paradox', *Far Eastern Economic Review*, 20 August 1992.

——'Young Turks on the Move', *Far Eastern Economic Review*, 30 September 1993.

Wark, McKenzie, 'Blunders of a Nation In Search of Identity', *Australian*, 1 December 1993.

White Paper 1991, *Shared Values*, Singapore National Printers, Singapore.

Wood, Alan, 'Pragmatism the Only Way for APEC', *Australian*, 28 June 1994.

Yeo, George, 'Democracy and Socialism, East Asia Style', *Straits Times*, 17 June 1994.

Zoohri, Wan Hussin, *The Singapore Malays: The Dilemma of Development*, Singapore Malay Teachers Union, Singapore, 1990.

Newspapers

Age, Melbourne
Asian Business Review (*ABR*), Sydney
Australian, Sydney
Australian Financial Review (*AFR*), Sydney
Business Times (*BT*), Kuala Lumpur
Canberra Times (*CT*), Canberra
New Straits Times (*NST*), Kuala Lumpur
Star, Penang
Sydney Morning Herald (*SMH*), Sydney
Far Eastern Economic Review (*FEER*), Hong Kong

Part II

'Asian' models of political and social organisation

4

Culturalisation of economy and politics in Singapore

Chua Beng Huat

When Australia decides to orient itself economically towards Asia, the representation of 'Asia' in Australia unavoidably becomes a contested ideological terrain. Each representation will promote a concept of 'Asia' that advances specific interests and world views. This chapter may be read as another representation in the contest. However, coming from Singapore and placed in the Australian context, its interests are somewhat ambiguous and has at least three possible speaking positions: First, it can maintain a privileged position and offer itself as an 'insider' version which will clarify non-Asian readings of Asia. Second, it can take the position of an 'Asian' seeking and invited to an outside space, in order to speak critically, presumably with greater impunity, about the 'Asia' that he inhabits. Third, it can insist on and 'essentialise' the differences between 'Asia' and 'non-Asia', and turn the critical focus on Australia. Each possible speaking position is, of course, further complicated by the equally ideologically interested multiple representations of 'Asia' by its own inhabitants in a process of 'self-orientalisation'; that is, the representation of 'Asia' is itself a contested terrain among 'Asians'.

This contest for 'Asia' is not limited to ideologically diametrically opposed believers of progressive liberal democratisation of Asia as part of the momentum of modernisation and those who subscribed to a so-called 'Asian' democracy. It is also contested through competing interpretations of the canons of the philosophical and religious texts that govern the everyday life of Asians across the vast continent, including Islam and Confucianism. For example, the competition for 'Islam' is institutionalised in Malaysia in the very core of contesting political parties themselves, between Party Islam Malaysia and the United Malay National Organisation. As for Confucianism, a leading figure in its revitalisation, not only in Asia but on a global scale, has consistently insisted on the need to be vigilant against the use of

Confucianism as veil for various modes of political practices, such as nepotism and authoritarianism. Indeed, he has further suggested that Confucianism can only flourish in the late twentieth century within a liberal democratic polity.[1]

Ironically, some of those most vocally concerned with the task of defining a 'self-representation of Asia' are to be found in Singapore. There are several reasons for this.[2] First, with a per capita income second only to Japan, it may be considered economically the most successful of the 'new' nations in Asia. Second, its political representatives are possibly the most articulate in English among leaders of East Asian states, giving them disproportional access and exposure in international press. Third, it is of strategic economic and political importance for this smallest state in Asia to assume for itself a larger Asian role. Asia may not need Singapore, but Singapore needs Asia. Fourth, by virtue of the constituent groups of Chinese, Malays and Indians in its population, Singapore is well placed to present itself as 'a composite' of Asian cultures. Thus, the Singapore state presents itself, to both its own citizens and others, as a multiracial 'Asian' nation, where the inheritors of three major Asian traditions—Chinese/Confucian, Malay/Islamic and Indian/Hindu-Buddhist—meet harmoniously, in spite of the overwhelming Chinese numerical majority.[3]

The above context generates certain demands that this chapter must fulfil. First, it will delineate how 'differences' between Singapore and the 'West' are constructed. Discussions of how some of the privileged 'Asian values' are put into social practice will then follow. Finally, aware of the political leadership's ideological motivations in promoting the 'Asianisation' of itself and those it governs, the process will be critically evaluated.

Before elucidating the 'differences', it is necessary to enter a conceptual note. All systems of representation are ideological and, as such, are derived from crystallising a selection of the historical experiences of their protagonists. The terms and concepts that the People's Action Party (PAP) deployed in its construction of Singapore as a 'nation', and in inscribing this construction onto its citizens, have undergone several configurations in the brief thirty-year history of the city-state, each time retaining some items, discarding others and adding new ones.[4] The current construction of Singapore as an 'Asian' nation is no exception. The PAP's terms for the representation of 'Asia' will, therefore, undeniably privilege those features that have been instrumental to its own success in the development of Singapore's economy. These elements provide the frame for the rationalisation of the concepts that the political leadership are proposing as the 'essential' qualities of Asians.

The emergence of the strong state

Singapore was a reluctant nation. Expelled from Malaysia, its very first day as an independent nation, 9 August 1965, was marked by dashed hopes and anxieties about the future, rather than jubilation of freedom.[5] This crisis had as one of its effects the consolidation of political support for the PAP-dominated government and the subsequent development of a strong state in Singapore. A brief account of these developments is thus in order.[6]

Although historically part of the Riau-Johore Sultanate, there was no royalty and its attendant political structure in Singapore because the island was 'sold' to the East India Company soon after Raffles had established a trading post, in 1819. The development of a trading economy under British tutelage left Singapore without a well-formed capitalist class, either in land or in industry. Nor was there an established structure of power among the capitalist trading sector.

The only politically organised interest was the coterie of Straits-born Chinese professionals who had constituted themselves as the Progressive Party in 1947. Given its narrow interest and membership base, its members were elected to office only under condition of limited franchise in 1948 and 1951. Its irrelevance to the general population and the reluctance of its members to promote the cause of independence for Singapore, in fear of losing their privileges in the colonial regime, led to its fatal defeat in the 1954 general election with an expanded electorate. In contrast the working class, penetrated by the communist party after the banning of communism in Malaya in 1947, was relatively well organised into radical trade unions. The unions were strategically supported by the associations of Chinese middle-school students, who were mobilised against the colonial regime, after the latter attempted to impose compulsory conscription on the students in 1950. These two relatively organised forces were captured by the PAP, which was established in 1954 by a coalition of a small group of English-educated professionals and leaders of the radical unions.

It may be argued that by the time the PAP decided to contest for the governing position in the 1959 general election it had no credible opponents. The Progressive Party was dead, there was no organised capitalist interests and the previous government, elected in 1954, had discredited itself with the Chinese by ordering the forced evictions of protesting Chinese students from their schools where they had encamped and detention of radical union and student leaders. With the support of the organised forces of labour, the mobilised students and general sympathy from the Chinese masses, the PAP had its first overwhelming electoral victory when it won 43 out of 51 seats contested. This was the beginning of the strong state that was to be constituted by the unbroken PAP government until today.

In 1968, the *Barisan* boycotted the general election. Its immediate effect was to leave the PAP to win the first of its 'clean sweep' elections, without opposition voices in parliament. As it is now apparent, this was a great tactical mistake that spelt the end of the two-party political system in Singapore; a consequence that could only be reversed, if at all, at great efforts by oppositional voices. The result is a polity governed, since independence, by a single dominant party, without effective parliamentary opposition; facilitating the establishment of a strong state under the PAP. Furthermore, the electoral legitimacy of this strong state enabled it to rein in the civil service into a concerted party-cum-bureaucracy directed towards economic development. The authority and legitimacy of this party-state bureaucracy coalition to govern was, and continues to be, based on its technical capacity to plan and manage the 'national' interest, especially on improving the material life of the population. It most certainly was not dependent on any reference to and/or reverence for any cultural traditions, Asian or otherwise.

Significance of ideological hegemony/consensus

The history of PAP's ascendancy to absolute power in Singapore was undoubtedly paved with instances of severe political repression. Critics are not only quick to point this out but often use this history as part of the evidence for the 'authoritarianism' of the PAP regime, and claim that it is this authoritarianism that is essential to the economic growth of Singapore in the last three decades. Here an ironic confluence of ideas can be located. That a strong (repressive) state is essential to economic growth appears to be a point of unwitting agreement between critics and the PAP. The difference is that the latter uses it as ground for state intervention while the former use it as ground for criticism or lament that it had to be so. Yet, such a suggestion is simplistic. In fact, there are more strong states that perpetuate underdevelopment through corrupt practices than those that are economically successful— the East Asian capitalist societies notwithstanding.

Undoubtedly, strong states may be conducive to economic growth by providing political stability, even if this stability were achieved through less than democratic means, but there are no guarantees. Singapore's economic success and the PAP's political success must be explained by more than just a single variable. The inscription of an ideological system on the collective orientation of the population is a crucial supportive variable to the strong state. Indeed, it may be argued that the successful inscription provides the population with a 'rational' ground for the continuing acceptance of the PAP government, in spite of occasional discomfort and disagreement with its specific policies or its general aloofness and even arrogance. An analysis of the PAP's ideological success must begin at a point at which a 'national interest' for Singapore was being formulated.

The ideological significance of winning the referendum on merger to the PAP government has until now been neglected by analysts. Apart from defeating the left for the first time after the split, it was also, more significantly, an ideological triumph. In a series of radio broadcasts, labelled the 'Battle for Merger', Lee Kuan Yew set out for the first time to delineate an idea of a 'national interest' in his promotion of the cause for merger. The national interest was defined in terms of the 'legitimate' interest of the different groups of Singaporeans, who collectively constitute the 'people':

> The English-educated want to be assured that merger does not mean that four to one ratio between Malays and non-Malays will apply in the Singapore section of the civil service. Businessmen, contractors and bus companies want to be assured that priority of tenders and licences will be as before, with no priorities or special rights for anybody. Workers want to be assured that our pro-labour policy will continue. Merchants want to be assured that our free port status and our free trade with all countries will continue, and that our trading links with the whole world will remain as they have been, free and easy. Every legitimate interest will be protected.[7]

Clearly, legitimate interest referred to 'economic' interest, into which all other interests were reduced: 'Political problems ultimately mean the problem of how we make our living, how we can give everyone a fair and equal chance to study and work and have a full life'.[8] Social and political issues are here conflated with economic development.

The national interest is ideologically rendered synonymous with the 'livelihood'—the material interest—of each Singaporean and, again ideologically, served as the cement that bonds the people in the nation. The PAP's victory at the referendum might be read, retrospectively, as indicative of the population's acceptance of its definition of the state of the nation, thus forging an ideological consensus between the two.

The emergent ideological consensus was further strengthened by the sudden expulsion of Singapore by Malaysia in 1965. As suggested earlier, independence brought with it dashed hopes and anxieties about the future of the new island nation. This condition was ideologically crystallised, by the PAP government, as an overall issue of 'survival'.[9] National 'survival' was again simplified to economic development; political, social and economic problems were again conflated. This

reduction continues to be central to the rationality of the state to serve
as the basis for rationalising social and political disciplinary strategies.

At the social attitudinal level, economic development requires
active transformation of the population into a disciplined industrial
workforce. This means, among other things, the induction of individuals into competition for comparative advantage in consumption which,
in turn, can only be maintained through constant striving to upgrade
one's education and training. That is, an attitude of materialism,
competition and hard work must be implanted in the population.
Improvements in material life of individuals so inducted in turn generate the internal dynamism that keeps the induction process in continuous motion. This induction is all the more effective when backed
by a tight-fisted attitude towards state disbursement of cash transfer to
any individual, thus denying anyone the possibility of escaping the
proletarianising/disciplining process.[10] Finally, the material improvements at the individual level further strengthen the ideological consensus between the population and the PAP, at the level of economic
rationality.

The truism that economic growth is facilitated by political stability
is ideologically deployed to 'naturalise' what was the historical development of a single-party dominant polity. The impressive economic
growth of the last three decades is now ideologically reduced to being
largely a result of such a polity. This is then used to reinforce a
self-serving conviction that a single-party dominant government is the
best possible form of government for a small state like Singapore
because its scant political talents should not be wasted on oppositional
or adversarial politics. Undoubtedly, the single dominant party should
remain the PAP in perpetuity. Unlike the economic level, this self-serving ideological argument is less able to generate consensus regarding
the development of the Singapore polity.

The idea that national survival depends on continuing economic
growth is still stressed. Political stability via single-party dominance
has become an abiding belief of the political leadership. A high level
of self-discipline, whether a result of fear of punishment or of genuine
ideological agreement, remains the norm among the bulk of the population. These ideological concepts and their manifestations not only
remain in place, they are now 'culturalised'.

Culturalisation of economics and politics

In Singapore, economic rationality remains hegemonic. However, 'sensible' social practices in terms of this rationality have been reframed
as 'essential' cultural traits of the population. Hard work, competition

and skills improvement through education, argued earlier as necessary attitudinal transformation of the population into a disciplined labour force for capitalist economic expansion, are now rendered as the 'essential' cultural inheritance of the population.[11] The, until recently, palpable ideological consensus between the electorate and the PAP, achieved through legalised repression and deep ideological penetration in the social body, is also reframed as a culturally determined desire for 'collective welfare', 'social harmony' and passive acceptance of hierarchical authority and one of its political manifestations, paternalism.[12]

The genesis of this culturalisation of economics and politics can be located in the early 1980s. At the time, internationally, mutually supporting neo-conservative academic and political discourses sought to explain the rise of capitalism in East Asia in terms of the Confucian ethics.[13] Locally, in Singapore, these discourses coincided with two emergent ideological concerns. First, the perceived 'creeping individualism' that had supposedly come in train with economic development and had invaded the moral basis of society. Second, the supposedly 'undesirable' state of moral education of students, discovered during a major review of the education program aimed at standardising curriculum, improving performance and reducing both financial and human wastage. The confluence of these two concerns gave rise to a multiplicity of government-sponsored promotions of Confucianism as an ethical system for Singaporeans.[14]

Confucianism was introduced, along with studies of other religions, as alternative subjects in moral education in secondary schools. Internationally known Confucian scholars were engaged to develop new curriculum material. The same scholars were used to propagate the Confucian ethics in public fora and television programs[15], raising concern among the non-Chinese population that there might be a hidden agenda to 'Sinicise' the public culture of Singapore as a whole. However, a government-commissioned study on religion reported, in 1988, that the teaching of religious knowledge had resulted in greater religious commitment and intensified the ethnic/religious divide among the multiracial and multi-religious population. The report further suggested that this process should be managed with care in future, lest it disrupt the balance of race and religion in the society.[16] For this and other reasons, all religious knowledge classes, including Confucianism, were abruptly terminated in 1990.

Having already raised concern for public morality, the government began to develop a 'national ideology' to 'evolve and anchor a national identity'. This was to lead to the institutionalisation of the 'Shared Values' as the guiding principle for future social and political development. The five values are:

1 nation before community and society above self;
2 family as the basic unit of society;
3 community support and regard for the individual;
4 consensus, not conflict, as the basis of national decisionmaking;
   and
5 racial and religious harmony.[17]

To avoid charges of 'Sinicisation', the government went to some
lengths to reassure the electorate that it was not its intention to use
the 'Shared Values' as 'a subterfuge for imposing Chinese Confucian
values' on non-Chinese Singaporeans; although the affinity of these
values to Confucian ideas are recognisable.[18] So, to achieve distance
from exclusive Chinese Confucianism, room is made for labelling the
'Shared Values' in ideologically more inclusive terms.

Although stated in an affirmative manner, the 'Shared Values' are,
nevertheless, only comprehensible in relation to its 'Other'. They are
derived in direct opposition to a fate that they seek to avoid. This is
a fate that is supposedly already the living present of Western developed
nations and has insinuated itself in the Singapore populace; namely,
individualism, liberalism and demand for extensive social welfarism.
Hence, it is this living 'West' that is to be avoided. Framed against
individualism is the privilege of collective welfare; against individual
rights is the raising of collective responsibilities; against individual
entitlements to state welfare is the institutionalisation of family and
community responsibility towards their respective individual members;
finally, against a conception of equality of individuals is the acceptance
of hierarchical social order. And as they are obviously 'anti-Western',
they are 'Asian' by fiat, where 'Asian' supposedly includes, as its
essential components, Chinese, Indian and Islamic legacies.[19]

Of course, questions regarding 'exclusivity' and 'authenticity' of
these values within Asian cultures can be raised. However, such questions are analytically problematic because they presuppose some notion
of cultural 'essence' to what is unavoidably an ideological phenomenon. A more appropriate analytic interest is to examine the effects of
'Asianisation' in the social practices of the PAP government. Indeed,
since the mid-1980s, it has translated the ideological commitment into
practices in different segments of social life. The following three
instances exemplify three different levels of practices.

Asianisation in social practice

1. Asset enhancement schemes

Decades of growth have generated a financially wealthy state both in
foreign reserves and as owners of highly capitalised government-linked

companies, many of which are monopolies. In line with increasing demand for privatisation of state enterprises in most capitalist nations, and following the recommendations of the 1985 Economic Committee, the government has embarked on divesting some of its holdings in the state-owned companies.[20] In each case, a substantial portion of shares of a company will be sold in the stockmarket, with the government continuing to hold the controlling shares and thus control over the company. The process is more appropriately characterised as 'corporatisation' than 'privatisation'. What is significant, is that the government appears to be using this 'corporatisation' process as a vehicle for social distribution—'sharing'—of the accumulated national wealth.

In contrast to earlier corporatisation of government-owned companies, Singapore Airlines being the prime example, in which only the employees were entitled to discounted shares, the shares of the corporatised Singapore Telecoms were distributed throughout the entire working population of Singapore. A two-tier distribution scheme was devised. First, every Singaporean who had $1000 in a social security savings account was entitled to $200 of direct subsidy from the government in order to purchase 600 shares at a discount price of $1.90 per share from its placement price of $3.60. Furthermore, if the purchaser did not sell the initially allocated shares, an additional 60 'loyalty' shares would be allocated for the first, second, fourth and sixth years. Second, every Singaporean who applied with cash to purchase second-tier discount shares was equally allocated 200 shares at $2 per share. In all about 1.42 million Singaporeans were allocated first-tier shares and about 790 000 obtained second-tier shares as well. The total exercise cost the government approximately 3 million dollars. Similar allocation procedures will likely be followed in future corporatisation efforts; the next in line will be the Public Utilities Board.

Another area of social distribution of the accumulated wealth has a more limited reach but in effect is perhaps more progressively egalitarian. In 1990, the government announced that in order to maintain comparable, and competitive, property values of old public housing estates, such estates will be upgraded over a period of fifteen years. The areas to be upgraded include changes to the flat itself and general improvements of common areas. Residents of each block targeted to be upgraded must vote on whether to participate; at least 75 per cent of the block must vote positively before upgrading is carried out. It is not mandatory for a flat owner to vote; however, failing to cast the vote is deemed to be in favour of the upgrading.

In this exercise, the government will absorb a substantively much larger portion of the cost than the tenants themselves; subsidies range from 50 to 90 per cent depending on the nature of the renovation. It is estimated that the total exercise will cost the government 15 billion dollars. Given the obvious benefits, the response of the residents has been good and the government has decided to speed up the upgrading process. Significantly, although this process only benefits those who live in public housing it, nevertheless, is popularly supported by those who live in private houses and do not stand to benefit.[21]

Undoubtedly, such processes of social distribution are one way in which the collective have benefited directly from the public enterprises. The government explicitly sees its social aim as the process of 'levelling up'; that is, improving the basic level of material life for all rather than increasing social welfarism through greater income equality. As the Prime Minister put it in announcing the Telecom scheme: 'It will help Singaporeans to learn, in the most direct way, that each of us is a part owner of Singapore, and that when Singapore prospers, so will all of us'.[22] Similarly, the housing upgrading program is viewed as a means of sharing the wealth Singaporeans have created together and strengthening the stake they have in the country. This idea of sharing accumulated national wealth appears to be widely held by Singaporeans; a survey by the *Straits Times* (18 Sept. 1994) showed that 93 per cent of those surveyed agreed that government subsidies is one way of 'giving everyone a share in Singapore's prosperity'. However, it should be noted that none of these redistributions is aimed at reducing income inequalities, which is emerging as an important social and political issue as the economy further expands.

2. Community 'self-help' organisations

As capitalist economic rationality remains hegemonic, consequential social inequalities resulting from market processes are unavoidable. Like all capitalist states, the legitimacy of the PAP government is dependent on its ability to ameliorate the effects of the inequalities.

In 1981, recognising the structurally determined disadvantaged economic position of Malays[23], the government sponsored, with an inaugural donation of ten million dollars, the establishment of MENDAKI, an acronym of a Muslim organisation, under the leadership of Malay MPs.[24] Its aim is to enhance academic performance of Malay students, and thus their long-term employment and financial prospects. A similar organisation, Singapore Indian Development Agency (SINDA), was set up in 1989 by Indians to help their own 'lower achievers'. Following the logic of multiracialism, the Chinese Development Assistance Council (CDAC) was established in April 1992. In the latter two cases, the government provided no funds.

These agencies are officially known as 'community self-help organisations'; 'community' refers to the three official races.[25] Ideologically, they can be rationalised within the 'Shared Value', 'regard and community support for the individual'. With these racially constituted organisations, each caring for the education of its own needy, race is centrally placed in the management of some aspects of national social welfare. This is a significant change from the encasing of race, with high public visibility, in the private spheres of religious and festival practices while keeping it politically ineffective.[26]

The funding method of these agencies is significant: every Singaporean worker contributes to improve the educational performance of children of needy families in one's 'own' racial group. Contribution is deducted monthly from the employee's compulsory savings in the government-managed social security fund, known as the Central Provident Fund. No cross-racial contributions are permitted in this basic deduction. In principle, contribution is voluntary. However, in contrast to conventional practice of charity, contribution is presumed unless one intentionally opts out. Given the obvious good cause and the paltry monthly contribution, few opt out.

Such a mechanism for enhancing the education of children of lesser able families may be considered an example of the practice of the 'communitarian' orientation of Asian tradition, where the collective well-being is everybody's responsibility.[27] However, that such a reading is not entirely satisfactory can be gleaned from the reasons given by some individuals who 'opt out' of the scheme. Some did so because they prefer to retain the right to decide whether and how much to contribute; such individuals can be dismissed as being 'contaminated' by Western liberalism. More significantly in the local context are those who argued that this method of caring for the lesser able will intensify racial divisiveness and jeopardise the generation of a Singaporean identity and national unity. They, therefore, prefer a national institution for the needy which defines 'community' in national rather than racial terms. In addition, they argue that such 'self-help' agencies are a means of reducing the state's responsibility to social welfare of the people; thus obliquely charging it with absence of communitarian attitude.

3. Disciplining the family

An area of direct effects of 'Asianisation' is in policies that adhere to the Shared Value of 'family as the basic unit of society'. These effects are most noticeable, until recently, in the public housing policies. There are several policies in place that encourage families to stay together as extended families either in the same flat or in close proximity.[28] On the other hand, singles are excluded from purchasing subsidised public housing. In 1981, they were excluded even from buying no-subsidy, executive-income-level housing built by state agencies; on the presumption that granting them housing causes the premature 'break-up' of their families of origin.[29] Under the 'Asianisation' process, the use of public housing as a means of disciplining the family has gone much further.

It is increasingly argued, by the government, that Asians have an unyielding belief in a 'traditional' family structure in which the 'man' is the 'head of household'. Desire for gender equality among the increasingly better educated and professional women population is seen as the unhealthy influence of Western liberalism.[30] The above noted Prime Minister's 1994 National Day Rally speech set out to 'correct' for this tendency: first, the estimated one thousand women who have children but never married are to be denied the possibility of purchasing subsidised public housing; second, the demand by women employees in the public sector for a fringe benefit package equal to their male counterparts' was pronounced dead by fiat, and third, all government benefits for the family, such as supplementary education funds for children, were to be channelled through the man. All these measures are aimed at reinforcing a male-dominant household structure.

The steps taken clearly contradict the increasing presence of two-income families which must by force of circumstance have become increasingly egalitarian in the familial division of labour; against the actual familial practices in which the women tend to manage daily household finances, and against the very audible protests from women and their organisations who correctly see these measures as anti-women.[31] In view of the protests and, perhaps, realising the risk of loss in popular support in the next general election, government ministers have been trying to reformulate the policies as 'pro-family' rather than anti-women.

What is apparent, however, is that the PAP government is willing to back its ideological commitment to a version of 'Asian' values in its public policies, even at the risk of weakening its political support. Its anti-liberal attitudes are, thus, more than mere strategic positioning in the sphere of international rhetorical exchanges. The effects of this determination to inscribe the 'Shared Values' as part of the idea of 'Asianisation' must thus be assessed.

Asianisation as difference

As argued earlier, the 'Asianisation' of Singapore derives its own substance from identifying the phenomenon that it seeks to avoid; namely, the 'West'. It is a discourse that insists on a difference between

Self and Other; it is part of the process of self-identity formation. This government-initiated process begins with a critique of a particular version of Western liberalism. It is argued that:

1 because liberalism embodies an imaginary, socially unencumbered, hyper-independent 'individual', it is difficult to develop a positive concept of 'collective' interest and responsibility in the social and political body;[32]
2 with the entrenchment of individual rights, the civil society appears to be no longer constituted morally, instead it has been reduced to one defined and determined by the competition of rights among individuals, settled only by litigation; and
3 failure to develop social responsibility accounts for current declines in civility and economic health in both public and private spheres of the liberal West.

It is these perceived tendencies that the PAP government wants to avoid. This led to the rejection of liberalism and the insertion of reinvented 'Asian' traditional values, which have as their cultural core the privileging of the collective, expressed in a version of 'communitarianism'.[33]

For Singapore, the moral critique and rejection of liberalism is particularly significant at the current global conjuncture, when the liberal democratic West appears to have no opponents. The demise of the centrally planned command economy of state socialism has indirect ideological and even practical consequences for the PAP government, in spite of the fact that Singapore has a thriving capitalist economy. The demise calls into question the mode of operation of the PAP government: absolute concentration of power in a few political leaders who control and deploy the state machinery in a highly interventionist manner throughout the polity, economy and society.

Yet, it is precisely because of its combination of a highly centralised and interventionist state with a willingness to subject itself to the discipline of the global capitalist market economy that makes Singapore an attractive model of development for the socialist states in Asia, which are trying to maintain their authoritarian political structures with capitalist economies, such as China and Vietnam.[34] Here an interesting conceptual point can be located: promotion of 'communitarianism' may enable the preservation of a concept of the 'social' that is central to 'socialism' and 'communism'. It is the insistence on the primacy of the social that provides socialism with a moral basis for offering itself as an alternative to the rapaciousness of capitalism. It is capitalism that requires for its proper functioning a concept of a 'free' individual, the better to commodify the social exchange between capital and labour as an activity contracted between such 'free' workers and capitalists.

Thus, in spite of its openly anti-communist pronouncements, the possible conceptual shading of communitarianism into socialism was revived by the current Minister of Information and the Arts and of Health, George Yeo. As Chairman of the Young PAP, he had on different occasions reminded its members of the Party's own social democratic beginning and insisted that, regardless of the demise of state socialism elsewhere, this commitment to social democracy or socialism should never be abandoned. In addition, he has attempted to ideologically realign socialism with the concept of 'Asian communitarianism' and the 'Shared Values'. He argued, 'Socialism will never die, of course, because it springs from the very nature of man as a social animal. At least, the family will always stay socialist'.[35] Thus, according to him, the social welfare policies of Singapore are aimed at strengthening the family and not at replacing it with agencies of the state as in the extensive state welfarism of Western developed nations.[36]

As discursive self-formation, 'Asianisation' has been socially productive. As a formulation of a post-colonial nation and subject people, 'Asianisation' avoids the reproduction in Singaporeans of a self-alienating image of their colonial past or the construction of themselves by negation of the colonial past but without resources to develop an alternative, new identity. 'Asianisation' allows the self-identity to be constructed in affirmation, to mould itself substantively in reinvented traditions. It also enables Singapore to position itself as in opposition to liberalism and the 'West'.

Australia as the 'other' to Singapore

However, the issue of Singaporean self-identity formation does not stop at the positioning of Singapore against the 'West'; it also exercises its effects on Singapore's own polity and society. Under the idea of the 'national interest' or 'collective well-being', the popularly elected PAP government is able to place itself in an exclusive position to decide on 'what is good for the nation' and intervenes accordingly as measures of good government. State and society, representation and governance are thus conflated behind a 'communitarian' face. These conflations risk the chance of the elected slipping into authoritarianism, whether in genuine belief of acting in the collective interest or merely using it in a self-serving manner. This likelihood explains why, while logically 'communitarianism' does not favour any form of government it, nevertheless, often spawns authoritarianism in practice. The issue that faces Singapore's political development under a single-party dominant government with a communitarian ideology is, therefore, one of developing political institutions that can hold off the possible imposition of authoritarianism. This is where Australia may play a role in the domestic political development of Singapore.

As argued above, embedded in the 'Asianisation' of Singapore as an ideological process is an anti-liberalism represented by Western developed nations, including Australia. This dichotomous juxtaposition undoubtedly lives off the current configuration of global capitalism; the rise of capital in Asia and the apparent economic decline in Western nations. Obviously, it is this relative position that lends some degree of credibility to the Singaporean political leadership's insistence on the superiority of supposedly 'Asian' values, such as beliefs in education, thrift, hard work and family relations, in the economic health of a nation.[37]

At one analytic level it is, of course, possible to delink the logic of global capital from the prevailing social values of a place. Indeed, in their more sober moments, members of the PAP government will admit to the tenuousness of substantive and/or logical connections between the social values they are promoting and the economic growth of Singapore itself.[38] Nevertheless, it is the intention of the PAP government to link the economic sphere with the effects of social values not only ideologically but also, as shown above, in its administration of the economy. This insistence on the linkage is, of course, politically useful, even necessary, to continue its rationalisations as a highly interventionist state.

In a sense, what is going on locally in Singapore may be treated as largely irrelevant to Australia, if not for the fact that different segments of the Australian population want to appropriate, for their respective selves, from Singapore an interested version of what Australia should be as a society. I am, of course, not in any position to comment on the multiple versions of Singapore in Australian public discourse. Thus, limiting myself to my own interested version: Australia should take its position as the Other to the 'Asianisation' of Singapore seriously. It should not engage in counter construction of the PAP government as an 'unchanging' authoritarian state. This can be, unwittingly, counterproductive because it shares the same conviction that an authoritarian state is essential to economic development.

The position for Australia *vis-à-vis* the PAP government should be to demonstrate that current economic difficulties are results of the logic of global restructuring of capital and that economic growth is not anathema to democratic polity. Furthermore, the freedom of individuals in such a polity provides the ideological conditions for greater creativity and productivity. At the social level, it should also counter the PAP's argument that democracy is incapable of generating social responsibility and taking care of collective welfare. In this area, there is perhaps a need to re-examine state welfarism as practised and to see that collective well-being can be achieved by greater income equality rather than accepting the inevitable inequalities of the market.

Greater individual freedoms, better distribution of incomes and greater social equality are problematic issues within the anti-liberal ideology of the PAP government. Income inequalities are emerging as an area that requires increasing administrative attention, as indicated by the earlier mentioned redistributive mechanisms channelled through public housing. The demand for greater equality is also apparent, especially in gender relations. Although desires for greater freedom to develop a range of conceptual approaches and images are particularly prevalent in the artistic community, such desires are also a generalised sentiment among the tertiary educated. Indeed, the formation of public opinions is no longer the exclusive business of government nor of the pro-government media, if it ever were. It is by now generally suggested that since the mid-1980s, the PAP government has been attempting to satisfy this 'middle class' demand.[39] These are specific desires that are difficult to articulate within the current ideological configuration in Singapore.

Economic success of Australia with a more democratic political system will make available an external reference point which will provide not only the necessary language but also moral support to Singaporeans who are concerned with issues of greater social equality and greater degree of individual freedom. I recognise that given Australia's current relative economic recession, influential segments of public opinion may be inclined to argue for the replication of parts of Singapore's 'success formula' in Australia itself, rather than having it serve as the external reference for the former. Nevertheless, I shall conclude by looking at an illustration to the suggestion.

Conclusion

Without traditional bases for power, the professionals that constitute the PAP leadership have always depended on economic rationality and performance as the basis for government and legitimacy, in addition to clean general elections. These elements are unlikely to change; although there may be legal redrawing of constituency boundaries to the PAP's own advantage, as it faces opposition challenges. However, in the last few years, influenced by strengthened faith in conservative values, derived from the apparent declines of Western developed liberal nations, it appears to have become more explicit in its anti-democratic sentiments beyond the formal strictures of election. The most recent manifestation is the attempt to reinscribe patriarchy in the family under the guise of 'Asian tradition'.

Significantly, among the recently more successful interest group organisations are the women's organisations; namely, the Singapore's Association of Women Lawyers (SAWL), the Association of Women for Action and Research (AWARE), and the Singapore Council of Women's Organisations.[40] Indicative of their success are their ability to keep women's issues in the public media and the appointment of a past-president of AWARE as a 'nominated' MP.[41] However, the reintroduction of patriarchy appears to radically reduce the influence of these organisations in public policy, leaving them at a quandary as to how to respond. The difficulties are compounded by the 1987 Amended Society's Act, introduced after the Law Society criticised legislation limiting the freedom of foreign press operating in Singapore. The Act disallows a voluntary association from making 'political' statements beyond the interests of its declared constituencies and delimits 'political' activities narrowly to the purview of political parties exclusively. It thus imposes severe limits on actions that can be undertaken by the women's organisations to challenge the institutionalisation of patriarchy, beyond public fora and press statements.

This development is rather surprising. Since 1984, the government had on several occasions conducted very extensive consultations with relevant individuals and organisations and public discussions, paying heed to suggestions that emerged in subsequent policy decisions. For example, the 1985 Economic Committee, which was to produce recommendations which involved changes of substance in economic strategy, consulted with more than one thousand individuals in various capacities. One would have deduced from such instances that the process of consultation is a step from which the PAP government would not retreat. Indeed, it cannot retreat because failure to consult obviously interested groups on actions that may be prejudicial to the latter will potentially lead to further erosion of electoral support.

Difficulties with directly politicising issues of equality have intensified frustrations among women, both individually and within organisations. This has led to suggestions that women should use their ballots in the next general election in their own interest, implying that they should vote against the PAP if the institutionalisation of patriarchy is not retracted. However, the government's determination to deny full equality for women suggests that it is willing to risk erosion of political support for its own ideological commitment. Ironically, it may therefore be said that the government's position on patriarchy is neither communitarian in intent nor in consequence.

It is in struggles like those of the women's organisations that liberal democratic polities outside Singapore, like that of Australia, will

continue to provide the language and moral support for those concerned
with democratisation of the political sphere in Singapore.

Notes

1 Tu Wei-Ming, 'Confucianism and Human Rights'. Inaugural lecture for
   the Wu Teh Yao Memorial Lecture Series, 21 March 1995, Singapore.
   Tu Wei-Ming was one of the experts invited by the Singapore government, in the early 1980s, to help in developing the secondary school
   curriculum on Confucianism and to establish the Institute of East Asian
   Philosophy, a research centre for Confucianism. Since 1990 the centre
   has been renamed the Institute of East Asian Political Economy when
   the idea that Confucianism is the essential cultural underpinning of the
   rise of capital in East Asia was abandoned.
2 Among the more vocal Singaporeans who espouse this position is
   Kishore Mabubani, Singapore's Permanent Secretary of Foreign Affairs,
   for example, see *Straits Times*, 16 September 1994.
3 Malaysia, which has similar constituent racial groups, could have represented itself in similar ways. However, the Malays have laid claim to
   being indigenous to peninsular Malaya, thereby rendering Malaysia a
   Malay nation, where Malay political dominance is irreplaceable. Furthermore, given the religious identity of Malay with Islam, the Malaysian
   leadership is keen to establish its own niche to represent the much larger,
   global Islamic nation.
4 Chua Beng Huat, *Communitarian Ideology and Democracy in Singapore*,
   Routledge, London, 1995.
5 Devan, Janadas, 'Why Singapore Always Looks to Future', *Straits
   Times,*12 August 1994.
6 For details of the by now much repeated story of this ascendancy of the
   PAP see Drysdale, John, *Singapore: Struggle for Success*, Times Books
   International, Singapore, 1984; and Bloodworth, Denis, *The Tiger and
   the Trojan Horse*, Times International Press, Singapore, 1986.
7 Lee, Kuan Yew, *The Battle for Merger*, Ministry of Culture, Singapore,
   1962, pp. 78–9.
8 ibid., p. 83.
9 Chan, Heng Chee, 1976, *Singapore: The Politics of Survival*, Oxford
   University Press, Singapore, 1971.
10 This is not to suggest that the PAP government is against welfare
   spending. Indeed, in spite of its grandstanding against social welfarism,
   the government spending in housing, public transport and matching
   grants to voluntary welfare agencies are substantial (*Straits Times*, 18
   September 1994), leading the neo-Marxist scholar, Manuel Castells, to
   suggest that Singapore is a 'welfare' state *sui generis*. See Castells,
   Manuel, 'The Development City-Sity in an Open World Economy: the
   Singapore Experience', BRIE Working Paper No. 31, University of
   California, Berkeley, 1988.

11 Koh, Tommy T.B., 'The Ten Values that Undergird East Asian Strength and Success', *International Herald Tribune*, 11–12 December 1993.

12 Confucianist cultural reading of the political behaviour of the Singaporean electorate is an ever present frame that lurks in the margin of academic analysis; for example, see Chan, op. cit., and Clammer, John, *Singapore: Ideology, Society and Culture*, Chopman Publishers, Singapore, 1985, pp. 91–104.

13 Genealogically, it is difficult to locate the point at which such an ideological trajectory was initiated; however, there is no doubt that the current discourse bears affinity to the critique of 'yellow cultures' in the late 1950s and earlier manifestations of fear of Westernisation of the population in the 1970s. See Seah, Chee Meow, *Trends in Singapore*, Institute of Southeast Asian Studies, Singapore, 1975.

14 See Chua, op. cit., 1995.

15 Kuo, Eddie C.Y., 'Confucianism as Political Discourse in Singapore: the Case of an Incomplete Revitalisation Movement', Working Paper no. 113, Department of Sociology, National University of Singapore, 1992.

16 Kuo, Eddie C.Y., Quah, Jon & Tong, Chee Kiong, *Religion and Religious Revivalism in Singapore*, Ministry of Community Development, Singapore, 1988.

17 White Paper, *Shared Values*, Singapore National Printers, Singapore, 1991.

18 Kuo, op. cit.

19 Although in the Singapore context this hierarchical social order is seen as Confucianist it should, however, be noted that a Western derived conceptualisation of Indian society is also one that is quintessentially hierarchical. See Ram, Kalpana, 'Modernist Anthropology's Comparative Project: the Construction of Indian Identity in Tradition', *Modernity and Identity: Asian Illustrations*, ed. A. Gomes, LaTrobe University Press, Melbourne, 1994.

20 The Economic Committee was constituted during the brief two years of recession of 1985–87, under the chairmanship of Deputy Prime Minister Lee Shien Loong. The Committee was instrumental in reorienting some of the economic policies of the government.

21 *Straits Times*, 18 Sept. 1994.

22 *Straits Times*, 18 Aug. 1993.

23 Zoohri, Wan Hussin, *The Singapore Malays: The Dilemma of Development*, Singapore Malay Teachers Union, Singapore, 1990.

24 Zoohri asserts, 'the inescapable fact is that the Malays have found themselves trapped within a definite vicious cycle. The absence of the right education had made them incapable of associating themselves with modern trade and commerce. They, therefore, had to opt for occupations of low economic status. This inevitably made them poorer than the other communities. It is this vicious cycle syndrome that had entangled them for over a century'. See Zoohri, op cit., p. 9.

25 David Brown has read this process of the constitution of racial groups as equivalent to the government-sponsored formation of interest groups which can then be given proper operating space within the inclusive

corporate sphere of the PAP regime. See Brown, David, 'The Corporatist Management of Ethnicity in Contemporary Singapore', *Singapore Changes Guard,* ed. G. Rodan, Longman Cheshire, Melbourne, 1993.

26 For discussion of the elaborate ideological work from side-lining race from political discourse to reframing and invoking it for some aspects of welfarism as a consequence of a larger ideological framework, see Chua, op. cit., 1995.

27 It should be noted that even MENDAKI, which was founded before the institutionalisation of the 'Shared Values', was justified by the Prime Minister in terms of its potential contribution to the welfare of all Singaporeans. According to him, 'If the money is seen to be in aid of communal ends, then no party, governing on the basis of one man, one vote, will be in a position to go out of its way to give more to a group which says it is going to be more loyal to its ethnic ties than to Singapore society' (Goh Chok Tong quoted in Zoohri, op. cit., p. 82).

28 Chua Beng Huat, 'Not Depoliticized but Ideologically Successful: the Public Housing Program in Singapore', *International Journal of Urban and Regional Research,* vol.15, 1991, pp. 24–41.

29 Chua Beng Huat, 'Singapore in 1981: Problems in New Beginnings', *Southeast Asian Affairs 1982,* Institute of Southeast Asian Studies, Singapore, 1982.

30 Thus, the Senior Minister, Lee Kuan Yew, laments publicly his 'youthful' enthusiasm in passing the Women's Charter which abolished polygamy and instituted gender equality. This reinterpretation of the Charter's history glosses over the fact that it was proposed, in the late 1950s, by the Chinese educated women in the PAP, who were influenced not by contemporary feminism but by progressive politics of mainland China.

31 See for example letters to the editor in the *Straits Times* (9 Sept. 1994) from the woman nominated MP, Dr Kanwaljit Soin, and ex-Minister of State, Dr Seet Ai Mee. On a more satirical note see the essay by leading Singapore writer, Cathrine Lim,'Oscar doesn't understand: things are changing too fast for some Singapore men' in *Asia Magazine* (2–4 Sept., 1994).

32 The hyper-independent character of the individual in liberalism is fully criticised by Bell. Bell, Daniel, *Communitarianism and its Critics,* Oxford University Press, London, 1993.

33 In the formulation of a communitarian ideology, Singapore is a latecomer in a trio of ASEAN nations; both Indonesia and Malaysia have enshrined a communitarian national ideology in their Constitution, namely *Pancasila* and *Negara Ku,* respectively.

34 The ageing Chinese leader, Deng Xiao Ping, had explicitly stated that Singapore is a model for China's opening up to capitalism.

35 Yeo, George, 'Democracy and Socialism, East Asia Style', *Straits Times,* 17 June 1994.

36 The idea that the family is at base 'socialist' is also the ideological beginning point for social welfarism in Scandinavia, such as Sweden. Accordingly, the nation is conceptualised as the 'social family' and the role of the state is to look after the welfare of the nation, hence the

extensive social welfarism. Yeo's argument that state welfarism under-mines the solidarity of the family seems to be supported by the long-term experience of Scandinavia. See Kemeny, J., *Housing and Social Theory*, Routledge, London, 1992, pp. 131–48.

37 It should be noted that there are Singaporean academic economists who do not accept this emphasis. Instead they see the apparent differences between East Asian capitalist economies and that of the United States as one of transition of the former towards the latter as capitalism matures in East Asia (*Straits Times*, 12 Oct. 1994).

38 See *Straits Times*, 8 Sept. 1994.

39 Rodan, Garry, 'The Growth of Singapore's Middle Class and its Political Significance', *Singapore Changes Guard*, ed. G. Rodan, Longman Cheshire, Melbourne, 1993.

40 ibid.

41 A nominated MP is one who is appointed rather than elected to Parlia-ment. This is a strategy, initiated by the PAP government, of introducing independent and potentially contrary voices into a PAP-packed Parlia-ment.

Further References

Chan, Heng Chee, 'Democracy, Human Rights and Social Justice: What Comes First ?', *Straits Times,* 22 November 1992.

Chua Beng Huat, 'Pragmatism of the PAP Government in Singapore: a Critical Assessment', *Southeast Asian Journal of Social Sciences* vol. 13, 1985, pp. 29–46.

——'Australian and Asian Perception of Human Rights', *Australia's Human Rights Diplomacy,* eds I. Russell, P. van Ness & B. H. Chua, Australian National University, Canberra, 1992.

5

Cultural relativism and democracy: political myths about 'Asia' and the 'West'

Stephanie Lawson

A myth's essential function is to create willing obedience.[1]

With one or two exceptions, the nature of political myth has rarely been the subject of detailed investigation in political studies. Yet myth often underlies a whole range of important beliefs and assumptions about political institutions and practices. In the West, for example, myths of white supremacy and a 'civilising mission' justified, for several centuries, a whole range of practices which many non-Westerners suspect have not altogether vanished from the political agenda. Others subscribe to the myth of the market in order to simplify, explain and justify certain economic trends and norms. In many ways, myth is tied closely to ideas about tradition, culture and identity. A recent media commentary noted that countries on the rise rarely care to cast their economic success in terms of some dull explanation of comparative advantage or a particular pattern of technological change, but rather through the identification of virtues unique to their particular culture: 'So the British believed that a special spirit of industry enabled them to turn the globe red and the United States saw its strength born of the rugged individualism of its pioneering spirit'. More recently, the spectacular economic successes of East Asian countries has led some to proclaim that this is due to 'the superiority of "Asian values" over those of the decadent West'.[2]

Myths that sustain a certain view of culture are also frequently linked to the appropriateness of any given set of political arrangements. Accordingly, myths based on cultural interpretations are often invoked to legitimate a certain political order while at the same time portraying others as lacking legitimacy because they do not appear to resonate with certain cultural 'givens'. This cultural component also allows regimes to depict internal critics as either traitors to their own 'cultures' or not 'real' members of the society. In addition, cultural myths can have a clearly instrumental political function and are often highly effective in mobilising support regardless of their substantive 'truth' content. Some of the current debates about a culturally derived Asian variant of democracy—a debate that has received additional impetus from Australia's 'engagement with Asia'—can be interpreted in this light. Against the 'self-appointed judges of "true" democracy' from the West, it is now common to hear and read about arguments put forward that draw sharp (but quite simplistic) contrasts between the achievements of 'Asian democracy' and the cultural values that support it, and some of the less attractive aspects of politics and society in the West:

> Singapore opposition parties do not get equal time on television, but disadvantaged minorities do not riot, loot and burn. Malaysia detains dissidents, but children are not gunned down at school. Taiwan does not allow free speech advocating communism, but its inner-city youths do not dissipate their energies on drugs. In South Korea one can be arrested just for publicly harbouring affection for Kim Il Sung, but may walk the streets without fear of muggers.[3]

The message seems to be that many of the values underscoring democratic practices in the West lead to all sorts of undesirable consequences. The logic of these formulations also seems to imply that because opposition parties in Singapore do not get equal media time, disadvantaged minorities refrain from rioting; that because Malaysian dissidents are often detained, children are safe at school, and so on. It would probably be impolite to point out the source of much of Australia's illegally imported drug cargoes on which some of our inner-city youths undoubtedly expend their energies.

'In one of the few discussions of the subject of political myth, it has been remarked that the widely held, but highly misleading, preconception that the term "myth" stands for any belief that has no foundation in fact, should be disposed of in the interest of greater intellectual rigour and subtlety'.[4] There is no doubt that myths and processes of mythmaking are much more complex than this preconception indicates, as the preceding discussion suggests. But the etymology of 'myth' leaves us with no doubt that its persistent meaning is related to fantasy. From the time that *mythos* was first conceptualised by the ancient Greeks to denote a fable or a fictional account of past events, it has retained its character as something 'devoid of historical truth and rational foundation'.[5] Furthermore, resort to 'facts', or the exposure of faulty premises, is certainly useful in destroying certain other preconceptions on which some myths are based. For example, the allegedly 'scientific' basis of the myth of white supremacy—which was undoubtedly a political as well as a scientific myth—was eventually destroyed by the illumination of biological facts that showed that earlier formulations of 'scientific racism' were empirically wrong.

The discussion that follows is therefore directed, to some extent, to exposing the fairly tenuous bases on which some versions of 'Asian democracy' have been constructed and used for certain political purposes, paying particular attention to Indonesia, Singapore and Malaysia, and to demonstrating that, when applied to this variant of democracy, the common understanding of 'myth' is quite appropriate. It should also be made clear that the democratising processes that have taken place in Taiwan and South Korea, for example, are not a subject for critique in this discussion. In other words, I am not suggesting that there is only one version of democracy in Asia, nor that there are no Asian countries in which genuinely democratic politics is being practised or developing. Rather, the critique of 'Asian democracy' in this chapter is concerned with the rhetorical flourishes that have been deployed by some Southeast Asian leaders in defence of instrumental interests. At the same time, it is important to acknowledge that what often passes for democracy in the West, especially the capitalist variant, can be subjected to a number of similar criticisms. In the final part of the discussion I shall therefore pay particular attention to the extent to which the United States has claimed the interpretive high ground on democracy, thereby relegating the elements of democracy concerned with community and social justice—which are more closely associated with the Western democratic socialist tradition—to obscurity, and confusing the debate on the legitimate issues that make up the broad agenda for human rights.

Democracy

A *pluralist approach*

Ideas of 'Asian democracy' propounded by some political elites in Indonesia, Singapore and Malaysia usually turn on the idea of relativism, especially as this relates to culture. The basic premise from which this discussion starts, however, is that democracy cannot mean all things to all people. More specifically, although the institutional shape of democracy may take a diversity of forms, and democratic polities may differ with respect to the value assigned to the various elements of democracy, there are nonetheless limits to the kinds of regimes that can legitimately be called a 'democracy'. This position stands in contrast to what I shall call dogmatic or rigid relativism, a point of view that implies that there are virtually no limits to what we may legitimately call a democracy. Although this seems, ironically, to be a more democratic epistemological position to adopt than one that prescribes conceptual standards and limitations, the rigid relativist position can (and does) in fact provide a protective cloak for various kinds of authoritarian stances—as many commentators on 'Asian democracy' have pointed out.

On the other hand, it should be stressed that the rejection of rigid relativism does not automatically entail the adoption of the opposite extreme, namely a rigid universalism that endorses a single authoritative standard of 'correctness' for democracy. Clearly, this would be an equally dogmatic, and certainly undemocratic, epistemological posture in so far as it works to silence alternative views and leaves little space for the legitimate diversity that characterises democratic politics. In other words, a rigid universalism is also inherently authoritarian in its implications for political rule. The position that best supports a genuinely democratic polity is one underpinned by a pluralistic epistemological position which in turn supports a sufficiently flexible approach to understanding democracy that is neither relativist nor universalist.[6] This position is not entirely unassailable—nor can it be if it is to serve as a democratic model. Indeed, given the fallibility inherent in the nature of a democratic model, it must remain open to criticism. In other words, whereas both the relativist and universalist positions logically entail a certain closure of discourse—and for that reason are dogmatic—the pluralist position must always remain open, while at the same time allowing that some interpretations of democracy may be better than others.

The contextual importance of these issues for the theory and practice of democracy has been sharpened by a number of trends in international politics over the last four decades or so. Although there are certainly many notable precursors to contemporary debates in earlier eras, the period since the end of World War II is especially significant because of the greatly extended scope for controversy stimulated by such developments as decolonisation, the Cold War, the post-Cold War era of 'democratisation' and ethnonationalist conflict and, above all, the rhetorical endorsement on a global scale of democracy as the most desirable form of political rule. Along with these broad developments, there has also been increasing international debate and disputation over issues concerning human rights (and whether certain categories of rights can or should be accorded priority), and the extent to which norms of inviolate sovereignty should be respected in cases where human rights abuses are perpetrated by repressive regimes, or where culturally defined groups claim the apparently democratic right to self-determination—sometimes in the form of a new sovereign state. These hardly exhaust the catalogue of relevant issues, but for the purpose of the present discussion, they provide an adequate point of departure.

A further broad contextual issue concerns an important conceptual division that has emerged in contemporary debates about democracy.

This is founded on the distinction that is frequently drawn between Western and non-Western cultures and the wide-ranging implications of this distinction for social and political structures in terms of their form, content and value base. It is from within this specific cultural context that some leading proponents of a distinctively 'Asian' version of democracy have launched their arguments. Furthermore, this stance has received implicit support from Western conservatives such as Samuel Huntington whose (in)famous 'clash of civilisations' thesis readily supports the cultural relativism on which the primary assumptions of 'Asian democracy' are based. Beyond this, it is important to note the extent to which there is actually an ideological *convergence* between conservatives from both the West and Asia (and elsewhere) that transcends the putative obstacle presented by 'culture'.[7]

As suggested above, there is no reason why democracy as a form of rule cannot assume various institutional forms, or operate in different modes to suit different contexts. It is not assumed, therefore, that Western countries have a monopoly over interpretation or practice when it comes to ultimately 'correct' forms or modes of democratic rule. Nonetheless, in accordance with the arguments outlined above, the position maintained here is that there are limits to the kinds of polities that can be called 'democratic'. I shall also argue that, in some cases, what is proposed as an 'Asian form of democracy'—usually by political elites and their supporters in a number of Southeast Asian countries—is not democratic at all and is used quite cynically as an attempt to justify continuing authoritarian political measures. Some attention will also be paid to the question of whether this form, or its constitutive elements, may really be described as authentically or uniquely 'Asian'—an issue that is especially interesting in terms of contemporary debates about 'invented traditions'.[8] As a background to some of the political aspects of the claims made by proponents of 'Asian democracy', we shall turn next to the emergence of democracy as the (apparently) most desirable form of political rule in the contemporary era.

The universalisation of democracy

One of the ironies about relativist approaches to defining democracy is that they imply support for the normative idea of democracy as a universal good. This is reflected in the very fact of democracy's current moral prestige and the extent to which it is employed by virtually all regimes as an agent of political legitimation in contemporary international discourse—at least in a rhetorical sense. Historically, the powerful legitimacy factor that now attaches to the name 'democracy' has much to do with the outcome of World War II which saw the triumph, not only of the Allied military forces, but also of their official political ideology. Geography and other factors, however, conditioned the nature of the various responses in the wake of the war, which in turn influenced the subsequent development of foreign policy stances among the Allied countries. At a general level, it has been argued that in Europe, where the experience with fascism was a very direct one, there developed a strong antipathy to right-wing authoritarianism. In the United States, however, the relative isolation from this experience, as well as a growing obsession with communism, led to a tacit endorsement of right-wing authoritarian regimes so long as they demonstrated 'their eagerness to cooperate in an American-led world order, and their reliability as opponents of the Soviet Union'.[9] In the process, the meaning of democracy was made sufficiently elastic so as to allow the United States to welcome into its circle of friends and allies 'an extraordinary variety of friendly but repressive regimes', and to defend 'democracy' in such places as South Vietnam under Diem, the Philippines under Marcos and more recently Kuwait.[10]

There is little doubt that these factors, apart from underscoring the near ubiquitous endorsement of democracy as the preferred form of political rule, have also contributed to the widespread disagreement as to what it actually means to have a 'democratic government'. In turn, this has given cultural relativists a very useful and important basis on which to stake their claims. Following the position outlined in the introduction, my argument here is that although it is certainly difficult to specify a precise set of jointly sufficient conditions for the full and actual expression of democratic political rule, let alone to identify empirically any real-world regime that lives up to all the ideals and principles of democracy in practice, it is not impossible (*contra* the relativists) to distinguish between those regimes characterised by various styles of authoritarianism and degrees of repression, and those that support more democratic, open practices. The importance of addressing these general issues has been highlighted in this volume's predecessor:

> It is argued by some . . . that democracy is a culturally relative term and indeed there is no regime that does not in some way describe itself as democratic. However, to accept this cultural relativist position is to deny any universal meaning to the word and, in the process, to indemnify the most scurrilous of dictatorships and to undermine the legitimacy of democratic and reformist oppositions.[11]

To argue adequately against the cultural relativist position requires that something be said about what democracy is—and is not. The next section therefore looks briefly at the broadly accepted basics of democracy.

Defining democracy

The approach outlined above recognises that various regimes may
measure up differently against the various criteria of democracy, and
that the most useful way of analysing the extent to which the political
institutions and practices of any given regime accord with democratic
principles is through the concept of a continuum from more democratic
to less democratic. Apart from the difficulty of securing widespread
agreement on the relative merits of all the democratic variables, this
approach also has its limits insofar as the qualitative assessment of
any regime cannot be achieved by a simple check of such constitutional
provisions as elective representation, universal franchise, or the presence of a number of political parties competing for office. In any given
state, the mere existence of a formally democratic constitution and, in
some cases, an accompanying bill of rights, is no guarantee that
democracy is flourishing. As one theorist has suggested, only a mod-
icum of insight is required to recognise that constitutional provisions
such as universal adult franchise and equal voting rights, even if strictly
abided by, do not serve to distinguish between a democracy and an
'elected dictatorship'.[12] Singapore's government, for example, has been
controlled by the People's Action Party (PAP) for well over thirty
years. Although the parliament there is elected and legally 'free'
political parties may compete for office—thereby satisfying some of
the formal mechanisms of democratic political procedures—the PAP
government has used a number of repressive devices to ensure that
genuine political competition for office remains very limited, thereby
ensuring its own continued electoral success.[13]

The most basic elements of contemporary political democracy,
including its formal mechanical structures and provisions as well as
an indication of some of the principles that underlie them, have been
summarised conveniently by Sørenson as follows:

- Meaningful and extensive *competition* among individuals and
  organized groups (especially political parties) for all effective positions of government power, at regular intervals and excluding the
  use of force.
- A highly inclusive level of *political participation* in the selection
  of leaders and policies, at least through regular and fair elections,
  such that no major adult group is excluded.
- A level of *civil and political liberties*—freedom of expression,
  freedom of the press, freedom to form and join organisations—sufficient to ensure the integrity of political competition and participation.[14]

This general statement of mechanisms and principles serves to identify the political and procedural aspects of democracy understood in terms of certain freedoms or liberties (namely, political and civil rights). It says very little, however, about other important aspects of democracy such as equality and community which, as foreshadowed earlier, are as important as the component of liberty and which are also integral to the Western democratic tradition (outside the United States). Some would no doubt argue that these find adequate expression through the guarantee of political and civil freedom. This is certainly true of mainstream American discourse, especially that emanating from the White House. The arguments about these issues are well worth considering, especially since they have assumed a certain prominence in recent debates concerning democracy and human rights in Asia, and we shall return to these at a later point in the discussion.

Another way of approaching the question of what democracy *is,* is to specify what it *is not.* For example, one democratic theorist has argued that although there are 'many uncertainties surrounding the term "dictatorship", it can nonetheless be understood structurally as a non-constitutional form of rule (and therefore a structurally undemocratic form) because the rulers in these cases either make a sham of an existing constitution or write their own document empowering themselves to do virtually as they please'.[15] It is further proposed that an even clearer contrast can be drawn by negatively elucidating the characteristics of democracy by way of contradistinction to the principles of autocracy. 'Through repudiation of the autocratic principle that personalised power can be held irrevocably, democracy can be seen as a form of rule under which no one can arrogate to him or herself unconditional and unlimited power'.[16] The key to qualifying and limiting the power of rulers over the ruled in a democratic system is to be found in the doctrine of constitutionalism. In its simplest formulation, this doctrine refers to limited government insofar as any government, including each and every one of its members, is as much subject to the rule of law as any other individual or group. The origins of this conception are to be found in the Greek *polis* where it developed synchronically with the notion that the legitimate exercise of political power lay not in the hands of a monarch or tyrant, an aristocracy or an oligarchy, but ultimately in those of the *demos*. In modern mass polities, where the idea of rule or power of the people has necessarily been translated into representative democracy, governments remain subject to the law of the constitution in both letter and spirit. And since democratic constitutions always provide for succession of government via a peaceful process of voting, it is clearly understood that the tenure of any particular government in office is strictly temporary and that it may legitimately be replaced by an opposing party.

This last point is especially important in assessing the extent to which the version of 'Asian democracy' proposed by some Southeast Asian leaders conforms to several basic requirements of contemporary democratic theory, and that is the problem of political opposition (both constitutional and non-constitutional), and legitimate succession of government. For underlying much of the debate about the virtues of this particular variant of Asian democracy, especially as explicated by holders of government power, is a marked hostility to the notion of legitimate political opposition and the idea of alternation in office. Yet the notion of free political opposition, and its assumptions about legitimate succession of government, is central to the democratic process, and its legal or constitutional institutionalisation is taken as a key distinguishing feature of democratic politics. If we refer to the three clusters of practices and principles outlined above, it is not difficult to see that these are ultimately dependent on acceptance of the legitimacy of open criticism and the entrenchment of legal political opposition. As a first step in understanding some of these issues, it is necessary to outline some of the basic features said to constitute the Asian variant of democratic rule, and how these relate to the idea of culture.

'Asian democracy'

The cultural dimension

As we have seen, the definitive elements of 'Asian democracy' are frequently elucidated through a process of positively contrasting certain (allegedly) Asian values with certain (allegedly) Western values. What is produced in this process is an inverted version of 'Orientalism' complete with its essentialist framework, and which is best described in this context as 'Occidentalism'. This provides the necessary basis for the assertion of a particular political identity—in this case a broad 'Asian' identity—which in turn serves as an important legitimating device for the particular account of 'democracy' that is put forward, especially to the extent that it is firmly connected to some kind of cultural base which in turn purports to lend authenticity to the model. Formulations of this kind are of course common to nationalist constructions of identity and in this respect the kind of 'regionalism' evident in the process of conceptualising an Asian identity and an Asian variant of democracy may be understood as an extension of the nationalist device.

Of the values proposed as constituting the 'essence' of Asian culture and identity and, by implication, Asian democracy, those that have received most emphasis are consensus, harmony, unity and community.

These are contrasted, favourably, with a number of values said to characterise Western polities, namely, dissensus, conflict, disunity and individualism. On the face of it, the former set of values appear to be quite admirable. With the possible exception of individualism, the latter of course appear to be just the opposite. As the old adage goes, however, appearances can be deceptive and on closer inspection, especially in terms of how each set of values operates in the political sphere, matters are not quite so straightforward.

Accounts of Asian democracy

There is no single authoritative account or canon of thought on what the basic constituents of 'Asian democracy' are—just as there is no single authoritative account of (Western) democracy. A general picture may nonetheless be gleaned from various statements delivered by leading proponents and commentators on 'Asian democracy'. The Southeast Asian leaders of Indonesia, Singapore and Malaysia have been most outspoken about this model, and the following discussion will therefore concentrate on their arguments.

One of the earliest accounts of 'Asian democracy' is to be found in the Indonesian version of 'guided democracy', a term devised in the late 1950s by Sukarno to describe the regime he instituted after a relatively chaotic period of unstable coalition governments earlier in the decade. Sukarno's regime was short-lived, but the successor regime of Soeharto's 'New Order', although purporting to represent a revolutionary change in Indonesian politics, built on much the same kind of official ideology that had underscored Sukarno's, namely, a strongly organic conception of the state. 'This provided the ideal basis for sanctifying conservative, authoritarian rule by denying the legitimacy of political activity outside state-controlled structures'.[17] Robison's analysis suggests that the Indonesian conception of organic statism emanated from two main sources, both of which incorporated distinct elements of the kind of Occidentalism described above:

> One source was a type of nationalist cultural relativism in which
> 'Eastern' society was viewed as one characterised by ideals of
> harmony and consensus, while 'Western' society was considered to be
> based on individualism, confrontation and materialism. A second
> source was the political culture of the Javanese aristocratic officials
> . . . order, authority and hierarchy balanced by the mythology of
> aristocratic obligation as contrasted to 'Western' or 'liberal'
> government which was seen to be the institutionalised conflict of
> vested interests.[18]

The further development of Indonesia's political system under Soeharto and the official state party, Golkar, was the adoption of a state ideology—Pancasila. Now, 'Pancasila Democracy' is held up in favourable contrast not only to the Sukarno version (from which it differs only marginally), but also to the decade before the introduction of guided democracy in which a more liberal order flourished briefly. As Feith reports, this period is depicted by proponents of Pancasila as 'one of pointless imitation of Western political forms, of persistently petty party bickering, of frustratingly deadlocked government, of primordial antagonisms and religious–ideological polarisation that benefited nobody but the communists . . .'.[19] Pancasila has also played a critical role in delegitimising forms of political organisation outside those sanctioned by the state. Robison points out that its policy content (which is largely a bland statement of fairly unremarkable and typically nationalistic goals) is relatively unimportant. Its real significance lies in the way in which it serves to legitimise authoritarian rule 'as a mechanism that achieves the common will of society through consensus under the tutelage of a state in the possession of its own officials'.[20] If democratic politics includes, as one writer has suggested, 'the distancing of dogmatic ideology (religious or secular) from the machinery of power',[21] then this aspect of Indonesian politics places it well outside the fold of democratic polities. The implications for democratic politics of delegitimising political organisation, and therefore opposition terms, outside government imposed limits, are also clear enough.[22]

A particular irony of Pancasila ideology and the version of democracy it supports, especially given that one of its principal thrusts was directed towards differentiating an 'Eastern' or 'Asian' value system from a 'Western' one in order to fortify its legitimacy for local consumption, is that many of the ideas underpinning its key value of organic statism are derived substantially from certain aspects of European political thought. The Western medieval worldview, for example, is generally characterised as 'embodying a belief in political and social order based on hierarchy and organicism together with an emphasis on personal and particularistic relations'.[23] European ideas of organic statism survived the feudal period and later became part of the ideologies of Western conservatism and fascism. A further irony is that conservative perspectives, complete with their organicist content, were often transported from their British/European environments to the colonies via officials who applied these perspectives in interpreting local sociopolitical structures. Conservative colonial doctrine, which received some intellectual respectability from early anthropological schools of thought, and which was often endorsed by local political elites who benefited from colonial systems of indirect rule, readily became incorporated as part of local 'tradition' and assumed the qualities of timelessness, authenticity, and legitimacy.[24] Furthermore, the elements of feudal political thought described above, and the kind of values they support, share much in common with certain other traditions of thought found in parts of Asia. This is especially so in the case of Confucianism which has found a place in the political mythmaking of one of Indonesia's closest neighbours.

Singapore is another country from which a version of 'Asian democracy' has emerged. Again, this has been constructed very clearly in opposition to 'Western values' in general, and 'Western' democracy in particular. In the case of Singapore, however, the specification of the cultural basis from which Asian democracy and its values emanates has been much more precise in that it is tied directly to a Confucian heritage. In this respect, some of the cultural arguments employed by Singaporean political elites in recent years are well worth assessing in terms of the 'invention of tradition' phenomenon. In addition, Singapore provides a clear example of how the existence of formal institutions associated with democratic rule provide no guarantee that substantive democratic practices, especially in relation to freedom of political expression and opposition, are in fact operative. As Rodan points out:

> Parliamentary elections constitute a stunted political expression—they are not the end products of broader contests over social and political power but rather the only contest. Contestation outside a narrowly defined formal politics is severely limited. But even in this sphere, the PAP sees little margin for opposition, continually arguing the importance of the 'dominant-party system'. This system is a critical element in what is effectively a one-party state.[25]

Through a variety of mechanisms, Singapore's PAP government has successfully maintained hegemony over the island state since it was first elected in 1959. This is also partially explained, however, by its impressive economic record and its ability to deliver a relatively high standard of living to a diverse population and with minimal levels of corruption. These factors are said to have instilled a significant level of 'pragmatic acquiescence'[26] among the population. But this acquiescence has been carefully engineered through repressive policies such as detention without trial and restrictions on various civil rights including free speech against which there are heavy sanctions. In response to complaints by US Congress about the detention of a number of activists in May 1987, the then Singaporean Minister for Home Affairs responded in the following terms:

> In our short history, Singapore has repeatedly encountered subversive threats from within and without. . . . To combat these threats to the nation, the usual procedures of court trials, which apply in Singapore to most criminal cases, have proved totally inadequate. The very secrecy of covert operations precludes garnering evidence to meet the

standards of the criminal law for conviction. In many cases of racial
agitation, the process of trial itself will provide further opportunity for
inflammatory rabble rousing . . . Singapore cannot be ruled in any
other way . . . Preventive detention is not a blemish marring our
record; it is a necessary power underpinning our freedom.[27]

In addition to these measures, the PAP has engaged actively in
bolstering acquiescence through the inculcation of certain 'Asian values'. The beginnings of such a program may be traced to the foundation, in 1983, of the Institute of East Asian Philosophies (IEAP).
Sponsored by the PAP, the purpose of the IEAP was 'to advance the
understanding of Confucian philosophy so that it [could] be reinter-
preted and adapted to the needs of present society'.[28] In addition, the
government instituted a secondary school program of religious education and Confucian ethics. The explicit purpose of these programs was
to counter the perceived trend in 'Westernisation' among the population, especially the large Chinese sector who were considered 'more
susceptible to other cultural influences'.[29] 'To the outsider, the idea
that the Confucian heritage is entirely appropriate for Singaporean
Chinese (if not for other Singaporeans) may seem obvious. After all,
Confucianism *is* Chinese. But this is to fall all too easily into the errors
of stereotyping, essentialism, and myth-making. It has been pointed
out that Singaporean Chinese do not in fact have a particular traditional
familiarity with Confucianism'.[30] The PAP's promotion of Confucian
values among its Chinese citizenry may therefore be seen as a fairly
cynical political exercise in the 'invention of tradition' mode.

By the end of the 1980s, the PAP government felt it was time to
formalise a 'national ideology' for Singapore as a counter to 'the
disintegrative impact of Western individualism'. Accordingly, a set of
'core Asian values', consisting of 'multiracialism, consensus, family
and society before self' were identified and promulgated.[31] These
values were further elaborated by one member of the IEAP team in a
new theory of 'democracy' which was to be based not on (Western)
ideals of free political competition between opposing parties—ideals
explicitly repudiated—but on (Asian/Confucian) ideals of harmony and
consensus. Accordingly, notions of political freedom were recast to
preclude open, public competition and to endorse instead existing
closed practices where any debate and criticism was conducted behind
closed doors and only among members of the government.

Democracy understood in such a manner may be likened to the two
sides of the same coin in government. In the Western parliamentary
form it is arrived at through open debate from within and without; in
an Eastern form of democracy it is arrived at through closed debate
with no opposition from without. In this dual and mixed form,

democracy is synthesized to become a new polity which may be called consencracy.[32]

What is noticeably absent from this neologism is the qualifier derived from *demos*—the people. In its place we find 'consensus'. Apart from appearing in most rhetorical statements on the virtues of 'Asian democracy', consensus also comprises an important theme in ideas about organic unity and harmony (and which also flourished in the dogma of classic Western conservatism). In the contemporary context, and especially in Indonesia and Singapore, it means a high degree of conformity with the wishes of those controlling the apparatus of the state.[33]

A third country in which the cause of 'Asian democracy' is now being championed is Malaysia. Again, the rhetoric of the Malaysian political elite in recent years has produced a vision of 'Asianness' that is directed clearly towards extolling the virtues inherent in existing social and political arrangements, while emphatically criticising alleged Western social and political values. In this respect Prime Minister Mahathir seems to have taken over the role of leading critic of the West from former Singaporean Prime Minister and PAP leader Lee Kuan Yew. While the West is a general target, democracy is naturally singled out for special attention. A classic statement in the now familiar genre of such criticisms is that: 'Too much democracy leads to homosexuality, moral decay, racial intolerance, economic decline and single-parent families'.[34] Moreover, Mahathir has claimed that: 'Values based on the spiritual, on peace of mind, and on belief in feelings loftier than desire, have no place in the Western psyche'.[35] At the same time Mahathir, like a number of other Asian leaders, has frequently asserted that 'autochthonous forms of political rule are quite obviously much more appropriate in cultural terms'.[36]

The rhetoric associated with these claims is usually directed at both internal and external audiences. For internal consumption, it operates to produce a unified, nationalistic rallying point—and it differentiates the unified 'us' from the external 'them'. This is despite the considerable internal social and cultural diversity that marks most Asian polities. For external purposes, and especially for the West, it serves as a useful defence—and sometimes an offensive defence—against criticism and prescription. One example of how these factors can come into play was the 'diplomatic incident' occasioned by the remarks of the Australian Prime Minister, Paul Keating, in November 1993 when he described his Malaysian counterpart as 'recalcitrant' for refusing to attend the APEC summit talks in the United States. Amid threats to Australian trade links and other economic activities, it was also made clear on the Malaysian side that Keating's remark was evidence of the lack of manners and respect in Australian culture—the obvious contrast

being 'Asian culture'. Mahathir's public posture throughout was one
of aloofness, and the general impression cultivated by the Malaysian
government was that it was the 'Malaysian people' who had been
offended by the remark rather than Mahathir personally. As I have
noted elsewhere, external criticism of authoritarian leaders is often
interpreted in a negative and exaggerated manner, and can easily be
depicted as an insult to the cultural values of the people as a whole.
External criticism can thus provide the domestic regime with an ideal
rhetorical weapon as well as·the moral high ground from which to
launch it. 'In this particular case Keating provided some very convenient material for an exercise in national political chauvinism on the
part of the Malaysian government which effectively targeted both
internal and external audiences'.[37]

Just as the 'recalcitrance incident' was finally fading away,
Mahathir engaged in a heated and bitter trade dispute with Great
Britain which had serious consequences for British trade and investment. This incident followed allegations in some British press reports
of corrupt links between a defence contract and British aid for the
construction of a Malaysian dam. This time, Mahathir became directly
involved in the public debate and very skilfully used the historic
images of British colonial racism. In a letter to London's *Financial
Times,* Mahathir reaffirmed a ban on British industries being granted
Malaysian government contracts, and added an inverted racialist attack
reported in the Australian press as follows: 'Of course Malaysians are
corrupt, Dr Mahathir wrote. "They must be, because they are not
British and not white" . . . Linking the general issues of the incident
with the broader debate on democracy and human rights, Mahathir
added: "Lies, damned lies are free. Redress isn't. This is what Western
democracy and human rights is all about. If this is not moral decadence, then what is?" '.[38]

Conclusion

To return now to some more general themes, it is evident that the idea
of a set of 'core Asian values' has been identified by a number of
Asian political leaders as deeply embedded in local culture (extending
over a conceptually homogenised Asian region), and therefore intrinsic
to the very nature of 'Asian society'. It also underscores the notion of
what should and must constitute the foundations of a genuinely Asian
polity. As a corollary, these values should and must inform a conception of democratic government that is acceptable, viable and ultimately
'authentic' in an Asian context. This, then, is a form of relativism that
basically constructs two opposing cultural models—both of which are

represented as monolithic and essentially incommensurable—and accords to each a kind of political authenticity, and therefore legitimacy, linked directly to the cultural component. In addition, the mode of argument from culture hinges on a classic form of cultural determinism which, put simply, implies that people are forever encapsulated in their 'own' culture and therefore doomed to follow the dictates of the socialisation processes in which they have been immersed from infancy.

These ideas also fit in very well with cultural incommensurability theses. Put briefly, these support the view that 'cultures' are like different species with distinct boundaries, whose essential components are not susceptible to establishing meaningful commonalities with another. They are also highly reductionist, by which is meant a conceptual exercise that effectively reduces the multiplicity of politically salient factors to a single, overriding, determining element— namely 'culture'. All this is so easily falsifiable that it seems scarcely worth making the effort to expose the errors. 'Asia', like 'the West', is a difficult enough region to define geographically let alone to cast in terms of a coherent cultural entity. Furthermore, culture itself is hardly inert—it is dynamic and creative, and is constantly changing, moving, accommodating, and syncretising. Yet the grand, monolithic and apparently eternal constructions described above, and the polarities and stereotypes they generate, are readily accepted by so many people, both in Asia and the West, and so easily brought into play in everyday politics, that they cannot be dismissed summarily as having no consequence. In their simplicity and accessibility to unthinking minds they are indeed the stuff of myths.

The minds of political elites, however, are rarely so unsophisticated. The kind of politics that deploys cultural myths to advantage is often a carefully and strategically calculated activity designed, above all, to maintain an elite in power by appealing to the most readily available as well as emotive symbols of legitimacy. These strategies, of course, are hardly the preserve of non-Western authoritarian elites, and the nationalistic devices on which they are based will often work as well in Western democratic polities as they do in non-democratic ones. This suggests, among other things, that there are probably as many universals in politics as there are particularities, which brings us back to some of the issues raised at the beginning of the discussion on democracy.

There is not and cannot be one fixed and finally 'correct' form of democracy. To believe that such a form can be identified, prescribed and implemented on a universal scale is to subscribe to a myth of equally erroneous (and authoritarian) proportions as some of those propounded by supporters of the relativistic and highly dubious 'Asian' variant of democracy discussed in this chapter. Democracy is about many things, but it is principally about the legitimacy of the power of ordinary people to exercise some kind of control over political elites and to judge the appropriateness of policy decisions made on their behalf that can vitally affect their lives. This is part of the moral, normative dimension of democracy that clearly has some universal implications insofar as all human beings are assumed to be equally worthy and entitled to exercise some power and control in this way. On the other hand, because of the assumptions about human diversity on which democracy is based, there is reasonable scope and space for people to pursue their different conceptions of 'the good', whether this is conceived in an individualistic fashion or in a way that is more oriented towards the community, or through some balance between these.

I have earlier stressed an important point that is too often forgotten in the debate between the values of individualism on the one hand and the ideals associated with community on the other. And that is that democracy, as it developed in the West, has historically incorporated notions of community as well as of individual freedom, and this has been one of the most significant elements of Western democratic socialism. Indeed, many of the claims made by some Asian countries about the importance of social and economic rights in fact derive from the Western socialist tradition. There is no doubt, however, that the value of liberty, especially when linked almost exclusively to notions of individualism, has received excessive emphasis—especially in the United States, but also in Great Britain under a Conservative government as well as among conservatives in Australia—and at the expense of the equally important democratic values of equality and community. This has much to do with the dominance of a particular strand of liberal political ideology[39] and the extravagant homage it has paid to market freedom and the virtues of capitalism (which, incidentally, have been embraced enthusiastically by many Asian elites regardless of the rhetorical importance attributed to collectivist values). It is testimony, too, to the domination of the United States in the international debate about democracy, democratisation and human rights, and the arrogant universalist assertion of its own version of capitalist liberal democracy which is, as Parekh has so eloquently demonstrated, 'just one of several variations on the democratic theme'.[40] And as any student of the sorry story of modern American history can tell us, its own founding myths of individual freedom and enterprise are themselves founded on the blood of millions, not only of Native Americans and African slaves, but on that of ordinary immigrant working people whose lives were sacrificed in the name of individual liberty, progress and manifest destiny.

Australians would also do well to reflect critically, if not a little cynically, on their own founding myths of egalitarianism, 'mateship' and giving everyone 'a fair go'—but which didn't of course include Aboriginal Australians or non-white immigrants, and have only been marginally inclusive of women. Furthermore, from the perspective of some Asian leaders, Australia's past record hardly serves as a moral high ground from which it can legitimately criticise its Asian neighbours for failing to uphold human rights: 'Australia, the former ally of imperial Britain, the recent lieutenant of imperial America—the "deputy sheriff" in Lee Kuan Yew's unflattering terminology—possesses an unfortunate history from the perspective of those who doubt the legitimacy and sincerity of human rights activism.'[41]

At the same time, Australia does have an important (although often subordinate) tradition of democratic socialism,[42] as well as social liberalism, both of which support the values associated with community and social justice and which therefore lend substance to a genuine concern with social and economic rights. Ironically, it is this tradition that is under attack from neo-liberals/conservatives in Australia who prescribe emulation of the 'Asian way' both in terms of economic restructuring as well as social and political control. For Australian conservatives, the slogan 'engagement with Asia' therefore offers a new banner under which an old agenda may be pursued. A further irony is that the success stories selected to provide the moral lesson are almost always based on individual achievements rather than on the communitarianism that purportedly characterises the 'Asian way'. A recent article, for example, selected two successful business entrepreneurs, briefly outlined their path to riches, and in the classic individualist/liberal rhetoric purveyed by Australia's New Right during its rise to prominence in the 1980s (but now somewhat muted by the spectacular crash of Alan Bond, Christopher Skase and others), surmised that:

> All these people have one thing in common: the will to succeed. They didn't sit around waiting for government handouts or make-work programmes or social 'benefits' that destroy jobs in so many countries. No government tried to limit the hours they could work or the wages they could earn. No government mandated their hiring because they were the favoured ethnic group of the moment. They wanted to work. And they did.[43]

Finally, a few words should be said about the present debate about democracy and human rights in Asia, especially with respect to the attempt to separate political and civil rights (construed as individual rights) from social and economic rights (construed as collective rights),[44] and their assignment to the cultural-political categories of 'Western' and 'Asian'. Apart from the hypocrisy evident in this exercise—as so clearly illustrated above—it is evident that in so doing, both 'sides' have committed the error of dissecting and separating the cluster of democratic values, which incorporates all of these rights, in order to support their own political agendas. This also effectively perpetuates the obnoxious racialist myths built on the Orientalist divide and encourages equally ill-founded prognostications about civilisational 'fault lines' and the future bases of threats to world peace. The irony is that whereas such constructions used almost always to be the preserve of Western colonising elites, they are now being wielded skilfully by post-colonial political elites and for much the same purpose—and that is the political subordination and repression of ordinary people. Finally, by taking issue with the notion of cultural relativism and critically assessing the poverty of its explanatory value, as well as its instrumental deployment as a political tool, we may be less likely to award the benefits of 'sensitivity to culture' to authoritarian elites in Australia's process of 'engaging with Asia'.

Notes

1 Delaisi, Francis, *Political Myths and Economic Realities*, Noel Douglas, London, 1925, p. 18.
2 *Australian*, 2 June 1994.
3 *Asiaweek*, 9 Feb. 1994.
4 Tudor, Henry, *Political Myth*, Pall Mall, London, 1972, p. 13.
5 Delaisi, op. cit.; Sinclair, T.A., *A History of Greek Political Thought*, Routledge & Kegan Paul, London, 1967.
6 The 'pluralism' emphasised here relates to the epistemological aspect of the approach to defining democracy, rather than to democracy *as* pluralism (although the two are related). Furthermore, this use of the term 'pluralism' should not be taken to imply endorsement of certain schools of thought, such as the English school of legal pluralism, or American 'pluralist' theories based on the work of A.F. Bentley, which have used it to describe particular (and rather narrow) approaches to understanding democracy. For a more detailed discussion of some of these points, see Stephanie Lawson, 'Conceptual Issues in the Comparative Study of Regime Change and Democratization', *Comparative Politics*, vol. 25, no. 2, January 1993, pp. 183–205.
7 See Rodan and Hewison (this volume). This point is also dealt with extensively in the South Pacific context as well as at a more general level in Stephanie Lawson, *Tradition Versus Democracy in the South Pacific: Fiji, Tonga and Western Samoa* (Cambridge, Cambridge University Press, in press).
8 Two of the earlier works dealing with this issue in the South Pacific and Africa respectively are Roger M. Keesing and Robert Tonkinson (eds), *'Reinventing Traditional Culture: The Politics of Kastom in Island Melanesia'* (special issue of *Mankind*, vol. 13, no. 4, 1982), and Eric

Hobsbawm and Terrence Ranger (eds), *The Invention of Tradition* (Cambridge, Cambridge University Press, 1983).

9 Whitehead, Lawrence, 'International Aspects of Democratization', *Transitions from Authoritarian Rule,* ed G. O'Donnell, P. Schmitter & L. Whitehead, The Johns Hopkins University Press, Baltimore, 1986, p. 39.

10 ibid.

11 Hewison, Kevin, Robison, Richard & Rodan, Garry, 'Introduction: Changing Forms of State Power in Southeast Asia', *Southeast Asia in the 1990s: Authoritarianism, Democracy and Capitalism,* eds K. Hewison, R. Robison & G. Rodan, Allen & Unwin, St Leonards, 1993, p. 5.

12 Mayo, Henry B., 'The Theory of Democracy Outlined', *Communism, Fascism and Democracy: The Theoretical Foundations,* Random House, New York, 1972, p. 573.

13 Lawson, Stephanie, 'Much Ado About Recalcitrance', *Pacific Research,* vol. 7, no.1, 1994, p. 24.

14 Georg Sørensen, *Democracy and Democratization* (Boulder, Westview Press, 1993), p. 13. See also Larry Diamond, Juan J. Linz and Seymour Martin Lipset (eds), *Democracy in Developing Countries,* vol. 2: *Africa* (Boulder, Lynne Reinner, 1988), p. xvi.

15 Sartori, Giovanni, *The Theory of Democracy Revisited,* Chatham House, New Jersey, 1987, p. 205.

16 ibid., pp. 206–7.

17 Robison, Richard, 'Indonesia: Tensions in State and Regime', *Southeast Asia in the 1990s: Authoritarianism, Democracy and Capitalism,* eds Hewison et. al, Allen & Unwin, St Leonards, 1993, p. 42.

18 Robison, op. cit., p. 42. See also David Reeve, 'Sukarnoism and Indonesia's "Functional Group" State: Implementing "Indonesian Democracy" ', *Review of Indonesian and Malay Affairs,* vol. 13, no. 1, pp. 53–115.

19 Feith, Herb, 'Constitutional Democracy: How Well Did it Function?', *Democracy in Indonesia: 1950s and 1960s,* eds D. Bourchier & J. Legge, Centre of Southeast Asian Studies, Monash University, Clayton, 1994, p. 17.

20 Robison, op. cit., p. 44.

21 Mirsky, Yehuda, 'Democratic Politics and its Culture', *Orbis,* vol. 37, no. 4, Fall 1993, p. 573.

22 Obviously, there are limits to the toleration of political opposition in Western democracies as well, which is why democratic theorists make a clear distinction between constitutional and unconstitutional political opposition. For a more detailed discussion of these limits and how they are delineated through the doctrine of constitutionalism, see Lawson, 'Conceptual issues'.

23 Waltzer, Michael, *The Revolution of Saints: A Study in the Origins of Radical Politics,* Atheneum, New York, 1974, p. 8.

24 For further discussion of this phenomenon, see Elizabeth Colson, *Tradition and Contract: The Problem of Order* (London, Heinemann, 1975); and Stephanie Lawson, 'The Politics of Tradition: Problems for Political

Legitimacy and Democracy in the South Pacific, *Pacific Studies,* vol. 16, no. 2, June 1993, pp. 1–29.

25 Rodan, Garry, 'Preserving the One-Party State in Singapore', *Southeast Asia in the 1990s: Authoritarianism, Democracy and Capitalism,* eds Hewison et. al., Allen & Unwin, St Leonards, 1993, pp. 77–8.

26 Rahim, Lily Z., 'Singapore: Consent, Coercion and Constitutional Engineering', *Current Affairs Bulletin,* January 1994, p. 21.

27 Quoted in Yash Gai, 'The Asian Perspective on Human Rights' (University of Hong Kong, unpublished manuscript, circa. 1994).

28 Tamney, Joseph B., 'Confucianism and Democracy', *Asian Profile,* Vol. 19, No. 5, October, 1991.

29 Lu, Martin, *Confucianism: Its Relevance to Modern Society,* Federal Publications, Singapore, 1983, pp. 71, 85.

30 Cotton, James, 'The Limits to Liberalization in Industrializing Asia: Three Views of the State', *Pacific Affairs,* vol. 64, no. 3, Fall 1991, p. 320.

31 Jones, David M. & Brown, David, 'Singapore and the Myth of the Liberalizing Middle Class', *The Pacific Review,* vol. 7, no. 1, 1994, p. 83.

32 Wu Tch Yao, *Politics East Politics West,* Pan Pacific Book Distributors, Singapore, 1979, pp. 57–8.

33 For further elaboration of this point see Lawson, Stephanie, 'Institutionalizing Peaceful Conflict: Political Opposition and the Challenge of Democratization in Asia', *Australian Journal of International Affairs,* vol. 47, no. 1, 1993, p. 24. Also, this is not to say that consensus has no place at all in democratic theory—see Lawson, 'Conceptual issues'.

34 *Canberra Times,* 31 May 1993.

35 *Asian Wall Street Journal,* 12–13 Nov. 1993.

36 Case, William, 'Semi-Democracy in Malaysia', *Pacific Affairs,* vol. 66, no. 2, 1993, p. 203.

37 Lawson, see note 13 above, pp. 21–2.

38 *Financial Review,* 18 March 1994.

39 It would be a mistake to cast liberal ideology itself as a homogeneous body of ideas as different strands emphasise different values. For example, social liberalism rejects extreme individualism and has been very supportive of state intervention in matters of human welfare.

40 Parekh, Bhikhu, 'The Cultural Particularity of Liberal Democracy', *Prospects for Democracy,* Polity Press, Cambridge, 1993, pp. 156–75.

41 Australian–Asian Perceptions Project, *Perceiving 'Human Rights',* Working Paper no. 2, University of New South Wales, Sydney, Academy of the Social Sciences in Australia and the Asia-Australia Institute, December 1993, p. 4.

42 Subordinated, according to some, even during times of Labor government. See Graham Maddox and Tim Battin, 'Australian Labor and the Socialist Tradition', *Australian Journal of Political Science,* vol. 26, no. 2, July 1991, pp. 181–96.

43 *Far Eastern Economic Review,* 24 Nov. 1994.

44 For a discussion of these issues see Ann Kent, *Between Freedom and Subsistence: China and Human Rights* (Hong Kong, Oxford University Press, 1993), esp. Chapter One.

Part III

'Asian' models of economic organisation

6

The neo-classical ascendancy: the Australian economic policy community and Northeast Asian economic growth

Trevor Matthews and John Ravenhill

The shift in the world's centre of gravity towards East Asia has brought with it large changes in the international economic and geo-political systems, as well as in the analytical and ideological prisms through which people all over the world view reality.[1]

The Australian economic policy community's interpretation of industrial policy in the Northeast Asian economies has been inextricably caught up in the debate over domestic economic policies. Advocates of the level playing field have been determined to ensure that their simple policy prescription should not be complicated by an acknowledgment that industrial policies have worked elsewhere. This is seen in a number of official reports. Take Ross Garnaut's *Australia and the Northeast Asian Ascendancy* (1989). This report firmly placed on the political agenda the importance to Australia of the phenomenally rapid and sustained rates of economic growth in Northeast Asia. By viewing the Northeast Asian success through a conventional neo-classical economic prism, the Garnaut Report is tellingly silent on the issue of state assistance to targeted industries.

This interpretation—viewing Northeast Asian success through the prism of neo-classical economics—is one that has been vigorously championed by the economic policy community in Australia. In official reports, academic papers, speeches, interviews and newspaper articles, the leading voices in that policy community have argued that the Northeast Asian economies demonstrate:

- that selective governmental assistance to targeted industries has been neither a necessary nor a sufficient condition for the economic success of those economies;
- that in cases where targeting could be considered to have been successful, the targeting was 'market-conforming'; and

- that attempts by government to promote and assist particular industries are as likely to be harmful as beneficial.

The policy community has also been at pains to refute claims being
made by Australian advocates of selective industrial intervention that
the Northeast Asian economies demonstrated that new developments
in international trade theory (strategic trade theory) could work in
practice. The policy community has argued

- that strategic trade theory rests on fragile assumptions unlikely to
  hold in practice and too intimidating to be a practical guide to
  action.

The most influential statement of these claims is the Industry
Commission's study *Strategic Trade Policy: The East Asian Experience*[2], and that is the study we will use to exemplify the economic
policy community's interpretation of Northeast Asian economic
growth. It is an appropriate text to use for that purpose. The Industry
Commission published the study to refute claims being made by
Australian advocates of selective industrial intervention that strategic
trade theory offered an intellectual justification for such intervention
and that the Northeast Asian economies showed that the new theory
could be effectively implemented as policy. Even though the Industry
Commission's study was entirely derivative and contained no new
empirical work, economists and economic commentators in Australia
have frequently cited the study as an authority to support *their* arguments that strategic industrial assistance contributed little (or nothing)
to the strong economic (and export) performance of the Northeast
Asian economies.[3] The study has also attracted attention outside of
Australia.[4] We first examine each of these four claims.

1 *That selective assistance to targeted industries has been neither a
   necessary nor a sufficient condition for the economic success of
   those economies.*

The IC study draws on the experience of five economies in the
region—Japan, South Korea, Taiwan, Singapore and Hong Kong. It
claims that strategic targeting cannot be taken as a common factor in
East Asia's economic success since it was not present at all in Hong
Kong, 'the most outstanding and robust example of the benefits of free
markets'. Hong Kong provides 'the most convincing evidence' that
exceptional economic performance can be achieved without the help
of government intervention.[5]

The report also refers to econometric and statistical evidence to
suggest a 'mixed picture' concerning the effectiveness of targeted
industrial policies in Japan and Korea.[6] It acknowledges that in Japan

in the 1950s and 1960s the output of the machinery industry, including the targeted motor vehicle and computer industries, grew at rates well above the manufacturing average. But it points to Japan's metal finished goods and the consumer electronics industries[7] to indicate that good performance is possible without assistance, and to the targeting in the 1950s of Japan's iron and steel industry—which experienced a growth rate below the manufacturing average in that period—to demonstrate that government assistance does not guarantee success.[8] The Industry Commission advances a similar case for Korea. Broadly based statistics are presented to show that several of the industries targeted during the heavy industrialisation drive of the 1970s were already growth leaders in the 1960s (such as transport equipment and iron and steel). While the growth in those two industries was greatly boosted following the extensive targeting of heavy industry in the 1970s, 'similarly high growth was also achieved in the same period by industries not included in the heavy and chemical industries drive, such as leather products, footwear, fabricated metal products, and electrical and scientific equipment'.[9] In short, econometric and statistical evidence is used to draw the conclusion that government intervention is neither a necessary nor a sufficient condition for achieving above average rates of growth: 'some assisted industries became international successes, others failed. And some industries succeeded without government intervention'.[10]

To the authors of the Industry Commission's study, the evidence points to the conclusion that strategic interventions to assist industries are 'unimportant in explaining success' compared with a number of other factors that each of the East Asian economies faced. They include:

- a period of crisis before the rapid growth phase;
- a strong social consensus in favour of growth;
- strong governments able to ensure that the legal, social and institutional frameworks necessary for the effective operation of markets were in place and to resist the pleas of special interests;
- an unusual opportunity to exploit technological catch-up;
- vigorous domestic and international competition;
- a plentiful, flexible and competitive labour force.

But even in the case of industries that succeeded with government intervention, the Industry Commission cautions that the existence of these common factors makes it difficult to isolate the contribution of state assistance.[11]

There are serious weaknesses in this account by the economic policy community of the role played by industry-specific assistance in the Northeast Asian capitalist economies.

First, in arguing that 'there is no convincing evidence that targeting was crucial to good economic performance', the Industry Commission's study reveals its own narrow notion of evidence. It places excessive reliance on a small number of neo-classical econometric studies while at the same time choosing to ignore much of the rich case study literature that challenges a neo-classical interpretation. Moreover, its reliance on growth rate indicators to compare the performance of sectors is questionable in that these are heavily dependent on the size of the base from which growth occurs. There is also a question of what is the relevant comparison: with the average growth rate of all industries or with what that industry might have achieved in the absence of intervention?

Second, by insisting that analysts must show that 'other factors were of minor importance' before they can conclude that governmental targeting was an essential ingredient, the Industry Commission's study not only wrongly requires a necessary condition to be a necessary and sufficient condition but also fails to consider the possibility of joint and cumulative causation. After all, policies of industrial targeting may well have been effective precisely because of the accommodating environment in which they were implemented. It is not necessary to deny the relevance of such factors as quiescent trade unions, a trading regime that encouraged exports, and a domestic consensus in favour of growth to argue that industry-specific policies were an important factor in the success of *some* industries in *some* of these countries. And it is quite beside the point for neo-liberals to point to the success of 'laissez-faire' Hong Kong as if that constituted a refutation of the claim that state intervention has played a decisive role in *other* countries at certain stages of *their* development.

2 *That in cases where targeting could be considered to have been successful, the targeting was 'market-conforming'.*

The Industry Commission makes much of the argument that industrial policy interventions in Northeast Asia were 'market-conforming'. Curiously, given the centrality of this concept to its interpretation, nowhere does it provide a definition of 'market-conforming' or an indication of the criteria by which policies might be judged not to have conformed to the market.

The closest the report comes to providing a definition is to suggest that 'industry assistance policies were combined with competition measures and intervention-induced distortions to prices were not allowed to go on indefinitely'.[12] We would agree with both components of this statement. Contests, to use the World Bank's terminology, were important either domestically as in the fierce rivalry among Japan's *keiretsu,* or internationally as in the Korean government's insistence that its targeted industries compete on world markets. And it is true that 'the government did not offer permanent protection'.[13] But neither of these statements addresses the issue of whether the policies substantially conformed to market signals in key periods of industry policy activism. Mercantilists would not be surprised that protectionism was not maintained indefinitely: to support an industry until it is sufficiently strong to compete on world markets in its own right would be a classic mercantilist strategy. Even on the issue of the length of time for which protection was provided, however, the Industry Commission's own evidence contradicts some of its claims. The report argues that 'where success was observed, any specific support was broadly market conforming and was normally withdrawn within a relatively short period of time'. But Table 20 of its report records that government intervention in Japan in the car industry was 'high' from 1952 to the early 1970s; in computers it is similarly listed as 'high' from the mid-1950s until the mid-1970s. Much obviously depends on the interpretation of a 'relatively short period of time'.

For another industrial policy sceptic, the World Bank, the market-conforming nature of economic policies in Northeast Asia is demonstrated by a comparison of domestic and international prices. The prices of traded goods in Northeast Asian countries, it suggests, were closer on average to international prices than those in other developing areas.[14] There are several problems with this analysis. First, the use of averages disguises considerable inter- and intra-country variation. Second, the data in the analysis are for 1985, reflecting the substantial liberalisation that had occurred in the tariff policies of the Northeast Asian countries since the industrial policy heyday. Again, the data provided elsewhere in the report undermine the 'market-conforming' argument. These show that in the late 1960s transport equipment, iron and steel, and textile products all received effective rates of protection in Japan in excess of 30 per cent. The Bank cites Robert Wade's data for Taiwan that show that in 1972 a significant percentage of items was subject to non-tariff barriers and two-thirds of potential imports faced nominal tariffs above 30 per cent: this figure had fallen only to 40 per cent of potential imports by the end of the decade. In Korea, the Bank concludes, even by 1983 'most sectors were still protected by some combination of tariffs and non-tariff barriers'.[15] Even if the divergence between domestic and international prices in Northeast Asia was not as great as in most less developed countries, the policies can hardly be termed 'market-conforming'.

Finally, consider another definition of market-conforming policies. This argument accepts that interventionist policies distorted some prices but asserts that offsetting measures such as exempting exporters from duties and taxes on components created a neutral trade regime.

Two points are relevant here. First, the evidence suggests that the Northeast Asian countries did not maintain *neutral* trade regimes but that the combination of export incentives and undervalued exchange rates, in the Industry Commission's own description of Korea, 'strongly favoured producing for export as opposed to domestic markets'. Second, even if one accepts the argument that the trade regime was neutral, in itself this does not refute suggestions that governments frequently intervened 'to get prices wrong' when pursuing sectorally specific policies including, for example, provision of subsidised loans or inexpensive land.[17]

3 *That government intervention to promote and assist particular industries is as likely to be harmful as beneficial.*

The economic policy community is highly sceptical of government intervention. This attitude is reflected in the Industry Commission's comment that one of the 'valuable lessons' that Australia can learn from the Northeast Asian experience is *that intervention to promote and assist particular industries is as likely to be harmful as it is to be beneficial.* And it is a 'lesson' that other Australian economists and economic commentators have echoed. As one economist asserts, government has been as much a hindrance as a help in developing the Northeast Asian economies.[18] Two arguments are advanced.

The first states that the Northeast Asian evidence shows that even in those 'miracle' economies 'government failure' exists and that governments lack the capacity to 'pick winners'. Here the Industry Commission and other Australian critics of industrial targeting make much of three stock examples to show that even Japan's Ministry of International Trade and Industry (MITI) has been associated with policy failures.[19] They mention MITI's misguided attempt to promote the production of a people's car, a single model to be manufactured by one officially designated company; MITI's aborted attempt to prevent Honda from entering motor vehicle production; and, unable to foresee the value of transistor technology, MITI's myopic attempt to hinder Sony's acquisition of that technology. Korea's heavy industrialisation drive is also offered as an example of gross government failure, a failure that 'left scars on the economy in terms of distorted credit markets, overly-indebted firms and a very high concentration of economic power'.[20] Helen Hughes[21] doubts whether governments can play any useful role in fostering strategic technologies: 'For every case of public sector success, there are hundreds of cases of failure, even in East Asia'. Hughes however does not trouble the reader with any examples of these 'hundreds of cases'.

The second line of argument rests on the belief that all forms of selective intervention impose costs on others—taxpayers and competitors—and that the costs will normally outweigh the benefits. In the words of a former chairman of the Industry Commission (and subsequent head of the Treasury): 'Increases in exports from assisted industries are offset by losses in exports from other industries'.[22] Similarly Ian McLachlan, when he was shadow Minister for Industry, frequently asserted that there was no evidence to show that a nation can protect or help one industry without harming another.[23] Hughes[24] has claimed that direct government intervention in East Asia did not offset market failures, but simply raised costs of production; moreover attempts to offset the costs of the distortions introduced by inappropriate policies 'led to many additional intra- and inter-sectoral distortions, rent seeking and corruption'. For that reason: 'government intervention can be a far more serious cause of market failure than domestic or international market imperfections'.[25] Even the Industry Commission's study, which concedes that the 'ultimate test' is whether a protected industry generates enough extra national income to compensate for the costs, falls back on static notions of allocative efficiency when questioning the success of particular targeted industries. It is unwilling to concede that POSCO, the Korean steel giant—'considered one of the world's most efficient producers'—could be considered an example of successful government targeting for it 'may not be efficient in an economic sense' because it was developed with highly subsidised capital.[26] Likewise it argues that it is wrong to cite Japan's targeting of steel as a success (despite Japan's later emergence as a major exporter of steel) for 'the policy was actually a failure when judged by more appropriate criteria', namely the rate of return achieved by the industry, 'which was relatively low compared to manufacturing in general'.

The critics link government failure to rent seeking. They believe that because industry policies provide rents for their recipients, they tend to be hijacked by the assisted industries. That, Arndt[27] asserts, is the reason why infant industries almost always never grow up. A clear expression of the unease with industry-specific intervention is seen in this warning by a senior economic bureaucrat: even when there is a clear case in principle for intervention to overcome an obvious market failure, 'the risk of government failure increases according to the extent of detailed intervention'.[28]

No proponent of industrial policies would claim that the state is infallible. But just as there are examples of state failure in Northeast Asia so there are plenty of illustrations of private failure both there and closer to home. Australian commentators need look no further than Australian banks' experience with bad debts following the private sector extravagances of the 1980s. There is no *a priori* case that the private sector will inevitably pursue more economically rational policies than the state. In concluding that 'in general, the assertion that the government can do no better than the market is simply false', the distinguished American economist, Joseph Stiglitz, suggests that the state has several advantages over private sector actors that enable it to play an effective role in overcoming market failures.[29] It is not enough for critics of interventionist policies to point to individual cases of failure as evidence that selective policies have hindered sectoral or national growth. Policy failures must be seen in perspective. How frequent and typical are the failures? Do the failures outweigh the successes? Is failure to be measured by the yardstick of static allocative efficiency or by the yardstick of dynamic efficiency (that is, in terms of the policy's effectiveness in promoting growth and technological innovation)? Again, there is a question of what is the relevant comparison—with the average rate of return on investments within the country, with the performance of the same industries in other countries, or a proper (but impossible to measure) counter-factor: the performance that the industry would have achieved without state intervention?

At one level, the argument that support for one sector comes at the expense of the rest of the economy is a truism. If a static snapshot of the economy is taken, government support to one industry through, for instance, research allowances or tariff protection, must penalise other sectors of the economy that are taxed for this purpose, or which suffer higher input costs. At any given point in time, economies are a zero-sum game: gains for one sector inevitably come at the expense of others. But economies are not static. Once we adopt a framework that examines the *dynamics* of economic growth, the fallacy of this economic rationalist argument is exposed. Taken to its logical conclusion, a position advocated by some extreme economic rationalists, there would be no role for the government in the economy whatsoever. For government provision of education, of health services, and of roads and railways requires that productive sectors of the economy be taxed (either immediately, or at some later stage as interest payments on government borrowings become due).

Not surprisingly, this extreme position is usually rejected. Maintaining an educated and healthy population and providing a country with good transport facilities are regarded as sound investments of current expenditure in that they provide the foundation for higher rates of economic growth in the future. It is often argued that these forms of government intervention provide public goods that benefit all sectors of the economy: governments are not attempting to pick winners by favouring some sectors over others. Historically, of course, this has often not been the case: technical education has been tailored to the perceived requirements of local industry; railways were built specifically to open up areas for wheat growing or to facilitate coal exports.

To tax existing productive activities to improve economic growth in the future provides a justification for other areas of selective government intervention. Again, to take a local example, Australia maintained its pre-eminence in world wool markets in part because of the support provided to the industry through the research conducted by the CSIRO, research funded in part by taxpayers' money; in other words, by other sectors of the economy. Australia, like all other industrialised economies, has a long history of selective intervention in support of some sectors of the economy in the expectation that the long-term returns will offset the immediate costs imposed on others. Some industries are expected to contribute more to future growth than others.

The Industry Commission itself provides an answer to arguments that industrial policies inevitably lead to state failure in which policy is captured by rent-seeking elements. In asserting that the success of industrial policy in Japan owed much to the temporary nature of protection, the Commission comments that 'the fact that the government was able to reduce support to industry significantly over a relatively short period also suggests that it retained considerable autonomy from the demands of special interest groups'.[30] In Northeast Asia, governments forced infant industries to grow up. Contrary to the arguments of some members of the Australian economic policy community, the World Bank's recent major study of the East Asian NICs concluded that their governments showed a remarkable degree of policy pragmatism, that they reversed course when policies did not bring the desired results, subjected domestic firms to performance criteria through various 'contests', and reduced assistance once firms became internationally competitive.[31]

4 *That strategic trade theory rests on fragile assumptions that are unlikely to hold in practice and which policymakers will find too intimidating to be a practical guide to action.*

Three distinct strands of strategic trade theorising have been developed within mainstream economics. The first is based on game-theoretic considerations of strategy and credible commitments; it suggests that governments can help domestic firms to establish a dominant position in international markets and so earn excess returns ('economic rents'). The second incorporates notions of increasing returns to scale, and is an elaboration of traditional arguments for infant industry protection. The third focuses on externalities. In addition to this work within the mainstream framework, a fourth strand of theorising has been developed which builds on the literature on technological change. This last strand, which we have labelled the strategic technology approach[32], places at the centre of its analysis the dynamic and cumulative impact of technological change on inter-country competitiveness and economic growth.

In its critique of the intellectual underpinnings of strategic trade theory, the Industry Commission questioned the policy relevance of economic rents and externalities. It cast doubt on whether significant economic rents exist and, even if they do exist in many markets, whether they are large enough to be a major object of national policy. Citing work by trade economist Avinash Dixit,[33] it argued that any excess returns not eliminated by competition probably reflect the higher returns necessary to compensate firms for higher than average risks in a market—and so are merely an ordinary component of production costs rather than an instance of economic rents.[34] This debate over the significance of rents has, however, remained inconclusive. Estimating the extent of industry rents is particularly difficult in that some of the abnormal profits may not show up in firms' accounting statements as profits must be retained within the firm and used for new investment, employment of new staff, increased research and development expenditure, etc.—the very elements that strategic trade advocates see as providing an advantage to oligopolistic firms. Studies that rely on firms' reported after-tax rates of profits to deny the extent of rents thus may fail to capture the concept. Indeed a large portion of industry rents may not go to shareholders but may instead be captured by labour. Evidence in support of this proposition is provided by studies that show that there are significant differences in the wages paid to labour for the same type of job in different sectors of the economy—and that these differences between industries are consistent across time and across countries.[35]

The Industry Commission also questioned whether externalities, even if they are generated by assisted industries, can be confined to national boundaries.[36] This criticism of externalities (also advanced by the Department of the Treasury[37] has, however, been blunted by the recent reassessment of the importance of externalities by economists who were once sceptics. Paul Krugman, for example, now emphasises:

> . . . that meaningful externalities occur not only when there are direct technological spillovers, but in any situation in which there are increasing returns and [*where*] market size matters. That means almost everywhere. In other words, the marginal social benefit of a dollar's worth of resources is not, as conventional theory would have it, equal in all activities except for a few exceptions. Divergences between social rates of return are pervasive. There are good industries and bad, good jobs and bad, and the optimal policy is to subsidise the good and tax the bad.[38]

Externalities and the dynamic gains from learning by doing are, however, not captured in the studies that the Industry Commission and the Treasury cite in support of their negative evaluations of strategic trade (and industrial) policies. These econometric studies (often using 'calibrated' models[39]) are cast within partial or general equilibrium frameworks that fail to factor into the equation links with other industries or gains over time. One such study, cited by the Treasury in arguing against the view that Japan offers an example of the successful use of strategic trade theory, models the effects of Japanese government support for the semiconductor industry. The study's authors, the US economists Baldwin and Krugman, examine Japanese policies to target the production and export of computer memory chips—through promoting strategic early entry into the industry by Japanese firms and assisting R&D in the learning curve stage—and conclude that the policies only served to reduce economic welfare by raising average costs and prices.[40] This study, one of several by these authors that are frequently cited as reasons for rejecting the policy implications of strategic trade theory, fails to address some of the most significant issues raised by the strategic trade literature, notably benefits derived from increasing returns to scale, from technological externalities and from the dynamic and cumulative impact of technological change on a country's competitiveness and economic growth.[41]

The case for intervention in economic theory

For neo-classical economists, government intervention is only justified when market failures occur. Even the Australian Industry Commission, one staff member notes, has itself made recommendations for intervention on such grounds.[42] But economists tend not to believe that such failures are extensive or that governments have the capacity to correct them without at the same time causing other problems. As an Australian economic rationalist has commented, intervention 'is fraught with the . . . danger that government failure will be worse than the supposed market failure the intervention is meant to overcome'.[43] Economic planners in Japan, Korea and Taiwan in the 1950s and 1960s evidently believed that market failures were more likely than neo-classical economists predicted.[44] Whether the possibility of market failure was the real reason for state intervention or whether this derived from more old-fashioned mercantilist concerns to promote rapid industrialisation for purposes of both security and wealth is debatable. But whatever the motives for state intervention—and those commentators who assert that industrial policy has played a significant role in the economic success of the Northeast Asian countries often note wryly that their economic planning agencies were staffed primarily by engineers rather than economists—Northeast Asian countries demonstrated that industrial policies that economists have only recently shown to work in theory could work in practice.

A number of economists have recently acknowledged that markets are far more prone to failure than was previously believed. Joseph Stiglitz[45] comments that whereas the traditional literature 'characterized market failures as exceptions to the general rule that decentralised markets lead to efficient allocation', a revisionist view suggests that 'it is only under exceptional circumstances that markets are efficient' . And market failures are even more common in less developed countries.[46] In recent years, neo-classical orthodoxy has come under attack not only for its views on the efficiency of markets. New theories of growth and trade have challenged other core elements of neo-classical theory including the assumption of constant returns to scale, the treatment of technology as exogenous (that is, that technology is static and freely available to all countries); and the supposition that the rate of growth cannot be increased by raising the investment rate. These alternative approaches suggest a role for state intervention that goes beyond the correction of market failures.

The assumption of constant returns is fundamental to the neo-classical model. Yet it is one that does not sit well with reality, as has long been recognised, for example, by Adam Smith and Alfred Marshall. For the most part, however, increasing returns were ignored by economic theory until a model was devised in the early 1980s that incorporated increasing returns to scale derived from specialisation.[47] Alfred Marshall much earlier had made the important link between scale economies and benefits accruing to other parts of the economy. He suggested that external economies take two forms: those that increased the size of the local market enabling the realisation of economics of scale in the production of an industry's inputs; and the spillover of knowledge and technology to other firms. Any doubts there might be about the importance of such external economies can be dispelled simply by observing the tendency for firms in the same industry to locate within a narrowly defined geographical region. This geographical concentration—not merely of high-technology companies as in Silicon Valley or in the North Carolina research triangle, but of many industries irrespective of technological sophistication—is clear evidence of the pervasive influence of localised externalities.[48]

The damage that relaxation of the assumption of constant returns does to the neo-classical model is difficult to exaggerate. For rather than there being a single equilibrium point on the production function, the presence of increasing returns opens the possibility of multiple equilibria. Consequently, the neo-classical model is unable to provide any guidance as to which combination of capital and labor is optimal for economic growth. And if multiple equilibria are possible, there is a variety of trajectories that an economy may experience. The actual development path that an economy takes may be determined to a significant degree by historical accidents and/or by expectations of its future growth path that become self-fulfilling prophecies. Companies and countries that are the early movers in a field may gain advantages that prove very difficult for rivals to overcome. As Paul Krugman[49] noted, 'small beginnings can have large consequences'.

The role of historical accidents and early mover advantages in shaping countries' growth trajectories points to the centrality of technology in economic development. The inadequate treatment of the role of technology is one of the principal weaknesses of neo-classical models of growth and trade. Technological progress is regarded as being exogenously determined, fortuitous and, when it occurs, freely available to all countries within the system. This inability to explain technological change is all the more unfortunate when studies conducted within the neo-classical framework found that a major contribution to the growth of national output came from the residual in the regression equations—which measures total factor productivity or technological progress.[50] The World Bank estimates that technological progress contributed more than a third of the growth of Japan, Korea, Hong Kong and Taiwan, a much larger percentage than in other less developed countries

Recent work within mainstream economics on endogenous growth models abandons the assumptions of the early neo-classical growth model by attempting to allow for imperfect competition and the role of technology.[51] The new growth and endogenous technology models thus bring the mainstream approach much closer to the studies that have been produced over several decades by theorists of technological change. These have demonstrated that, contrary to the neo-classical model, technology cannot be considered as a commodity that is universally available as if it is embodied in a set of blueprints. Rather, technological knowledge is often specific to individual firms, is dependent upon the prior expertise they have built up, often evolves through a process of learning-by-doing, and comprises much tacit (that is, uncodifiable) knowledge that is embodied in the personnel employed by a particular company.[52] That companies spend a larger percentage of their research and development budgets on developing products than on research is seen as indicating the importance both of learning-by-doing, and the tacitness of technology.[53]

To the extent that techniques are company-specific and cumulative in nature, a country's economic trajectory will be heavily influenced both by the past performance of its companies and by the extent to which the necessary competence for the exploitation of scientific and technological opportunities has been developed. As firms and countries alike vary greatly in their accumulated competence and therefore in the range of technical choices that they may feasibly adopt, the international diffusion of technology does not keep pace with the generation of innovations. In consequence, a relatively wide productivity gap develops between countries. Intersectoral differences in technological levels within countries are smaller than such differences between countries. Consequently, absolute advantages are more important in explaining international trade than the concept of comparative advantage, much beloved in neo-classical theory.[54]

The emphasis in the new theories of growth and trade on the importance of technology and on how growth trajectories are determined by what goods a country produces is similar to the nineteenth century arguments of List and Hamilton that emphasised the advantages of specialising in the production of manufactures rather than primary products. The new arguments suggest a role for government that goes beyond the protectionism/free trade dichotomy that too often dominates the industry policy debate in Australia (although protection *was* pervasive in Northeast Asia at critical stages of some industries' development, and important in providing companies with a domestic market in which they could realise economies of scale and learning-by-doing advantages).

With the acquisition of technology being the key determinant of a country's growth trajectory, there is in the strategic technology literature a central role for governments to implement selective measures that foster the development and application of new technologies. Here particular emphasis is given to 'leading' industries, ones that 'drive and mold economic progress across a broad front';[55] in other words, industries that generate pervasive technological externalities for a broad spectrum of other sectors. The target should be industries judged to be in the country's long-term comparative (and absolute) advantage, those whose products have high income elasticities of demand. Nelson terms them 'strategic' industries, for it is upon their strength that a country's economic progress and its international competitiveness depend.

But why should government intervention be necessary? Why would a rational profit-maximising firm not pursue strategies that maximise the possibility of innovation and technological dynamism? The answer lies in market imperfections. First, imperfections in capital markets can give rise to 'short-termism'—the desire to see immediate high returns on investments. This myopia may flow from the structure of capital markets. In countries where companies are more dependent on equity than on long-term bank lending to finance major investment projects, corporate managers will be under pressure from their shareholders to deliver high returns in the short term. It may also flow from the highly uncertain and risky nature of high technology R&D, and the tendency of the market to discount heavily the possibility of future profits from technological breakthroughs. Uncertain about the technological feasibility of a project and the time it will take, about its total cost, and about the commercial viability of the planned new product, private capital markets are often unwilling to invest in high technology R&D. This unwillingness will be the greater if a country lacks a vigorous market in venture capital. Second, in imperfect product markets characterised by increasing returns, current market signals can be misleading indicators of future profitability.[56] Third, as Scitovsky pointed out many years ago, underinvestment from market failures also occurs because market signals do not reflect the 'untraded interdependencies' that exist among investment decisions when reciprocal externalities are present. Future profits in one industry may be inseparable from the successful establishment of another industry and vice versa—but as the market does not consider the two together, the necessary investments are not made.[57]

The possibility that market signals may fail to yield socially optimal outcomes for the nation is a strong justification for government intervention to target 'strategic transformative' technologies. For the targeting of strategic industries, even if it is temporary, may have permanent effects on the future trajectory of a country's economic development and its technological progress. In Northeast Asia, policies to promote high technology industries have been motivated by just such a Schumpeterian perspective. Governments have played a critical role in establishing institutions that have helped to overcome market failures and to set their economies on a favorable technological trajectory.

Strategic intervention in Northeast Asia

In this section we present evidence to show that the state in Northeast Asia has intervened decisively at various times over the last forty years to change the structure of incentives for particular industries in a manner that has significantly affected the pattern of economic development in those economies. This evidence, we contend, fits better the interventionist rationales of strategic trade and new growth theories than it does the so-called market-conforming rationale of neo-classical economic theory. Indeed much of the evidence is consistent with an interpretation that suggests that these governments have used trade and industrial policies (and deliberately 'got prices wrong') so as to achieve two ends:

1 to assist domestic firms to become internationally competitive by enabling them to realise scale and learning economies; and
2 to generate externalities that benefit a wide range of leading-edge industries.

Import protection as export promotion

One strand of strategic trade theory demonstrates that protection of the domestic market may enable firms to capture scale and learning economies sufficient to give them a cost advantage on foreign markets.[58] The assumption is that the protected industry is characterised by economies of scale whereby unit costs of production fall as output rises. If a government closes off its domestic market to foreign competition the domestic producer will enjoy longer production runs than would otherwise be the case and thus reap economies of scale. These 'static' economics may be reinforced by a firm's ability to 'learn by doing'. The larger the domestic market, the greater the potential for realising such benefits. The lower production costs that are gained from exploiting a protected domestic market—or that come from subsidies to the domestic industry—may then enable the domestic producer to compete more effectively in foreign markets.

Because of its large domestic market, Japanese companies have tended to benefit more than their Korean counterparts from such policies, and Korean companies in turn have benefited more than Taiwanese firms. It should be noted, however, that whereas in Japan vigorous competition has characterised most protected industries, in Korea and Taiwan governments have sometimes allowed monopolies in protected infant industries. Assistance given to the Japanese steel, automobile and colour television industries illustrates the way in which protection of the rapidly growing home market enabled those industries to achieve impressive scale economies and to be well placed to capture export markets when capacity began to outstrip domestic demand.

Promotion of the steel industry lay at the heart of Japan's postwar program of 'heavy and chemical industrialisation'.[59] In 1950 the Ministry of International Trade and Industry devised a policy for the development of a modern and internationally competitive steel industry. Under that plan, MITI (and the Ministry of Finance) intervened directly during the 1950s to boost the capital that the industry had for investing in the most advanced steel-making technology. The government ensured that the banking system made available to the industry ample capital at favourable rates; provided steel producers with generous depreciation allowances; allocated scarce foreign exchange to the industry for the purchase of the latest equipment and technology from abroad; and extended preferential low-interest loans to the industry, which acted as a green light to other lenders. Although governmental subsidies declined in importance after 1960, the government continued to guarantee much of the private lending. Investment poured into the industry, resulting in a massive increase in gross crude steel capacity. MITI was determined that the Japanese mills be of optimal size to exploit the economies of large scale characteristic of the industry. In targeting the industry, MITI favoured the very largest firms. Under the first steel plan (1951–55), 70 per cent of government funds flowed to only four of the forty-four steel firms.[60] It feared that left to themselves, competition between the six major steel companies would result in an excess of new projects below the optimum size. To prevent this form of market failure, MITI encouraged investment coordination among the largest companies to enable them to 'take turns' in building completely new integrated mills.[61] As a result of this official encouragement of huge new 'greenfields' facilities, Japanese mills were soon among the largest and most technologically advanced in the world. By the mid-1970s Japan led the world in the use of large capacity furnaces, continuous casting techniques, and computer-controlled production processes. There is little doubt that MITI's intervention in investment decisions greatly assisted Japan to exploit early-mover advantages to enable it to become by 1970 the world's most efficient steel producer.

Having made these massive investments, Japan's oligopolistic steel producers needed some assurance of market stability. The government provided that assurance, by allowing the formation of recession cartels and by protecting the domestic market from imports. In fact, throughout the entire postwar period the import of steel products into Japan has been almost negligible. In the 1950s and early 1960s, the 'extremely high' levels of tariffs and the system of rationing foreign exchange for imports were effective import barriers.[62] In later years, private non-tariff barriers effectively discouraged imports. As a result, the protected and rapidly growing home market enabled the industry to achieve impressive scale economies and to be well positioned to capture export markets when, by the late 1960s, capacity began to outstrip domestic demand. In addition, Japan reaped two other benefits: a falling domestic price for a crucial intermediate input and, because of steel's relatively large share in export demand, a rise in national income relative to its trading partners.

Policies to assist the Japanese automobile industry during the high-growth era also illustrate the mechanism whereby import controls can act as export promotion measures.[63] As in the case of steel, the automobile industry was designated in the early 1950s as a strategic infant industry to be fostered by the government. From then until the late 1960s, the industry benefited from a bundle of promotional and protectionist policies.[64] Among the former, the government supplied low-interest loans through government-affiliated financial institutions, granted subsidies for technological development, exempted necessary machinery and equipment from import tariffs, and, despite the severe foreign exchange restrictions, approved the import of essential foreign technology. And to secure efficient mass production, MITI subsidised the Nissan–Prince, Toyota–Hino and Toyota–Daihatsu mergers.[65]

At the same time the government sheltered the industry from foreign competition. It did so by means of protective tariffs, an excise tax that discriminated against foreign cars, foreign exchange controls on imports, and severe restrictions on direct foreign investment. Sheltered from foreign competition, the domestic industry—a competitive oligarchy characterised by product differentiation—was able to entrench itself in the home market. Because the protection was known to be temporary, designed to give the local industry just enough time to prepare for liberalisation, the threat of future competition spurred the local manufacturers to accelerate their investment in ever-expanding productive capacity and to avoid excessive price competition. Faced with an expanding domestic demand, investment surged, permitting the manufacturers to exploit considerable static and dynamic scale economies and to engage in further capacity-expanding investment. By the time passenger car imports were liberalised in 1964, the Japanese automobile industry was internationally competitive in terms of costs and quality. And by the time foreign investment restrictions were lifted in the 1970s, foreign producers found that the high-capacity domestic firms had pre-empted the market. When domestic demand began to slacken in the early 1970s, the irreversible effects of these time-bound protective measures were strong enough to give the Japanese producers a decisive competitive advantage in foreign markets.[66] That exports were able to leap from 100 000 in 1965 to over 1.8 million units in 1971 indicates the success of the government's strategy.[67]

Of Japan's achievements in the high-growth period, one of the most dramatic was the rapid emergence of the colour television industry and its swift capture of export markets. As already noted, some observers see the success of the Japanese colour television industry on world markets as owing little to government targeting. One Australian economist even asserts that a firm like Sony owes 'nothing whatever to bureaucratic promotion, but everything to innovation, rivalry and low cost'.[68] But to depict the industry in that way is to disregard the degree to which the surge of colour television exports was made possible by a combination of government policies: import tariffs and quotas, controls on direct foreign investment, lax enforcement of antitrust measures, tax incentives for exports, and a government-coordinated and financed R&D program. As a leading specialist in Japanese industrial policy has argued, these unique policy incentives 'cannot be ignored' in any explanation of the Japanese producers' success in capturing a large slice of the American market.[69] In fact, policies to protect and financially assist the industry served also to develop the industry's capacity to succeed in capturing export markets.

The fledgling industry benefited greatly from import protection. Tariff rates ranged between 20 and 30 per cent until 1968. Despite trade liberalisation after that date, imports in 1980 amounted to no more than a minuscule 0.1 per cent of the domestic market.[70] As in the case of automobiles, the industry also benefited from another form of effective market closure: restrictions on direct foreign investment.[71] Those restrictions prevented US firms from establishing subsidiaries in Japan or from acquiring the smaller Japanese producers and using their facilities for manufacturing portable sets.

The closed market enabled the seven major Japanese manufacturers to reap the advantages of scale economies, especially for small sets. It enabled them to cartelise the domestic market and to collude in setting high domestic prices. The closed market also compelled the US manufacturers, who were excluded from the Japanese market, to license their technology to the Japanese, a move that speedily closed the technology gap between the two industries. Special governmental grants and long-term low-interest loans made it easier for the Japanese companies to purchase this foreign technology, as did the high domestic earnings.

The scale economies and the high-profit base not only permitted the Japanese manufacturers to upgrade their production processes and incorporate new technological developments, they also 'provided the firms with the motivation and means to sell their products on world markets at prices below those commanded at home—possibly below the cost of production'.[72] The Japanese manufacturers sold on the American market at prices far below those charged in Japan. This dumping occurred with the connivance of MITI, which sanctioned the industry's legal export cartel and its system of common minimum prices for exports.

The importance of the Korean experience is that it shows that import-substitution policies need not be incompatible with an export-oriented development strategy. By providing firms with a protected home market and by using subsidies to socialise the risk of large-scale investments, the Korean government enabled firms to achieve scale and learning economies based on large and expanding production volumes. This in turn allowed firms to exploit their falling cost curves to capture export markets from foreign competitors. It also made it possible for the government, once export markets had been staked out, to wind back its subsidies and the level of protection. Korea in this respect followed the Japanese model: it supported at any one time only a 'narrow moving band' of infant industries, providing protection until a targeted industry was internationally competitive, then moving on to the next target. Exporting, in turn, enabled further economies of scale to be exploited, thus further reducing unit costs of production and leading to lower domestic prices than would occur in its absence.[73]

Neo-classical economists frequently depict Korea as a pre-eminent exemplar of export-oriented industrialisation.[74] They argue that because the Korean government maintained the exchange rate near the free-trade level, exempted intermediate inputs and export sales from indirect taxes, and granted exporters unrestricted and tariff-free access to imported inputs, it provided a virtual free-trade regime for exporters. But to depict Korea's industrialisation strategy as essentially one of export-promotion based on non-selective policies of 'unshackling exports' is to tell but half the story. It fails to acknowledge that the Korean government has since the early 1960s actually pursued *two* proximate industrial objectives.[75] These have been:

1 to encourage exports from industries where Korea has an established or readily attainable comparative advantage, and
2 to promote infant industries.

While measures without any discernible trade or industry bias were used in attaining the first objective, protection and other selective measures, including many genuine subsidies,[76] were used to attain the second.

Protection was the main promotional incentive for designated infant industries. In the early 1960s, these industries included cement, fertilisers, synthetic fibres and oil refining. They were followed in the late 1960s by steel and petrochemicals. In the 1970s, under the plan to promote self-sufficiency in the 'heavy and chemical' industries (HCI) and to upgrade Korea's export potential in capital and intermediate goods, import protection was extended to non-ferrous metals, shipbuilding, heavy machinery, transport equipment, motor vehicles and, although they were neither heavy nor chemical, consumer durables and electronics. Although the HCI drive was abandoned in 1979, the automobile and electronics industries continued to be protected. Import restrictions were still used as late as 1987 to protect high-tech products such as computers, electronic amplifiers, cameras, VCRs, integrated circuits, teleprinters and colour TVs.[77]

The selective allocation of credit, however, has had the most impact on Korea's industrial structure. Through its control of the entire credit system (the banks were not privatised until the 1980s), the government has been able to direct the commercial banks to accord designated 'strategic' industries preferential access to 'policy loans' at substantially subsidised rates. In this way, and because of the highly leveraged nature of Korean industry, the government has been able to determine not only the level and rate of industrial investment but also its direction. In the 1970s, for example, investment was directed into the export sector, the chemical and heavy industries, and the large conglomerates (known in Korea as *chaebol*). The government also used the credit system to increase Korean ownership and control in key sectors. By favouring the *chaebol,* the government's planners hoped to set up a small set of very large, domestically owned and controlled, diversified enterprises amenable to governmental direction and capable of surmounting the high entry barriers in the HCI sectors and of maximising scale economies in production, R&D and exporting. For example, the *chaebol* were given preferential access to concessionary credit to establish general trading companies modelled on Japan's *sogo shosha* in order to achieve scale economies in exploring new markets and in establishing overseas sales networks.[78]

In fact, what is quite distinctive about these various measures to protect and promote domestic industries is that they have been crafted in such a way as to be export promoting. The government required assisted infant industries to meet closely monitored export targets; it allocated preferential credit on the basis of export performance; and it allowed exporters to practise discriminatory pricing at home as a means of subsidising export sales. Its closely monitored export targets virtually compelled established export industries and assisted infant industries alike to keep expanding their exports.[79] The result, as Westphal writes, is that 'infant industry' has been a less apt characterisation in Korea than 'infant exporter'.[80]

It was this insistence on making exports 'a compulsion rather than a choice'[81] that enabled the Korean planners to elicit from the recipients of governmental subsidies progressive increases in production volumes, in quality and in productivity. The insistence that infant industries compete in international markets also helped the planners to achieve the elusive balance between economies of scale, often requiring monopolised or oligopolistic market structures, and competition.[82] Targeted industries soon became leading export industries. This group includes a number that were direct beneficiaries of the HCI drive, such as steel, shipbuilding, electronics and automobiles.[83] Even the export success of the semiconductor industry, often said to have been the result of private initiatives, stems in part from the policy of the HCI years to promote the large diversified conglomerates: by the mid-1980s they had attained the market power to internally cross-subsidise the development of the semiconductor industry, to surmount the high entry barriers, and to provide the marketing know-how.[84]

Externalities and transformative technologies

In Northeast Asia, governments have turned the market failures associated with technology to the advantage of their economies. These failures include the public good nature of technology, and imperfections in the international market for technology, in the market for risk capital, and in the flow of information between firms. Intervention to facilitate the acquisition, adaptation and diffusion of technology has been pervasive. All three have targeted industries and technologies perceived to be strategic for the economy's future growth—industries that were expected to generate pervasive externalities for a broad range of other sectors and which would set their economies on a favourable technological trajectory.

Consider first the acquisition of technology. The international market for technology is often characterised by oligopoly and monopoly. In all three countries, the state used its controls over direct foreign investment and over foreign exchange to improve the bargaining position of domestic corporations *vis-à-vis* foreign owners of technology. Direct foreign investment was discouraged, the state preferring instead to force foreign companies to license their technology to domestic producers. Where foreign investment was permitted, the foreign corporation was usually required to enter a joint venture with a local company, assuring that technology and production skills would be transferred. Wholly foreign-owned enterprises were extremely rare in Japan and Korea.[85] Where a licensing agreement was to be arranged, the state sometimes insisted that local firms be represented by a single negotiator, sometimes a single licensee, to maximise the domestic bargaining leverage.[86] The Taiwanese state has been less hostile towards direct foreign investment than its counterparts in Japan and Korea but, like them, has limited the access of foreign corporations to key sectors and imposed obligations on foreign investors to transfer technology, establish linkages with local suppliers, and meet export targets.[87]

Because capital market failures are a major barrier to technological development, the state in Northeast Asia developed a variety of mechanisms for financing technology acquisition. These included loans at concessional rates; equity participation by the state (especially in Taiwan[88]); and the establishment of institutions to fund high risk, high technology R&D by the private sector. Examples of the latter include the Japan Key Technology Centre (JKTC) and the Korean Technology Advancement Corporation (KTAC), and the Taiwan Bank of Communications'. The JKTC lends government and private funds at preferential rates to consortia and firms conducting R&D in 'key technologies', primarily microelectronics, telecommunications, new materials and biotechnology. The KTAC funds the commercialisation of technologies developed by government research centres. The Bank of Communications is Taiwan's government development bank and has a division for venture and risk capital which underwrites high technology investments.

Consider next the adaptation and diffusion of technology. In neoclassical economics, one of the most pervasive market failures is the externalities arising from the inability of companies to exclude others from the benefits of their private research and development activities. Competitors are able to mimic improvements by reverse engineering; and knowledge of new production processes often leaks from the originating firm. Since firms fail to capture all the benefits of their research, the tendency is for underinvestment in such activities. Rather than attempt to strengthen the private ownership of technology, governments in Northeast Asia have acted to reinforce its collective good status. They have done this by promoting industry associations and encouraging them to share facilities. They also created regional technology centres,[89] established government research laboratories, and encouraged research consortia. Samuels notes that since the 1970s every government program in Japan designed to promote technology development has included incentives for collaborative research.[90] Moreover, when the government issues contracts for high-technology research or goods, it ensures that the unsuccessful bidders are awarded part of the contract as suppliers to the primary contractor. In that way 'winners and losers "take all" *together*—though in different measure'.[91]

The export-orientation of the developmental strategies of the three governments has also assisted those economies to acquire and diffuse technology. The emphasis on exports is in accord with arguments found in the new theorising on trade and growth that claims that substantial externalities for the domestic economy arise from the experience of producing for foreign markets. These spillovers arise in particular from impetus that international competition gives to improving quality, introducing new products, and keeping up with new technology. Evidence from Korea indicates that exporting has been a particularly important mechanism for acquiring technological mastery.[92]

The rise of the semiconductor industry in Japan, Korea and Taiwan illustrates the way the state has forced the pace of technological learning. Over the last decade, semiconductor production has become the archetypical strategic industry. Countries covet a flourishing semiconductor industry not only because its technology spills over to other advanced industries but also because it is seen as essential for a nation's economic, technological and military strength. Because it is characterised by steeply rising scale and learning economies, by extremely short product cycles, by highly expensive R&D, by pervasive external economies, and by enormously costly start-up costs, 'the semiconductor industry is about as far as one can get from the classical model of a perfect market'.[93] Little wonder the industry is regarded by many as the ideal target for strategic trade policy.

In its 'vision' statement of how Japan's industrial structure should change in the 1980s, MITI advocated a shift to a 'knowledge-intensive industrial structure' based on advanced technology. Woven through the text of MITI's vision for the 1980s was a clear understanding of the major long-term 'ripple effects' of 'epochal technological innovation', of the bargaining leverage that possession of this technology will give Japan, and of the need for the government to promote these technologies when their development is 'urgently needed by the economy and society' and when it requires massive investment, R&D coordination among firms, and a long gestation period before results can be marketed.[94] Central to this vision was the recognition of the semiconductor as just such a strategic transformative technology whose national importance demands state promotion. A similar recognition of the strategic importance of semiconductors occurred in Korea and Taiwan. Although Korea had no comparative advantage in the production of semiconductors in the mid-1970s, the Korean government targeted semiconductors in 1976 as a 'strategic industry' for promotion. In the mid-1980s, Taiwan's government mapped out a strategy to shift the Taiwanese economy towards high technology industries. The promotion of the semiconductor industry became a central aspect of that strategy.

The erosion of US technological leadership in semiconductors has been ascribed in large part to 'the mobilizing, coordinating and rallying role of the Japanese government'—particularly the use of government-backed collaborative R&D projects.[95] The goal of many of the earlier projects was to match or surpass the technical capabilities of the leading foreign firms, notably IBM. For example, the 1966–71 super-high-performance electronic computer (SHPEC) program was to catch up to IBM's System 360 series; the 1972–76 3.5 Generation Project was in reaction to IBM's 370 series; the 1976–79 Very Large Scale Integration (VLSI) Project targeted the expected use of VLSI memory circuits in IBM's Future Series.

In the 1980s, MITI based a further series of joint R&D programs on the VLSI model. These projects targeted certain new technologies such as optoelectronics, supercomputers and future electronic devices. Having reached the technological frontier in many areas of computers and semiconductors, the problem facing Japanese companies at that stage was the uncertainty and risk inherent in 'over the horizon' R&D. MITI helped reduce these uncertainties. It did so by socialising the risk, by reducing the transaction costs of collaborative research and, by selecting in close cooperation with industry the technologies for development, MITI's funds not only acted as a magnet attracting additional corporate investment into the selected areas, they were also important in their own right. Around 20 per cent of the research resources spent by certain firms on R&D projects with a time horizon of ten years or more came from MITI.[96] But MITI shrewdly left the commercialisation of the technological advances to the firms. In this way MITI avoided the pitfalls of attempting to pick winning products and ensured that competition would have to centre on improving quality and lowering costs. Further, by providing the institutional context in which semiconductor producers could work with the producers of semiconductor fabrication equipment, the VLSI project helped to generate the technical synergies to be derived from 'learning by using'.[97]

Observers generally credit the 1976–79 Very Large Scale Integration (VLSI) project with enabling Japan to close the technology gap with the US, and indeed to achieve technological superiority in areas such as non-silicon products, new materials, and high-density memory devices. They doubt that Japanese firms would have been able, without the catalytic effect of the VLSI project, to commercialise the 64K dynamic random access memory (DRAM) chip as early as they did, or to capture 70 per cent of the world market for 64K chips by 1981–82.[98]

By providing incentives to encourage the leading semiconductor firms to participate in joint research, MITI and Nippon Telephone and Telegraph (NTT) were able to overcome the collective action problem deterring firms from collaborating on R&D. But given the fierce rivalry among the largest firms, cooperation was often difficult to secure. One incentive was the mechanism of 'distributed cooperation', where research is carried out independently in each firm's own laboratory, with the patents then shared. This enabled the participating firms to keep their competitors at arm's length yet at the same time it permitted the diffusion of technological knowledge.[99]

In a careful study of R&D consortia for superconductivity and engineering ceramics, Hane emphasises technological diffusion, rather than dramatic scientific breakthroughs, as the chief goals of the projects. Among these goals were: diffusing information about state-of-the-art to industry; establishing databases that would help eliminate blind alleys and contribute to the codification of knowledge that had a strongly tacit character; allowing sufficient time for firms to take the technology through several generations of iteration for greater commercial attractiveness; and coopting end-users by lowering their risks through subsidies and incorporating them into the development of the technology.[100]

By bringing together technical staff from the participating firms, the joint research projects also checked the tendency of the lifetime employment system, with its low labour mobility, to hinder the diffusion of technical knowledge among firms. Fransman singles out the synergistic effects of the improved flow of information among the participating firms and the economies of joint R&D (from pooling technical information, sharing costly non-divisible equipment, and avoiding wasteful duplication in research), as a distinct benefit that flowed from the VLSI project. To counter the argument that the market could have been relied upon to produce these benefits, he points out that not only did MITI have to force the firms to participate in the joint projects but that in the whole postwar period there were only two cases of spontaneous research cooperation among Japan's major electronic firms not prompted or assisted by the government or a government agency such as NTT.[101]

In Korea, the government has emphasised the role of public research institutes and collaborative R&D to enhance its own technological capacity in microelectronics. And as in Japan, it has given priority to raising the competence and competitiveness to a small number of the biggest firms in the industry, all of whom belong to three major conglomerates: Samsung, Goldstar and Hyundai. In 1976 the government established a public research institution, the Korea Institute of Electronics Technology (KIET). Its mission was to plan and coordinate semiconductor R&D, to import, adapt and disseminate foreign technologies, and to provide technical assistance to firms. KIET established contact with US semiconductor firms and created a network among Korean scientists working in US semiconductor companies. It took an active part in all technology transfer agreements between Korean and foreign firms. The government has continued to use its de facto influence over foreign investment—influence obtained through foreign requests for tax benefits—to induce technology transfers from foreign to Korean companies.[102] KIET also pioneered the fabrication of silicon wafers in Korea. By taking the initiative and backing those initiatives with sizeable funds, the Korean government 'got different results than had the firms that received no such guidance'.[103]

Once the *chaebol* began to produce semiconductors and to conduct their own applied research, the government's role changed. It took on more of a follower role. KIET's role (and name) changed. Now known as the Electronics and Telecommunications Research Institute (ETRI), it focused more on promoting parallel basic research in semiconductors, computers and telecommunications and setting its R&D agenda in consultation with the major Korean companies. In the mid-1980s, ETRI was associated with subsidising and coordinating the VLSI Project, a Japanese-style R&D consortium to develop a Korean design for a four-megabyte chip. It then moved on to target the development of 16M and 64M DRAMs through government–industry cooperation. Recognising the importance of spillovers and linkages, the government has in more recent years been using subsidies and administrative guidance to build a local supply infrastructure for semiconductor materials and an indigenous semiconductor equipment industry.[104]

The dominance of small and medium sized enterprises in Taiwan, and their reluctance to enter the semiconductor business, explains the leadership role taken by the state in Taiwan in creating a semiconductor industry. The Electronics Research and Service Organisation was set up in 1975 with a government grant to design and produce integrated circuits. Focusing on application-specific integrated circuits, it provided a series of spin-offs for the whole information industry. In 1980 the state created Taiwan's first semiconductor enterprise, United Microelectronics Corporation. A public corporation in which the government held a 44 per cent equity stake, UMC had the task of commercialising microelectronics technology developed in the public research laboratories. The government also established the Taiwan Semiconductor Manufacturing Corporation, a foundry manufacturing semiconductors on a contractual basis for other companies, in which it held a 40 per cent stake. The government has set up state-owned technology research institutes to acquire and adopt foreign technology. Given the capital constraints and coordination difficulties faced by Taiwan's proliferation of small-sized firms, and considering the high entry barriers resulting from short product cycles and steep learning curves in high technology sectors, government-supported R&D has been a particularly important measure in promoting 'strategic technologies' in Taiwan. Studies of government-initiated R&D in the machine tools and 'informatics' industries—computers, semiconductors, telecommunications—indicate the crucial role played by the state in assisting these strategic industries rapidly to master, improve, disseminate and commercialise the new technologies and to achieve international competitiveness.[105] As Biggs and Levy[106] observe, 'externality-creating investments promoted (and sometimes undertaken directly) by government appear to have been unusually important in Taiwan's successful industrialisation'.

Many of Taiwan's selective trade and industrial policies can be interpreted as efforts by the Taiwanese authorities to stimulate the generation of external economies.[107] By initiating investment in and directing capital towards consecutive sets of basic upstream industries, the government's planners provided new profit opportunities intended 'to spark an endogenous downstream expansion of private firms as a result of its initiatives'.[108] These initiatives helped generate sequential externalities that contributed to the economy's productivity and growth over and above the profits earned by the targeted upstream industries. These investment initiatives also generated simultaneous externalities—benefits that are contingent on the complementary and simultaneous decisions of interdependent actors, and which are often lost if left to the uncoordinated investment decisions of private agents—by ensuring the concurrent expansion of related industries. Certain trade policies, such as the law of similars, fostered technological acquisition through 'learning by using': this measure, which prevented manufacturers importing particular intermediate products, in effect brought downstream users and local suppliers together and encouraged the latter to upgrade their production processes so that their products would meet the specifications demanded by the users.

Conclusion

The interpretation of the Northeast Asian industrial policy experience by Australia's economic policy community has been inextricably caught up in the debate over domestic economic policies. Advocates of the level playing field have been determined to ensure that their simple policy prescription should not be complicated by an acknowledgment that industrial policies have worked elsewhere. At best they have been unable to conceptualise intellectually the dynamics that occur outside the paradigm in which they operate. At worst they have shown a marked reluctance to acknowledge and confront contrary evidence. This is evident in their deliberate silence on the role of sectorally specific policies in the success of the Northeast Asian economies, and through their distorted accounts of such intervention.

With the publication of the World Bank's *East Asian Miracle* (1993) it is very difficult for even the most hard-line of economic rationalists to deny that the state played a role in the success of the Northeast Asian economies. Two of the principal contributors to the Bank's report, which in general was hostile to industrial policies, summarise its findings as follows:

> . . . government interventions in many cases have not had the dire consequences that many would have predicted . . . the country studies leave no doubt that government intervention in picking winners was prominent in some East Asian countries.[109]

Not only was it prominent, our evidence for Japan, Korea and Taiwan shows many examples where government intervention in the form of sectoral trade and industry policies has occurred with the intention of realising externalities, of changing technological trajectories, and of shaping comparative advantage. None of the governments has been content to trust the course of economic development exclusively to the market. All three have consciously targeted industries that were perceived to be strategic for the economy's future growth—industries that were skill- and capital-intensive, industries that were expected to generate technological spillovers and other externalities, and industries whose products were identified as having high income elasticities of demand. A similar set of industries was identified in all three countries for government support—steel, heavy and chemical industries, automobiles, electrical and electronics, semiconductors, and most recently, biotechnology. The similarity in the industries assisted is unremarkable given, first, the importance of these sectors to modern industrialised economies and, second, the fact that both Korea and Taiwan consciously set out to emulate the Japanese model.

Various policies have been used to overcome the market failures, particularly coordination and information failures, that prevent externalities from being realised. Again, there are great similarities across the three countries. Governments have sponsored research and development activities designed to acquire and disseminate foreign technologies; they have used their powers over foreign investment to require technological transfer and/or to insist that foreign investors take on local joint venture partners. The net result has been to shift production to the local economies, production that would otherwise have been carried out overseas.

Northeast Asian governments have pursued various policies consistent with the variant of strategic trade theory that builds on the infant industry argument. This suggests that government intervention, through protecting the domestic market and through facilitating exports, may enable firms to capture the benefits of scale and learning economies. The larger the domestic market, the greater the potential for realising such benefits. Japanese companies thus have tended to benefit more than their Korean counterparts, which in turn benefited more than Taiwanese firms, from having a secure home market (although it should be noted that in most industries in Japan there has been vigorous competition in the protected domestic market between a number of companies, whereas Korea and Taiwan in some sectors have granted companies domestic monopolies). Governments in all three countries have also, however, used various policy instruments to enable domestic firms to realise scale and learning economies through penetrating foreign markets.

In short, the state has intervened decisively in Japan, Korea and Taiwan at various times to change the structure of incentives for particular industries in a manner that has significantly affected their patterns of economic development. The evidence cannot sustain the *a priori* case against government intervention that many Australian economists and economic commentators have presented. Conclusions about the replicability elsewhere of the East Asian experience with strategic trade policies must, however, be drawn cautiously. The success of the policies pursued by these states depended on the political and institutional contexts in which they were applied. To avoid state failure in the pursuit of similar policies in political systems that lack the normative consensus, the exclusionary characteristics, and/or the weak legislatures of Japan, Korea and Taiwan will be much more difficult. Similarly, to reproduce the elite planning agencies of these countries elsewhere, without the supporting political and economic environments, is to invite very different results. The distinctive features of the Australian economy (not to mention the different political and bureaucratic context) cautions against any simple application of the Northeast Asian experience with strategic trade policy to Australia.

The Industry Commission makes several persuasive arguments why strategic trade policies may not work in Australia:

> Even if significant economic rents exist, the small size of the Australian market places a major constraint on attempts to achieve international cost competitiveness by closing the domestic market. Further, while small size does not preclude the possibility that subsidies could enable Australia to dominate some markets, . . . the importance of a country being at the frontier of competitiveness before intervention is attempted. . . raises the question of whether, in many of the industries identified by the proponents of strategic policy as worthy of assistance, Australia is too far behind for market domination to be feasible. Also, Australia's relatively small market size means that the cost of (inevitably some) failed attempts at intervention would be substantial.[110]

In addition, Australia has (outside the resources sector) few major firms in world-scale oligopolistic industries where there are significant barriers to entry and economic rents to be earned.[111] In fact, very few firms that are large by Australian standards are large players by world standards. Apart from mining companies, only one manufacturing company, BHP, is an exporter of world class. Australian manufacturers lack the market power needed to participate in international strategic games in which the trick is to threaten to boost their size and output. Not only that, a large number of Australia's top exporters are actually the affiliates of major foreign-owned multinational corporations and have limited autonomy to develop and market high value-added products outside of Australia.

All of this suggests that the Northeast Asian experience with policies designed to assist targeted industries to capture economic rents or to realise scale and learning economies has very restricted relevance to Australia. The industries that come closest to meeting the characteristics needed for such policies include value-added processing of resource and agricultural commodities, custom-designed computer software (e.g. for banks), and specialist equipment for mining and agriculture (where the Australian market is relatively large). Other Australian firms may be able to carve out niches in specialist markets, gain first-mover advantages and earn rents, But as the entry barriers to such industries are unlikely to be significant for large overseas rivals, and the products may well be vulnerable to reverse engineering, such advantages may prove to be transitory.

While policies aimed at shifting economic rents to domestic firms may not succeed in the Australian context, these are but one small part of the strategic trade policy agenda. There are positive lessons for Australia from the Northeast Asian experience with other parts of the agenda. These are most notable in success of governments in changing technological trajectories in Japan, Korea and Taiwan through the pursuit of policies consistent with what we have termed a 'strategic technology' approach. In Northeast Asia intervention to facilitate the acquisition, adaptation and diffusion of technology has been extensive. All three countries have adopted policies to correct market failures—particularly the difficulties posed by imperfect and asymmetric information—hindering R&D activities. The use of government-sponsored R&D consortia illustrates how governments can overcome the collective action problem deterring firms from collaborating on R&D, can bring the potential users of a high-tech product and the manufacturers together in the R&D process, and, by involving a number of industrial sectors in the process, can promote more effective 'technology fusion'.[112] Moreover, all three have targeted industries and techniques that were expected to generate pervasive externalities for a broad range of other sectors, to lead to increasing returns at the economy level, and to set their economies on a favourable technological trajectory. Given Australia's poor R&D performance, particularly by the private sector, government intervention can play two roles: to help overcome the market failures that have resulted in too little R&D; and, as the Bureau of Industry Economics[113] has argued, to induce an attitudinal and behavioural change among Australian firms, 'such that R&D becomes an ongoing element of company strategy'. With evidence that R&D, innovation and competitiveness are empirically linked[114], such a change is essential if Australia is to improve its international competitiveness.

Notes

1 Garnaut, Ross, *Australia and the Northeast Asian Ascendancy* , Australian Government Publishing Service, Canberra, 1989, p. 5. The authors

thank Robin Ward for tracking down many of the references cited in this paper, Gillian Evans for locating articles in the Australian press, and Richard Robison for thoughtful comments and suggestions.

2 Industry Commission, *Strategic Trade Theory: The East Asian Experience*, Information Paper, Industry Commission, Canberra, 1990.

3 For example: Anderson, Kym, 'International Trade and Australian Protectionism', *Economic Rationalism: Dead End or Way Forward?*, eds S. King & P. Lloyd, Allen & Unwin, St Leonards, 1993; Anderson, Kym & Findlay, Christopher, 'The End of Tariff Protection', *Current Affairs Bulletin*, vol. 70, no. 3, August 1993, pp. 12–18; Blandy, Richard, 'A Panel of Views: Economic Rationalists and Anti-Economic Rationalists', *Economic Rationalism: Dead End or Way Forward?*, eds S. King & P. Lloyd, Allen & Unwin, St Leonards, 1993; 'Rational Policies Made Asian Nations Prosper', *The Age*, 3 February 1993; McGuiness, P. P., 'Counting the Cost of Export Subsidies', *The Australian*, 23 Nov. 1990; 'Industry Policy Won't Protect Us', *The Australian*, 1 Nov. 1991; 'The Price We Pay for Pathological Protectionism', *The Australian*, 21 Oct. 1991; Wood, Alan, 'Targeting Shoots Wide of the Mark', *The Australian*, 13 Nov. 1990.

4 Ostry, Jonathan, 'Are Growth Strategies in East Asia Relevant for New Zealand?', *Finance and Development: a publication of the IMF and the World Bank*, vol. 31, no. 1, 1994, pp. 13–15.

5 Industry Commission, op. cit., p. 63.

6 ibid., pp. 54–6.

7 The report (p. 57) cites Wolfgang Kasper's claim that 'names like Sony, Honda, Canon or YKK owe nothing whatever to bureaucratic promotion, but everything to innovation, rivalry and low cost'.

8 Arndt also mentions motor cars and consumer electronics as examples of successful Japanese industries in the 1960s that 'succeeded on their own without special government support'. See Arndt, H.W., *Industrial Policy in East Asia*, Reprint Series, National Centre for Development Studies, Australian National University, Canberra, 1989, p. 41.

9 ibid., pp. 55–6.

10 ibid., p. 59.

11 Few in the policy community were as extreme as Ian McLachlan: 'Japan's success is due more to plain hard work than to any miraculous government intervention'; op. cit., 1991.

12 Industry Commission, op. cit., p. 40.

13 ibid., p. 15

14 World Bank, *The East Asian Miracle: Economic Growth and Public Policy*, Oxford University Press for The World Bank, New York, 1993, p. 301.

15 ibid., p. 297.

16 Industry Commission, op. cit., p. 22.

17 Ironically, given the distaste with which his work is viewed by the Australian economic policy community, Chalmers Johnson was one of the first commentators to suggest that Japan's industrial policies have been 'market-conforming'. For Johnson, market-conforming methods of

intervention refer to 'a government-business relationship that both enabled the government to achieve genuine industrial policy and also preserved competition and private enterprise in the business world'. See: Johnson, Chalmers, *MITI and the Japanese Miracle: The Growth of Industrial Policy, 1925–75*, Stanford University Press, Stanford, 1982, p. 29.

18 Garvey, Gerald T., 'From Corporate Strategy to Interventionist Trade Policy: Two Critical Missing Links', *Australian Journal of Management,* vol. 17, no. 1, 1992, p. 198.

19 See: Arndt, op. cit., Gittins, Ross, 'Japan's MITI Success is a Heavyweight Myth', *Sydney Morning Herald*, 6 Dec. 1989 and 'MITI Didn't Make Japan', *Sunday Age*, 10 Dec. 1989; Kasper, Wolfgang *'Competition and Economic Growth: The Lessons of East Asia'*, Egon Sohmen Foundation, Tegernsee, Germany, 1990; Mellor, John, 'Interview with Ian McLachlan', *The Australian*, 27 August 1992.

20 Industry Commission, op cit., p. 24.

21 Hughes, Helen, 'Catching Up: The Asian Newly Industrializing Economies in the 1990s', *Asian Development Review,* vol. 7, no. 2, 1989, pp. 128–44.

22 Cole, A.C., 'Still Looking for Free Lunches: a Review of The Global Challenge: Australian Manufacturing in the 1990s', Centre for International Economics, Canberra, mimeograph, 1990, p. 4.

23 McLachlan, op. cit., 1991; also Mellor, op. cit.

24 Hughes, Helen, *Is There an East Asian Model?*, Working Papers, no. EA 93/4, Economics Division, Research School of Pacific Studies, Australian National University, Canberra, 1993, p. 22.

25 ibid., p. 5.

26 Industry Commission, op. cit.

27 Arndt, op. cit., p. 33.

28 Keating, Michael, 'The Influence of Economists', *Economic Rationalism: Dead End or Way Forward?*, eds S. King & P. Lloyd, Allen & Unwin, St Leonards, 1993, pp. 71–2.

29 Stiglitz, Joseph. E., *The Economic Role of the State*, Basil Blackwell, Oxford, 1989. These include its powers to tax, to proscribe, and to punish far more severely than penalties in private contractual arrangements. In addition, the state may be better equipped to overcome transaction cost problems.

30 Industry Commission, op. cit., p 15.

31 World Bank, op. cit. Contrast the comments of Helen Hughes (1989, p. 141): 'The exploitation of technological opportunities requires imagination, risk taking and speedy decisions. Because some technological judgements will be wrong, some firms will go bankrupt. For all these reasons the public sector, which cannot take risks and where bankruptcy is almost impossible to implement, cannot play a useful role in this area.'

32 Matthews, Trevor & Ravenhill, John, 'Strategic Trade Policy: The Northeast Asian Experience', *Business and Government in Industrialising Asia*, ed. A. Macintyre, Allen & Unwin, St Leonards, NSW, 1994.

33 Dixit, Avinash, 'International Trade Policy for Oligopolistic Industries', *Economic Journal Supplement,* vol. 94, (supplement), 1984 pp. 1–16.

34 Industries Assistance Commission, 'Appendix 5: Strategic Trade Theories', *Annual Report 1988–89*, Australian Government Publishing Service, Canberra, 1989, pp. 81–2.

35 Dickens, William T. & Lang, Kevin, 'Why it Matters What We Trade: A Case for Active Policy', *The Dynamics of Trade and Employment*, eds L.D.A. Tyson, W.T. Dickens & J. Zysman, Ballinger, Cambridge, Mass., 1988; Dixit, Avinash, 'Optimal Trade and Industrial Policies for the US Automobile Industry', *Empirical Research in International Trade*, ed. R. Feenstra, The MIT Press, Cambridge, Mass., 1988; Katz, Lawrence F. & Summers, Lawrence H., 'Industry Rents: Evidence and Implications' *Brookings Papers: Microeconomics,* vol. 1, 1989, pp. 209–90; Thaler, R.H., 'Anomalies: Interindustry Wage Differentials', *Journal of Economic Perspectives,* vol. 3, no. 2, 1989, pp. 181–93.

36 Industries Assistance Commission, op. cit.

37 Department of the Treasury, 'Strategic Targeting for Industrial Development', *Economic Round-up*, January 1990, pp. 3–13.

38 Krugman, Paul, 'Does the New Trade Theory Require a New Trade Policy?', *The World Economy,* vol. 15, no. 4, 1992, p. 438.

39 Calibration refers to a technique whereby assumed behaviour and the empirical data are made mutually consistent. According to Paul Krugman, it is a 'gimmick' whereby the data are 'not given a chance to reject the model'. (*Economic Policy*, vol. 3, no. 1, 1986, p. 661.) See also David J. Richardson, 'Empirical Research on Trade Liberalization with Imperfect Competition', *OECD Economic Studies,* no. 12, 1989, p. 19. The economic policy community continues to cite these studies despite Krugman's admission that 'Nobody really believes in the calibrated results' (Krugmen, see note 38).

40 Baldwin, Richard & Krugman, Paul R., 'Market Access and Competition: A Simulation Study of 16K Random Access Memories', *Empirical Research in International Trade*, ed. R. Feenstra, The MIT Press, Cambridge, Mass., 1988.

41 As is acknowledged by one of the authors in a subsequent reflection on this work: see Baldwin, Richard, 'High-Technology Exports and Strategic Trade Policy in Developing Countries: The Case of Brazilian Aircraft', *Trade Policy, Industrialization, and Development: New Perspectives*, ed. G.K. Helleiner, Clarendon Press, Oxford, 1992.

42 Banks, Gary, 'A Comment on Determining Industrial Policy', *Australian Journal of Management,* vol. 17, no. 1, 1992, pp. 188.

43 Anderson, op. cit., p. 109.

44 Okimoto, Daniel I., *Between MITI and the Market: Japanese Industrial Policy for High Technology*, Stanford University Press, Stanford, 1989; Soon, Cho, *The Dynamics of Korean Economic Development*, Institute for International Economics, Washington, DC, 1994.

45 Stiglitz, op. cit., p. 42.

46 Stiglitz, Joseph E., 'Markets, Market Failure and Development', *Ameri-*

can *Economic Review, Papers and Proceedings,* vol. 79, no. 2, 1989, pp. 197–203.

47 Ethier, Wilfred J., 'Decreasing Costs in International Trade and Frank Graham's Argument for Protection', *Econometrica,* vol. 50, no. 5, 1982, pp. 1243–68.

48 Krugman, Paul, *Geography and Trade,* The MIT Press, Cambridge, Mass., 1991.

49 ibid. See also Helpman, Elhanan, 'The Noncompetitive Theory of International Trade and Trade Policy', *Proceedings of the World Bank Annual Conference on Development Economics 1989,* World Bank, Washington, DC, 1989; Matsuyama, Kiminori,'Increasing Returns, Industrialization, and Indeterminacy of Equilibrium', *Quarterly Journal of Economics,* vol. CVII, no. 2, 1991, pp. 617–50.

50 Denison, Edward F., *Why Growth Rates Differ: Postwar Experience in Nine Western Countries,* Brookings Institution, Washington, DC 1967, and *Trends in United States Economic Growth,* Brookings Institution, Washington, DC, 1985; Solow, Robert, 'Technical Change and the Aggregate Production Function', *Review of Economics and Statistics,* vol. 39, no. 3, 1957, pp. 312–20.

51 Grossman, Gene M. & Helpman, Elhanan, *Innovation and Growth in the Global Economy,* The MIT Press, Cambridge, Mass., 1991; Romer, Paul M., 'Growth Based on Increasing Returns Due to Specialization', *American Economic Review, Papers and Proceedings,* vol. 77, 1987, pp. 56–62 and 'Increasing Returns and Long-run Growth', *Journal of Political Economy,* vol. 94, no. 5, 1986, pp. 1002–37.

52 Dosi, Giovanni, Pavitt, Keith & Soete, Luc, *The Economics of Technical Change and International Trade,* Harvester Wheatsheaf, Hemel Hempstead, 1990; Mowery, D.C. & Rosenberg, N., *Technology and the Pursuit of Economic Growth,* Cambridge University Press, Cambridge, 1989; Nelson, Richard R., *High-Technology Policies: A Five-Nation Comparison,* American Enterprise Institute for Public Policy Research, Washington D.C., 1982.

53 Dosi, Pavitt and Soete (op. cit., p. 81) estimate that 60 per cent of companies' R&D budgets is devoted to product development.

54 In other words, the 'dominant difference between countries rests in the "different production functions" that they have, and not in "different factor combinations" along the same production function' (Dosi, Pavitt & Soete, op. cit., p. 63, emphasis in original; see also pp. 11, 151). For a further discussion see MacDonald, Glenn N., & Markusen, James R., 'A Rehabilitation of Absolute Advantage', *Journal of Political Economy,* vol. 93, no. 2, 1985, pp. 277–97.

55 Nelson, Richard R., *High-Technology Policies: A Five-Nation Comparison,* American Enterprise Institute for Public Policy Research, Washington DC, 1984, p. 1.

56 Dosi, Giovanni, Tyson, Laura D'Andrea & Zysman, John, 'Trade, Technologies, and Development: A Framework for Discussing Japan', *Politics and Productivity: The Real Story of Why Japan Works,* eds C. Johnson,

L.D.A. Tyson & J. Zysman, Ballinger Publishing Company, Cambridge, Mass. 1989, p. 17.

57 Scitovsky, Tibor, 'Two Concepts of External Economies', *Journal of Political Economy*, vol. 63, no. 2, 1954, pp. 143–51.

58 Krugman, Paul, 'Import Protection as Export Promotion: International Competition in the Presence of Oligopoly and Economies of Scale', *Monopolistic Competition and International Trade*, ed. H. Kierzkowski, Clarendon Press, Oxford, 1984.

59 Imai, Ken'ichi, 'Iron and Steel', *Industry and Business in Japan*, ed. K. Sato, M.E. Sharpe, Inc., White Plains, NY, 1980; Magaziner, Ira C. & Hout, Thomas M., *Japanese Industrial Policy*, Policy Studies Institute, London, 1980; Yamawaki, Hideki, 'The Steel Industry', *Industrial Policy of Japan*, eds R. Komiya, M. Okuno & K. Suzumura, Academic Press, Tokyo and San Diego, 1988.

60 McCraw, Thomas K. & O'Brien, Patricia A., 'Production and Distribution: Competition Policy and Industry Structure', *America Versus Japan*, ed. T.K. McCraw, Harvard Business School Press, Boston, 1986, p. 96, footnote 40.

61 Howell, Thomas R. et al., *Steel and the State: Government Intervention and Steel's Structural Crisis*, Westview Press, Boulder and London, 1988, pp. 215–18; Imai, op. cit., pp. 206–12.

62 Yamawaki, op. cit., p. 289; Yamazawa, Ippei, *Economic Development and International Trade: The Japanese Model*, East-West Center, Honolulu, 1990, p. 176.

63 Itoh, Motoshige et al., *Economic Analysis of Industrial Policy*, Academic Press Inc, San Diego, 1991, ch. 11.

64 Mutoh, Hiromichi, 'The Automotive Industry', *Industrial Policy of Japan*, eds R. Komiya, M. Okuno & K. Suzumura, Academic Press, Tokyo and San Diego, 1988; Ueno, Hiroya & Hiromichi Muto, 'The Automobile Industry of Japan', *Industry and Business in Japan*, ed. K. Sato, M.E. Sharpe, Inc., White Plains, NY, 1980.

65 Ueno & Muto, op. cit.

66 Itoh et al., op. cit., ch. 11.

67 Ueno & Muto, op. cit., p. 161.

68 Kasper, op. cit.

69 Yamamura, Kozo, 'Caveat Emptor: The Industrial Policy of Japan', *Strategic Trade Policy and the New International Economics*, ed. P. R. Krugman, The MIT Press, Cambridge, Mass., 1986, p. 179.

70 Yamamura, Kozo & Vandenberg, Jan, 'Japan's Rapid-Growth Policy on Trial: The Television Case', *Law and Trade Issues of the Japanese Economy: American and Japanese Perspectives*, eds G.R. Saxonhouse & K. Yamamura, University of Washington Press, Seattle, 1986, p. 253.

71 Peck, Merton J. & Wilson, Robert W., 'Innovation, Imitation, and Comparative Advantage: The Performance of Japanese Color Television Set Producers in the U.S. Market', *Emerging Technologies: Consequences for Economic Growth, Structural Change and Employment*, ed. H. Giersch, J.C.B. Mohr, Tübingen, 1982, p. 209.

72 Yamamura & Vandenberg, op. cit., p. 249.

73 Pack, Howard & Westphal, Larry E., 'Industrial Strategy and Techno-logical Change: Theory Versus Reality', *Journal of Development Economics*, vol. 22, no. 1, 1986, pp. 87–128.

74 Balassa, Bela & associates, eds, *Development Strategies in Semi-Industrial Economies*, Johns Hopkins University Press, Baltimore, 1982; Krueger, Anne O., 'Export-Led Industrial Growth Reconsidered', *Trade and Growth of Advanced Developing Countries in the Pacific Basin. Papers and Proceedings of the Eleventh Trade and Development Conference*, eds W. Hong & L.B. Krause, Korea Development Institute, Seoul, 1981; Little, I.M.D., 'The Experience and Causes of Rapid Labour-Intensive Development in Korea, Taiwan Province, Hong Kong, and Singapore and the Possibilities of Emulation', *Export-Led Industrialization and Development*, ed. E. Lee, ILO Asian Employment Programme, Singapore, 1981.

75 Westphal, Larry E., 'Industrial Policy in an Export-Propelled Economy: Lessons from South Korea's Experience', *Journal of Economic Perspectives*, vol. 4, no. 3, 1990, pp. 41–59.

76 The reliance on subsidies sits uneasily with the neo-classical depiction of the Korean economy. These subsidies included tax reductions on export earnings; accelerated depreciation allowances on capital used in export production; generous wastage allowances on duty-free imports of raw materials; preferential rates on electricity and rail transport; and, most importantly of all, preferential access to short- and long-term credit for exporters. Korea pursued its outward-oriented strategy by following the export-subsidy not the free-trade route—see Nam, Chong-Hyun, 'Export Promotion Strategy and Economic Development in Korea', *Export Promotion Strategies: Theory and Evidence from Developing Countries*, ed. C. Milner, Harvester Wheatsheaf, Hemel Hempstead, 1990.

77 World Bank, *Korea: Managing the Industrial Transition. (Volume I: The Conduct of Industrial Policy)*, The World Bank, Washington, DC, 1987.

78 Rhee, Yung W., Ross-Larson, Ross & Pursell, Garry, *Korea's Competitive Edge: Managing the Entry into World Markets*, The Johns Hopkins University Press, Baltimore, 1984, p. 65.

79 ibid.

80 Westphal, Larry E., 'The Republic of Korea's Experience with Export-led Industrial Development', *World Development*, vol. 6, no. 3, 1978, p. 375.

81 Amsden, Alice H., *Asia's Next Giant: South Korea and Late Industrialization*, Oxford University Press, New York, 1990, p. 90.

82 Green, Andrew E., 'South Korea's Automobile Industry', *Asian Survey*, vol. 32, no. 5, 1992, p. 307.

83 For a positive assessment of the HCI drive see the report by the World Bank's Operations Evaluation Department (1992).

84 Howell, Thomas R., Bartlett, Brent L. & Davis, Warren, *Creating Advantage: Semiconductors and Government Industrial Policy in the 1990s*, Semiconductor Industry Association in association with Dewey Ballantine, Santa Clara, 1992; Mody, Ashoka, 'Information Industries in

the Newly Industrializing Countries', *Changing the Rules: Technological Change, International Competition, and Regulation in Communications*, eds R.W. Crandall & K.Cramm, The Brookings Institution, Washington, DC, 1989, and 'Institutions and Dynamic Comparative Advantage: The Electronics Industry in South Korea and Taiwan', *Cambridge Journal of Economics*, vol. 14, no. 3, 1990, pp. 291–314.

85 Encarnation, Dennis J., *Rivals Beyond Trade: America Versus Japan in Global Competition*, Cornell University Press, Ithaca, 1992; Mardon, Russell, 'The State and the Effective Control of Foreign Capital: The Case of South Korea' *World Politics,* vol. 43, no. 1, 1990, pp. 111–38.

86 A case in point was MITI's insistence that Nippon Kokan become the only Japanese licensee of basic oxygen furnace technology. To ensure that the new technology was disseminated to other steel producers, MITI arranged for them to share in paying the royalty costs in return for having access to the technology. This arrangement enabled the Japanese steel industry to gain access to the BOF technology at a considerably lower cost than their American competitors.

87 Wade, Robert, *Governing the Market: Economic Theory and the Role of Government in East Asian Industrialization*, Princeton University Press, Princeton, 1990, pp. 149–57.

88 Two of Taiwan's leading semiconductor producers, United Microelectronics Corporation and the Taiwan Semiconductor Manufacturing Corporation were created with the government holding a large equity stake. The Bank of Communications holds an equity position in the Taiwan Masking Corporation, which produces semiconductor masks. See Howell, Bartlett & Davis, op. cit., p. 198.

89 Friedman, David, 'Phantom of the Paradise: Unresolved Issues in Japanese Industrial Governance Research', The MIT Japan Program: Science, Technology, Management, Center for International Studies, Massachusetts Institute of Technology, 1993.

90 Samuels, Richard J., *'Rich Nation, Strong Army': National Security and the Technological Transformation of Japan*, Cornell University Press, Ithaca, NY, 1993, p. 51.

91 ibid., p. 313.

92 Dahlman, Carl J., Ross-Larson, Bruce & Westphal, Larry E., 'Managing Technological Development: Lessons from Newly Industrializing Countries', *World Development,* vol. 15, no. 6, 1987, pp. 759–75; Pack & Wesphal, op. cit.; Rhee et al., op. cit.; Westphal, Larry E. & Kwang Suk Kim, 'Korea', *Development Strategies in Semi-Industrial Economies*, ed. B. Belassa, et al., Johns Hopkins University Press for the World Bank, Baltimore, 1982; Westphal, Larry E., Kim, Linsu & Dahlman, Carl J., 'Reflections on the Republic of Korea's Acquisition of Technological Capability', *International Technology Transfer: Concepts, Measures and Comparisons*, eds N. Rosenberg & C. Frischtak, Praeger, New York, 1985; Westphal, Larry E. et al., *Exports of Capital Goods and Related Services from the Republic of Korea*, World Bank Staff Working Paper no. 629, World Bank, Washington, DC, 1984; Westphal, Larry E., Rhee, Yung W. & Pursell, Garry, *Korean Industrial Competence: Where It*

Came From, World Bank Staff Working Paper no. 469, World Bank, Washington, DC, 1981.

93 Krugman, Paul, 'Targeted Industrial Policies: Theory and Evidence', *Industrial Change and Public Policy: A Symposium Sponsored by the Federal Reserve Bank of Kansas City*, FRB of Kansas City, Kansas City, 1983, p. 147.

94 MITI, *The Vision of MITI Policies in the 1980s: Trade and Industrial Policy for the 1980s*, MITI, Tokyo, 1980, pp. 136, 145, 148.

95 Howell, Bartlett & Davis, op. cit., p. 138.

96 ibid., p. 288.

97 Stowsky, Jay S., 'Weak Links, Strong Bonds: U.S.-Japanese Competition in Semiconductor Production Equipment', *Politics and Productivity: The Real Story of Why Japan Works*, eds C. Johnson, L.D.A. Tyson & J. Zysman, Ballinger, Cambridge, Mass., 1989.

98 Among economists who have judged the projects as economically worthwhile see: Fransman, Martin, *The Market and Beyond: Cooperation and Competition in Information Technology Development in the Japanese System*, Cambridge University Press, Cambridge, 1990; Goto, Akira & Wakasugi, Ryuhei, 'Technology Policy', *Industrial Policy of Japan*, eds R. Komiya, M. Okuno & K. Suzumura, Academic Press, Tokyo & San Diego, 1988; and Shinjo, Koji, 'The Computer Industry', *Industrial Policy of Japan*, eds R. Komiya, M. Okuno & K. Suzumura, Academic Press, Tokyo and San Diego, 1988.

99 Levy, Jonah D. & Samuels, Richard J.,'Institutions and Innovation: Research Collaboration as Technology Strategy in Japan', *Strategic Partnerships: States, Firms and International Competition*, ed. L.K. Mytelka, Frances Pinter, London, 1991, p. 129.

100 Hane, Gerald Jiro, 'Research and Development Consortia in Innovation in Japan: Case Studies in Superconductivity and Engineering Ceramics', PhD dissertation thesis, Harvard University, 1992, p. 541.

101 Fransman, op. cit., p. 279.

102 Howell, Bartlett & Davis, op. cit., p. 359.

103 Wade, op. cit., p. 318.

104 Howell, Bartlett & Davis, op. cit., pp. 361–2.

105 Fransman, Martin, 'International Competitiveness, Technical Change and the State: The Machine Tool Industry in Taiwan and Japan', *World Development,* vol. 14, no. 12, 1986, pp. 1375–96; Mody, op. cit.; Schive, Chi, 'The Next Stage of Industrialization in Taiwan and South Korea', *Manufacturing Miracles: Paths of Industrialization in Latin America and East Asia*, eds G. Gereffi & D. Wyman, Princeton University Press, Princeton, 1990; Wade, op. cit., pp. 106–8.

106 Biggs, Tyler S. & Levy, Brian D., 'Strategic Interventions and the Political Economy of Industrial Policy in Developing Countries', *Reforming Economic Systems in Developing Countries*, eds D. H. Perkins & M. Roemer, Harvard Institute for International Development, Cambridge, Mass., 1990.

107 ibid., pp. 353–4.

108 ibid., p. 383.

109 Leipziger & Vinod Thomas, eds, *Lessons of East Asia: An Overview of Country Experience*, The World Bank, Washington, DC, 1993, pp. 3, 29.
110 Industries Assistance Commission, op. cit., 1989, p. 83.
111 Hamilton, Clive, 'Strategic Trade Policy and Its Relevance to Australia', *The Economics of Australian Industry*, ed. C. Hamilton, Allen & Unwin, North Sydney, 1991.
112 Kodama, Fumio, *Analysing Japanese High Technologies: The Techno-Paradigm Shift*, Frances Pinter, London, 1991, and 'Japan's Unique Capability to Innovate: Technology Fusion and its International Implications', *Japan's Growing Technological Capacity: Implications for the U.S. Economy*, eds T.S. Arrison et al., National Academy Press, Washington, DC, 1992.
113 Bureau of Industry Economics, *R&D, Innovation and Competitiveness*, Research Report 50, Australian Government Publishing Service, Canberra, 1993, p. 20.
114 For evidence, see ibid.

Further References

Matsuyama, Kiminori, 'Increasing Returns, Industrialization, and Indeterminacy of Equilibrium', *Quarterly Journal of Economics,* vol. CVII, no. 2, 1991, pp. 617–50.
Westphal, Larry E. et al., 'Republic of Korea', *World Development,* vol. 12, no. 5/6, 1984, pp. 505–33.
World Bank, *World Bank Support for Industrialization in Korea, India, and Indonesia: World Bank Operations Evaluation Study*, World Bank, Operations Evaluation Department, New York, 1992.

7
Sources of the East Asian advantage: an institutional analysis

Linda Weiss

Whether geography requires that one look North, East, or West, the rise of high-performance market economies in East Asia is, from any vantage point, one of the most important events of the contemporary age. Though too early to draw firm conclusions, one increasingly clear consequence of that transformation has been a general (but not universal) softening of authoritarian rule and transition towards a more democratic polity. As a consequence, for many observers *inside* these societies, the key emerging issue is whether or not a high-performing economy can be maintained *in combination with* a newly liberalised and democratised polity. Ironically, this issue finds its mirror image Down Under in the social-democratic concern that Australia's welfare democracy might be compromised by increasing engagement with Asia and the primacy placed on economic performance.

Evident in both these Asian and Australian concerns is the supposition that welfare democracy and economic prosperity are in some sense deeply in tension. It is remarkable that the very same assumption is shared by neo-liberal economists who, like social-democratic welfarists, are prone to juxtaposing equity and growth, democracy and development as necessary tradeoffs.[1]

This understanding of the issue has provided the dominant point of departure for debate over Australia's economic integration with Asia. But it has generated two very different sorts of conclusions. For welfare democrats, Australia's continuing engagement with Asia is to be resisted, since it is most likely to bring only negative-sum outcomes, weakening its social-democratic traditions without strengthening its economic base. For the economists however (who have exercised most influence in policymaking circles), economic engagement is to be applauded and promoted, but can only bring success at a price. That price, according to the economists, is to adopt the set of economic policies that would help create the allegedly leaner-government, free-market system of our Asian neighbours to the north.

Which voice rings true in this debate? Posed in these terms, the choice seems to be *either* to become more industrially dynamic *or* to preserve our democratic welfare traditions. But this way of posing the problem is unfortunate, for it sets up a choice between false alternatives. The choice is not between a generous welfare system (as in 'the West') *or* a dynamic industrial economy (as in 'the East').[2] In an internationalised economic environment, the real issue must surely be: How can democratic Australia create an industrially dynamic economy that can generate rising standards of living and employment opportunities for all its citizens?

Posing the question in this way forces one to recognise that the solution may be neither as socially unpleasant nor, indeed, as economically simple as the regnant economic orthodoxy suggests. That is the message of this chapter. Its purpose is not so much to show that East Asia has a set of policies *quite different* from the minimal government-free market theory which has informed so much economic decisionmaking within the Australian community. That is a point amply developed in the chapter by Matthews and Ravenhill. This chapter adds to that by way of an overview of the research findings on East Asian development, which suggest *inter alia* that Australian economists are somewhat out of step with their counterparts abroad. But the central task of the chapter lies elsewhere: It takes a step back from the character of the policies themselves in order to explain why East Asian governments (specifically Japan, Korea and Taiwan, the most industrialised of the region) have been able to produce policies that have for the most part effectively transformed their industrial portfolios. Whether to establish new industries, create new products, or upgrade quality, technologies and skills, the East Asian experience has emphasised the advantages of a publicly coordinated approach to industrial innovation.

This chapter argues that the more *enduring* sources of East Asia's advantage lie neither in low wages and welfare parsimony nor in an imperfect or underdeveloped democracy (such claims themselves being either inaccurate or very difficult to substantiate). Rather, the sources of its transformative advantage are fundamentally *institutional* in character. The key institutions are principally, *but not only*, a set of high-grade public agencies involved in general task-setting with an eye to the nation's long-term industrial performance. More to the point, East Asia's institutional advantage lies in the emergence of 'developmental' or 'catalytic' states which coordinate and institutionalise networks of centrally organised public and private actors. Such linkages or networks make it possible for autonomous bureaucracies to enter into cooperative relations with industry in order to pursue collective goals, and thus to minimise the 'privatisation' of public policy. East Asian states, in short, have been relatively more capable in coordinating industrial change because they have been able to maintain political *insulation* while simultaneously avoiding economic *insularity*, a point to be developed later.[3]

The main discussion focuses on the institutional capabilities that underlie effective coordination. However, since this presupposes that East Asia's developmental success has not been 'market-led', the chapter begins by summarising the main contributions to that debate. Discussion then turns to the institutional features that enhance the policymaking capabilities of East Asian bureaucracies. The results of these institutional capacities for state–economy relations and industrial performance are examined in section 3. Finally, the chapter considers why, in spite of strong external (and some internal) pressures for the liberalisation of their political economies, East Asia's institutional advantage is more likely to strengthen than unravel (although this must be qualified for Korea). Some implications of this analysis for a relatively uncoordinated market economy like Australia are teased out in the conclusion.

1. Theories of East Asian development: The decadence of an orthodoxy

It is hardly surprising that the sources of East Asian dynamism have constituted the pre-eminent issue for so many commentators. Whether 'success' is measured in terms of manufacturing exports, growth rates, unemployment levels, per capita income, living standards or income distribution, or some combination of these, the industrial development of East Asia has been strikingly successful. Comparisons with the once richer Latin American region merely serve to dramatise the region's strength.[4] But the Asian experience also stands up surprisingly well to comparisons with many advanced industrial countries, including Britain, the USA and Australia, which have performed much less well on several of these economic indicators.

The ensuing debate has spawned a vast literature in which a handful of pioneering, path-clearing contributions can be noted.[5] There is wide agreement that the key to Japanese, Korean and Taiwanese performance was the rapid development of a manufacturing sector capable of exporting. The core disagreement has arisen over how that development took place. Neo-classical commentators have long insisted that the process was market-led, meaning dependent on low price distortions, free trade and minimal (or 'self-cancelling') government intervention.

But after exposure to more than a decade of careful empirical scrutiny, the economic orthodoxy of market-led development is now in disarray. This is one outcome of the debate that can be clearly discerned. Gradually emerging as the more credible alternative is an institutional understanding of how East Asia has produced a cluster of fast-growth, high-performance industries. No attempt is made to reproduce that debate in all its complexities. The main objective is to provide a bold outline of the major positions and what they have contributed to the 'sources of success' debate. The three main contributions are represented in Figure 7.1.

Free market theory

In the market-led account of East Asia's dynamic development, the character of the trade regime is all important. Of the various policy 'reforms' deemed to liberate markets and produce export success in the region (e.g. international alignment of exchange rates, adjustment of interest rates, control of inflation), neo-classical analysis has traditionally attributed most explanatory power to 'trade liberalisation'. The reduction of tariffs and other restrictions on imports is posited as the linchpin of economic success.

This account has evolved in two guises. First-wave neo-liberals present a simple 'free market' (FM) theory which relies heavily on a before-and-after picture of the trade regime. In the 'before' picture, the Korean and Taiwanese governments intervened heavily and their economies stagnated. In the 'after' picture, the extensive political controls have been lifted and rapid growth ensues. Representative of this simple FM approach is the statement that:

> . . . in South Korea and Taiwan, growth did not really start until
> around 1960 when, in both countries, there was a far-reaching
> redirection of economic policies away from regulation and
> interventionism over to a reliance on market mechanisms.[6]

Three claims are involved here; they concern the timing of growth and the extent of policy reform. The first is that the NIC economies stagnated prior to policy reforms; second, that the reforms were extensive, opening the economy to foreign competition; and third, that domestic industry was left to its own devices. On each count, there is now ample evidence showing this to be a gross distortion of what really took place.[7]

Confronted with so much evidence to the contrary, economists have been forced to take a different tack, neatly encapsulated in Robert Wade's term, 'simulated free market' (SFM) theory.

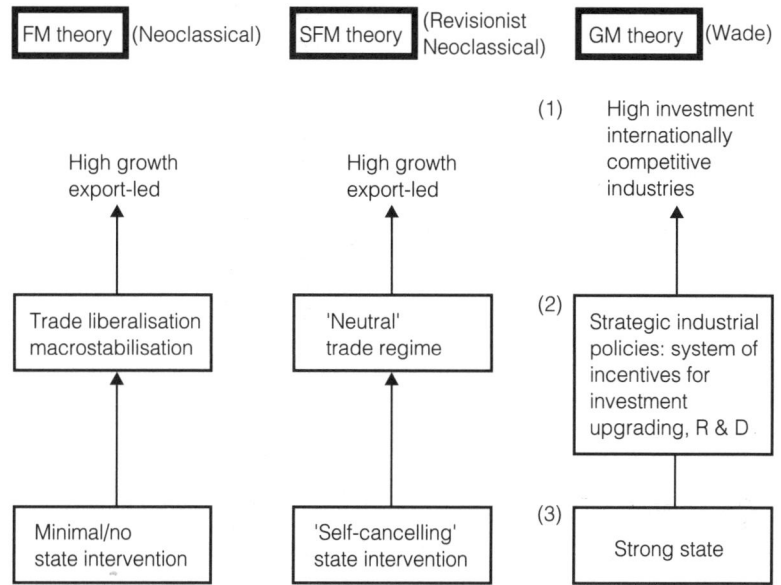

Figure 7.1 Theories of East Asian development

Simulated free market theory: 'self-cancelling' state intervention

SFM theory, associated in particular with the work of Anne Krueger, attempts to save the main proposition of FM theory, namely, that a liberal trade regime is central to the East Asian success story. It does this by acknowledging the fact of extensive 'intervention', but then seeks to reinterpret the character of that intervention. Thus, according to SFM theory, East Asian states do indeed 'intervene' extensively in their economies, but intervention does not fundamentally alter 'natural' market forces.[8]

The key claim of SFM proponents is that the various government measures aimed at promoting domestic industry and exports had a self-cancelling or 'neutralising' effect.[9] The lists of banned products, the high tariff walls around certain industries, the tax breaks and credit subsidies for favoured industries, the granting of domestic privileges to star exporters are accordingly interpreted as 'neutral' policies. They merely 'levelled the playing field' between the home and export markets. The thrust of this argument is that active trade and industrial policy were equivalent to no intervention at all; neutrality was thus established and development can therefore still be seen as 'market-led'.

Subsequent tests of this proposition show the SFM account to be without foundation. First, the neo-classical methodology used to measure and compare effective subsidy rates is seriously flawed.[10] Second, the evidence against neutrality is considerable.[11] The state has been extremely active in building up a production and trade system tilted firmly towards exports. Of the many important findings in this regard, it is worth mentioning at least one fundamental point overlooked by SFM theory. Promotion of import substitution and export production generally went hand in hand. But the result was not a neutral trade regime because the state ensured that much of the output of protected industry was destined (directly or indirectly, sooner or later) to strengthen export performance. The state's establishment of a petrochemical industry in the 1950s that could serve Taiwan's number one export industry, textiles, is a typical example of such complementarity. Here, up-stream producers supplied cheap inputs for mid-stream producers who ultimately provided the synthetic materials crucial to down-stream manufacturers of artificial fibres and fabrics.[12] The policy aim was to leverage the benefits of domestic protection in such a way as to promote or subsidise exports. This is a typical example of creative protectionism. It highlights one of the ways in which protection has been used throughout East Asia to promote international competitiveness, rather than to shelter domestic producers.[13]

Thus in the less doctrinaire literature, it is now an open secret that the East Asian Three created anything but a neutral trade regime. Inducements to export were so extensive, and the penalties against imports so heavy, that producers were pushed and pulled to focus on foreign markets. Far from 'removing obstacles' to exports, what the East Asians created had a powerful, built-in 'bias towards' exports and against imports. Throughout most of the high-growth period (roughly 1960–1980), these economies banned or severely limited imports of consumer goods. Those items allowed in were, by and large, only those essential to the export drive (e.g. raw materials and certain producer and intermediate goods). The Korean importer who in 1980 still had to submit some 250 documents in order to engage in trade would find it difficult to take seriously the claim that Korean policy approximated a free-trade (or trade neutral) environment. In the 1990s one may not readily find the hugely subsidised loans, the lucrative licensing privileges, or the special political recognition that East Asian exporters once enjoyed. But the legacy of their powerful impact over many decades has done little to 'level the playing field' between the home and export markets.

The main outcomes thus far can be summarised. First, the facts of East Asian development are at odds with both versions of 'market-led' theory. Second, the empirical evidence not only fails to support the neo-classical theory of 'virtual' free trade and market-driven development; it is *positively damaging* to its central propositions. It will be shown in due course how this has produced further shifts in the neo-classical position, as evidenced in recent research reports of the World Bank.

Governed market theory

It is one thing to demolish, another to build. 'Governed market' theory is an attempt to build an alternative theory of East Asian development. Pioneered by Robert Wade (1990), GMT advances three main propositions (see Figure 7.1).

First, the superior performance of Japan and the newly industrialised countries (NICs) is the result of heavy investment in internationally competitive, high-growth industries. Moreover, the patterning and level of investment are different from what would have been the case if market mechanisms alone had operated. Second, the exceptional levels of investment in increasingly high-technology sectors is the deliberate outcome of a set of 'strategic industrial policies'. Third, at a deeper level of causality, these policies were pursued with more consistency, and were relatively more effective than in other developing countries, because of a particular set of institutional arrangements, in this case a strong 'autonomous' state.

The main objections to GMT are of three kinds. One is the claim that industrial policies are not capable of producing success all on their own. Although an obviously true statement, this is not a valid criticism. GMT does not exclude the need for other things, such as a good education system, a well-developed public infrastructure, or sensible macroeconomic policies which affect investment and savings. As Lester Thurow has remarked, one cannot build a high-grade economy out of low-grade parts. The point is industrial policy is not the whole story and that East Asian governments are not oblivious to the levels of inflation, exchange rates, interest rates, or other aspects of economic fine-tuning, as is well recognised in World Bank studies. But in the absence of some form of coordination, there is no guarantee that savings and investment will be channelled towards productive rather than speculative activities, or that technological upgrading rather than cost-cutting strategies will prevail. Though it uses different language, governed market theory highlights this aspect of the state's coordinating role in the region. Industrial strategies seek to ensure the industries essential to the nation's long-run welfare, rather than merely reward short-term consumption.

Another criticism of GMT points to the existence of so-called 'policy failures'. The inability to create an export-oriented automotive industry in Taiwan is a favoured example. So too is the Korean heavy and chemical industry strategy of the 1970s, though recent reassessment of this policy does not concur with the 'failure' interpretation.[14] What seems to be implicit in this policy failure criticism is the assumption that error-free economic management is a useful criterion of effectiveness. If this were the case, neither public nor private sectors would qualify. What really matters from a comparative perspective is the incidence of policy success, that is, whether or not the achievement of policy objectives outweighs the mistakes.[15]

Finally, critics of GMT worry about the possibility of 'targeting' or selecting specific industries for promotion. There is more to be said on this issue below. For now, let it merely be noted that 'strategic' industrial–technology policies are not reducible to the practice of 'targeting'. Strategic policies generally involve three arms: an investment banking arm for promoting exports and/or particular sectors; a restructuring arm for streamlining or upgrading sectors in decline; and an R&D arm for developing and disseminating new products and technologies. All three are interconnected, but the importance of each will vary according to different phases in the development process. Thus, for example, in the 1990s, Korea, Japan and Taiwan give much more prominence to the R&D arm (promotion and diffusion of technologies) than to that of investment banking (export and sectoral promotion).

The approach adopted here differs from GMT in two key respects, as can be seen in Figure 7.2. This approach, referred to as 'Governed Interdependence Theory', is explained below.[16]

Governed interdependence theory

Governed interdependence theory (GIT) elaborates upon and differs from Wade's approach in two respects. The first difference to note concerns the larger 'system' nurtured by public policies, which institutionalises a dynamic response from industry. The argument is that the success of East Asian firms and industry on the whole is based on a system that socialises risk and thereby coordinates change across a broad array of organisations—both public and private.

In this system, firms are relieved from bearing the entire burden of four major 'risks': raising capital; developing new products and technologies; finding new markets; and training skilled engineers and workers. A significant proportion of the costs of upgrading technology, new product development, industrial training, market expansion, and so forth, are shared by, or embedded in, a thick network of state-informed (i.e. public–private) institutions.

This system is perhaps the most tangible byproduct of the state's strategic industrial policies (the latter being the focus of Wade's analysis). But beneath that system, what makes the policies so effective

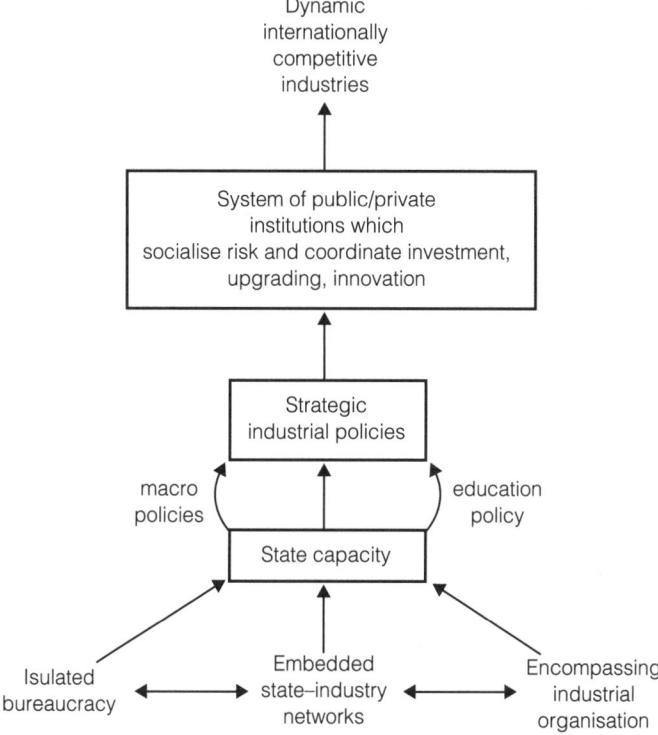

Figure 7.2 Governed interdependence theory: explaining East Asian development

is a particular kind of state structure and a particular kind of relationship between the state and industry. This institutional arrangement is here referred to as 'governed interdependence' (discussed in more detail in section 3). It describes a system of central coordination based on the cooperation of government and industry. Policies for this or that industry, sector or technology are not simply imposed by bureaucrats or politicians. Nor are they simply decided by powerful private interests. They are the result of regular and extensive public consultation and coordination with the private sector.

It is this institutional level of analysis (discussed at length in section 2) that remains the least developed or convincing aspect of governed market theory. Its main shortcoming is the failure to explain the capacity for coordinating industrial change, or what Wade and others refer to as 'strategic industrial policy'. Why have the Taiwanese, Koreans and Japanese been able to pursue 'their' developmental projects so effectively? Wade, like many other analysts, relies heavily on the idea of a hard state, able and willing to impose its own objectives and decisions, regardless of private opposition. He is therefore led to emphasise the authoritarian corporatist character of the East Asian state.

By contrast, governed interdependence theory rejects the notion that the state's ability to 'impose' its decisions is central to its effectiveness. Unilateralism is more likely to be a developmental minus than a plus. It implies the capacity to act, but not necessarily to act effectively. Of central importance is the state's ability to use its autonomy to consult and to elicit consensus and cooperation from the private sector. This is not the kind of power 'over' society that one associates with authoritarian government; it is power 'through' society, which is much more potent in developmental terms (see also section 4).

Governed interdependence encompasses both the coordinated and cooperative quality of that power. As will be shown through an examination of particular policy measures, governed interdependence can take a variety of forms, sometimes appearing more 'top-down' in character, yet at other times (especially in recent years) involving more private-sector initiative.

Decadence of an orthodoxy? The World Bank's shifting position

The weaknesses, distortions and inaccuracies of the neo-classical account of East Asian development have by now been very ably exposed by a large and growing number of studies.[17] As a result of this impressive challenge, the idea of institutional capacities and effective intervention has begun very gradually to be canvassed within the neo-classical community.[18] Indeed, a much more toned-down version of free-market orthodoxy can be found in the most recent series sponsored by the World Bank, 'The Lessons of East Asia'. Just a glance at some of the titles of the country reports in this series tempts one to venture that the hey-day of the neo-classical account is over, at least in its application to East Asia.[19]

These reports no longer emphasise the role of trade 'liberalisation' as key to East Asian development (the extent of trade openness having varied so greatly within the region). Instead, emphasis has shifted to 'macrostabilisation' as the more common feature of the policy environment. But even 'getting economic fundamentals right' is no longer presented as the whole story. Gone too is the emphasis on 'market-driven' development and minimal state intervention. Indeed, a novelty of these reports is the insistence on distinguishing 'government interventions' from 'market distortions', and on arguing that intervention does not necessarily distort growth for this depends on its scope, quality and scale.

In what amounts to something of a revolutionary *volte face*, we are told that 'the main reason for East Asia's superior performance was not that governments there intervened less', nor that their interventions were self-cancelling, but rather that they intervened more 'efficiently'. As the concluding statement from one of the summary reports—*Government Policy and Productivity Growth: Is East Asian an Exception?*—puts it:

> . . . the region does seem to be an exception in getting the most from its reforms and in making public expenditures work to promote growth rather than hinder it. *East Asian countries have been effective in blending the roles of market and state.* The combination of modest distortions, macroeconomic stability, and effective government spending, together with various intangibles such as consensus building, and efficient bureaucracies, has made possible the rapid productivity and economic growth of the region.[20]

Other reports in the same series similarly concede that active governments and competent state bureaucracies have made a difference. Leipziger and Thomas, for example, in summarising the conclusions of their 1993 report, *An Overview of Country Experience*, note in another context that:

> More often than not, the key to the policymaking process was the positive role of government in charting a development course, creating a longer-term vision shared among key participants, and fashioning an institutional framework for effective policy implementation.[21]

This new wave of World Bank research on East Asia comes as close as it possibly can to the 'new political economy'[22] without thereby merging and completely discarding its neo-classical trappings. Active 'interventionist' policies to promote exports or to acquire, develop and upgrade technologies are clearly acknowledged as a 'crucial' component of industrial success in the East Asian Three.[23] The one clear remaining disagreement would appear to be over the extent to which 'selective industrial policies' (i.e. targeting specific sectors) were necessary for successful industrialisation. But this disagreement is really over whether or not second-generation NICs can or should follow the first generation. Based on the cases of Indonesia and Malaysia, some economists conclude that selective industrial policies were not necessary, and that, where attempted in the second-generation NICs, they failed because of institutional shortcomings. Whether these countries have 'successfully' industrialised is, however, not at all clear.[24] Nonetheless, the main point is surely that the thrust of these reports is much more consistent with a version of governed market theory than it is with any version of the neo-classical account. One outcome to this debate can therefore be discerned. It is no longer possible to ignore the importance of state activism in East Asian dynamism. Economic fundamentals matter to industrial success, but so too do active policies to 'guide' firms in investment decisions, to promote exports, and to constantly renew technologies, and thus upgrade the industrial portfolio.

It is a question of some importance as to whether or not economic orthodoxy in Australia has begun to adjust its policy recommendations in line with the quite dramatic revisions reflected recently in World Bank research. By all indications, however, the more nuanced understanding of the East Asian experience emerging from that neo-classical body appears to have raised not a ripple of recognition among our doctrinally pure economists.

The consequences of that neglect are far from insignificant, for a whole new series of questions emerges from this recognition. Primary among these is the question of how and why government 'intervention' has worked in the region. Effectiveness in each of the areas outlined above depends on institutional arrangements. It is time to turn to a discussion of such arrangements in Korea, Taiwan, and Japan.

2. Institutional capacities for coordinating the market

How then did Japan and the NICs do what they did so well? What helped to make active industrial policies relatively effective in the region, especially in the light of neo-classical predictions about rent-seeking and information gaps?

The general argument highlights key features of the organisation and interaction of government and business, which make effective coordination of the market a more likely outcome in the East Asian Three. These include the character and organisation of the industrial bureaucracy, the linkages between state and industry, and the organisation of industry. The result is not a monolithic 'East Asian model', but different ways of achieving a coordinated outcome.

Bureaucratic structures of coordination

Most studies of the East Asian experience highlight at least one essential condition that enables state policies to be consistent with developmental and growth-oriented goals. Aside from bureaucratic competence, this is the condition that the state's key policymaking agencies be sufficiently *insulated* against special interest groups and clientelistic pressures generally. Three main features of the East Asian state's internal organisation are significant in this regard, in so far as they preserve policymaking from domination by special interests: the quality and prestige of the economic bureaucrats; a strong in-house capacity for gathering information; and the appointment of a key agency charged with the task of policy coordination.

(a) High-quality bureaucrats: In East Asia, government service has traditionally conferred high status. The stress on merit in recruitment and promotion of officials has served not only to minimise political manipulation of the bureaucracy but also to attract the most highly qualified individuals. The combination of talent and prestige has in turn made for a highly motivated and cohesive bureaucracy which has internalised national objectives.[25] In matters of trade and industry, bureaucratic expertise is also enhanced by a tendency to appoint engineers rather than economists. Bureaucrats are thus able to communicate easily with companies and do so with great frequency.[26]

(b) In-house expertise: The second, related feature of the core economic ministries is their powerful in-house capacity for marshalling and analysing economic information. In Japan, MITI's dedicated research institute yields much of the data, analysis and conceptual equipment that make possible the Ministry's powerful 'think-tank' role.[27] Striking parallels can be found in Korea and Taiwan. The Economic Planning Board's capacities are outstanding in this regard. More generally, Korea's key economic ministries each maintain an efficient information network of their own—from the research institutes attached to particular ministries, like KIET (Korean Institute for Economics and Technology) which serves the Ministry for Trade, Industry and Energy, to state agencies like KOTRA (Korean Trade Promotion Corporation) whose role has been crucial to the export drive of Korean firms. Indeed, in its knowledge of product demand, quality standards and foreign market trends generally, KOTRA has often been better informed than the private sector.[28]

Similarly, in Taiwan, the web of public research agencies surrounding the state sector provides both firms and individual ministries with a range of vital information that feeds into both private production and public policy. The public research institutes like ITRI (Industrial Technology Research Institute), for instance, are the crucially important implementation arms of the Industrial Development Bureau within the Ministry of Economic Affairs. ITRI, which houses the highly innovative and industry-dedicated laboratories such as ERSO (for electronics) and CCL (for computing and communications), mediates between industry and bureaucracy, monitors the new technologies, products and production processes of international competitors, organises technology transfers, and coordinates new projects in alliance with local firms. Hence, in addition to 'implementation'—carrying out R&D and diffusing the practical results to the private sector—these agencies form part of the policymaking process itself. The highly successful 'technology alliances'—joint public–private projects coordinated by ERSO and CCL, discussed in more detail below—are among the most recent policy outcomes of this information-saturated public sector.[29]

The contrasting case is where the public sector 'contracts out' most or a large part of its research and information requirements, as occurs in the Australian and American settings. (In Australia, for instance, it appears that even the definition of national 'visions' is something better left to a commercial consultancy firm like McKinseys!) The significance of these differences can be seen in the differential impact on state capacity. Two important consequences follow from the development of an in-house information-oriented capacity. One is that it gives state agencies a formidable *competence* in areas normally left to the private sector. The other is that it nurtures bureaucratic *independence vis-à-vis* sectoral interests within the business community. As is well known, none of the Anglo-American economies can boast similar attributes.

(c) Insulated pilot agencies and policy coordination: The third main condition for effective policymaking in the region is the existence of what Johnson has referred to as 'pilot agencies' charged with the task of coordinating economic change. MITI's horizontal bureaus, Korea's Economic Planning Board (EPB), and the Council for Economic Planning and Development (CEPAD) in Taiwan can all be seen in this light. While structurally divergent, they can be viewed as functional equivalents of the idea of a superministry in the economic policymaking apparatus. The key feature in common is that each agency engages in the task of policy coordination, and each has an insulated and 'encompassing' character, in so far as it is removed from direct contact with special economic constituencies.

This applies quite strikingly to the EPB which stands outside and astride the individual ministries and has no direct relationship with the private sector.[30] It is also the case for Taiwan's institutional 'equivalent' to the EPB, the Council for Economic Planning and Development (CEPAD), which operates independently of the ministerial bureaucracy by integrating the leadership of the individual ministries. Finally, MITI's so-called 'horizontal' agencies are functionally, if not organisationally, quite similar to the Korean and Taiwanese pilot agencies. These horizontal agencies have the task of integrating policies advocated by all vertical divisions (which represent specific industries), and balancing the needs of one industry against those of others. As in the case of the Korean EPB, this structure provides a degree of insulation—or 'built-in safeguards'—against the tendency (very noticeable in Anglo-American economies) to respond politically to particular business demands that so frequently have harmful effects for long-term production.

The key point to be emphasised in this context is that all three countries have an institutional advantage at governmental level: in the existence of a talented, technically able and prestigious public service, which is charged with a broad institutional mission and relatively insulated from special interests, and which has developed an impressive in-house capacity for acquiring and managing production-relevant information. This situation contrasts not only with the porous bureaucracies of developing countries, such as the Latin American NICs, but also with the lower status and narrow competence of public administration in some of the more mature industrial economies such as the USA and Australia.

State-industry linkages: insulation but not insularity

Bureaucratic 'autonomy' or insulation is hardly a sufficient explanation for the state's coordinating capacity in the Asian Three. History is strewn with examples of autonomous states that have proved either inept or diffident (or both) in matters of industrial management. Tsarist Russia and twentieth-century Britain offer two such examples at different points on the developmental spectrum. One important feature lacking in such cases of 'autonomy without capacity' can be described as industrial 'connectedness' or what others refer to as 'embeddedness'.[31] In practical terms, 'embedded autonomy' implies the existence of 'policy networks' linking government and industry.

In all three countries, various state agencies have established an elaborate set of linkages to the private sector. These linkages can be thought of in terms of policy networks since they provide a vital mechanism for acquiring adequate information and for coordinating agreement with the private sector. Somewhat surprisingly, the East Asian Three provide many more venues and networks for joint decisionmaking than one would expect in relatively 'youthful' democracies. (And rather more than compared with the older democracies.)

Japan boasts the most extensive set of institutional arrangements for reaching agreement between government and industry. MITI can count on some 250 or so deliberating councils—forums for public–private consultation on key policy issues—which give government the power of consultation and coordination with the private sector that is relatively smooth and rich in vital industry-related information.[32]

Taiwan has instituted joint 'industry task forces' which meet at two-monthly intervals. These have flourished especially since the Economic Innovation Commission (composed of government, business and academic leaders) was set up in 1985 as a provisional advisory organ to help draft industrial and economic policies to deal with Taiwan's international economic difficulties. Korean policy linkages have functioned most effectively in the famous monthly meetings held at the Presidential Blue House to propel the export drive. But in an era when export success has made such meetings irrelevant, the Korean bureaucracy is seeking to revive the 'private councils for industrial development' as a means of encouraging more intra-industry coordination and private initiative.

Why are such institutional linkages important? In a nutshell, because it is about the state doing things not in isolation from the private sector, but in concentration with industry. In so far as public and private decisionmakers get together to exchange information and to coordinate actions, information gaps are minimised and each generally ends up making better decisions than if trapped in isolation. Rather than engaging in purely top-down decisionmaking, abstracted from the real conditions of production, the economic bureaucracy therefore has a vital mechanism for acquiring production-related information and for coordinating agreement with the private sector in order to better design and implement policies. Moreover, decisions are more open to public scrutiny, thus reducing the risks of corruption or political favouritism. Being 'in daily contact' with industry experts, having formal meetings on a regular basis with industry representatives, establishing performance monitoring systems that provide constant feedback to enable policy adjustments—these are among the more tangible features of institutionalised public–private cooperation, which make for an effective policy apparatus. Moreover, as we shall see, the organisation of industry itself is by no means incidental to this outcome. Okimoto,[33] an astute observer of the Japanese system, has put the case concisely, as follows:

> Through its extensive network of contacts with the private sector,
> MITI can regularly tap into a vast system of up-to-date information.
> (Rigorous discussions with 'people in the know'—industry leaders,
> researchers, financial analysts, engineers—put MITI in a strong
> position) . . . to find out where technology is headed, and where the
> most promising commercial opportunities lie. The information it
> collects and processes is about as thorough as could be obtained.
> National research projects thus emerge from an ongoing process of
> national consensus building based on extensive give and take between
> government and the private sector.

This section has made two points that are important to the argument. First, on a general note, in addition to being insulated in certain areas, other parts of the bureaucracy need to be closely connected with organised industry. Both insulation and connectedness are important conditions of coordinating capacity. Second, public–private cooperation is much more institutionalised in the East Asian Three than in most other countries. One major consequence of these institutional capacities is the enhancement of policy effectiveness. Phrased in more theoretical terms, cooperative coordination (which I have earlier referred to as 'governed interdependence') is a source of enhanced state capacity. The question of whether such institutional capacities are adaptable to other environments, such as Australia's, is one that must be considered at a later stage.

Industrial organisation: The role of encompassing institutions

The third condition of coordinating capacity turns on the organisation of industry itself as a means of facilitating the linkages between government and industry. In spite of very diverse business structures—embracing the giant diversified groups in Korea, the specialised industrial corporations of Japan, and the thriving small and medium-sized firms of Taiwan—the organisation of industry in these settings exhibits a number of common features that facilitate its relationships with government.

One striking organisational feature is the encompassing rather than fragmented nature of business representation in the region, which is a legacy of statism. Industry or trade associations tend to be highly centralised and increasingly active in the design and implementation of policy. This participation has long been true across industry as a whole for Japan where the *gyokai*, or industry-specific manufacturing trade associations, provide the basic level for execution of policy.[34] It has also been the case in specific sectors for Taiwan, notably the Taiwan Electrical Appliances Manufacturer Association (TEAMA) which encompasses electronics, and the powerful Taiwan Textile Federation (TTF) which, since 1974, has overseen quota management in one of the country's top two export industries. Indeed, due to Taiwan's peculiar geopolitical and diplomatic situation, the role of TTF has for the past two decades been that of a quasi-government agency, empowered to undertake direct trade negotiations with foreign governments and to administer export quotas for the industry at home. This experience has imparted a competence in representing the industry and a confidence in undertaking tasks in the 'national' interest, resulting in an active role in the policymaking community. In particular, TTF has convinced the government of the advantages of upgrading rather than bypassing a traditional industry beset by low-cost competitors.[35]

In the Korean setting, the *chaebol*, which organise so much economic activity, have operated as functional equivalents to the encompassing trade associations. It is only in the past decade or so that trade associations have begun to acquire greater significance in the policy community, as the government seeks to enhance the role of organised industry in economic management. The aim is to sustain a disciplined approach to capital and a coordinated approach to industrial affairs, which the *chaebol*, having left behind their adolescent dependence on government nurturing and having become so diversified, increasingly resist. The obstacles however should not be underplayed. A key test for sustaining Korean competitiveness is whether the conglomerates can be sufficiently 'streamlined' and the trade associations sufficiently strengthened in order to prevent the collapse of public policy into private interest politics. The Korean case may therefore be seen as pushing at the limits within which governed interdependence remains possible in an economy that is not only highly concentrated, but whose business structures are highly diversified.

In Taiwan at least the trend is much clearer. Government is embedding its autonomy in a wider array of industry-related institutions, and industry is developing a capacity for policy input that strong organisational coordination makes possible. In this respect, Taiwan is following the path of Japan more closely than that of Korea.

In this section we have discussed the significance of industrial organisation, both in principle and as it is instituted in the East Asian Three. The central point is that cooperative coordination between state and industry is easier if industry is represented by encompassing organisations like trade associations, rather than partially organised or fragmented among several competing bodies. Where the latter situation prevails, as in Australia, Britain and the United States, intra-industry consensus has been far more difficult to construct and individualised lobbying has tended to override a more collective approach to an industry's problems. A similar situation can also occur if too much economic activity is organised by a handful of giant groups. This, as mentioned, is the present danger faced by Korea.

The more general point that emerges from this analysis is that close ties between government and industry are not in themselves an explanation for the state's effectiveness. In some contexts, such ties are more likely to invite rent-seeking than commitment to competitive behaviour. The Latin American case is often cited in this regard. Cooperation seems to work well only if the state is sufficiently insulated, as discussed earlier. Governed interdependence requires a state that is paradoxically both distant and close. Connectedness without insulation breeds rent-seeking and distributive policies that can smother development. By contrast, insulation without connectedness widens information gaps that encourage policy failure. But states that combine both insulation and connectedness by embedding their autonomy are equipped with greater institutional capacities for minimising these dangers and for achieving policy success.

3. State 'power' in East Asia

This chapter has argued that capable states are a key ingredient of East Asian competitiveness and that their capacity has been honed by a combination of institutional features that facilitate 'governed inter-dependence'.[36] The major theoretical point in this context regards the nature of state power that emerges from that combination. The latter refers to a cooperative relationship with industry that does not entail government's subservience, but rather a definite capacity to set broad goals and to coordinate policies and resources to that end. Governed interdependence is a way of capturing a set of relationships between government and industry that help to explain why some states are more effective than others at coordinating economic change. That relation-ship may be enhanced by long-standing *cultural* traditions (as is sometimes suggested for Japan), but first and foremost it has an *institutional* underpinning. The major theoretical point in this context regards the nature of state power.

To appreciate why Australia, Britain and the United States appear to have so little domestic state capacity to coordinate industrial change and why the East Asian Three have so much, we need to distinguish between two notions of state power, 'despotic' and 'infrastructural'.[37] East Asian capacity for coordinating change rests not on greater despotic, or *arbitrary*, power (i.e. the capacity of A to impose her or his own wishes over B regardless of B's desires); it rests above all on greater infrastructural, or *negotiated,* powers (the capacity to *cooperate* with others *from a position of autonomy* and to coordinate responses to achieve outcomes).

As argued at length in a different context, there is much more to the East Asian state's autonomy and capacity than can be gained from the reductionist notion that autonomy is simply tolerated by capital so long as it achieves desired outcomes.[38] Today, one of the biggest threats to state coordinating power (and thereby long-term growth) stems from the rise of American trained neo-classical economists to influential positions in the governments of Taiwan and Korea. Their growing significance in policymaking circles has led to increasing efforts, especially within the Korean government, to let markets do the job of coordination. The current difficulties confronting the Korean economy however strongly suggest that 'Anglo-Saxonisation' may be highly inappropriate for these economies.[39]

Current tendencies notwithstanding, East Asian bureaucracies have on the whole been effective coordinators because they have used their organisational insulation to develop networks. Through these linkages to the industrial sector, they have encouraged cooperative responses to economic change and converted autonomy into capacity. In practical terms, Japan is the country where such institutional capacities have been developed to the highest degree. Contrary to expectations, Taiwan is looking rather more like Japan than is Korea, thus disproving the idea that an industrial structure based largely on small and medium-sized firms is incompatible with coordination. Somewhat in contrast, Korea is the least stable of the three cases. Coordination is proving more difficult to sustain not so much because of the lack of 'policy instruments', as is sometimes claimed, but because of the peculiar features of Korea's industrial organisation and structure. Public–private cooperation has taken place largely through the *chaebol,* which worked well for a time. It is not simply that Korean groups are now financially independent enough to thumb their noses at the state that made them strong (a highly debatable point in itself). The problem is fundamentally structural rather than political. Extraordinary levels of diversification have begun to hamper coordination so that government is now working on two fronts. One is to streamline *chaebol* operations through a variety of measures that require them to concentrate on core activities; the other is to stimulate business and organisational initiatives outside the *chaebol* structures, hence an emphasis on small-industry promotion and on industry representation in policy deliberation councils.[40]

To the extent that these initiatives succeed, governed interdependence will be strengthened. But the task is by no means a simple one. Korea is in fact pushing at the limits in which it is possible for the state to engage in cooperative coordination with the private sector, owing partly to the sheer proportion of economic activity organised by a handful of concerns, but mostly because the activities of those concerns themselves are now so diversified. How Korea resolves this problem will have a significant effect on its future competitiveness.

In short, the East Asian economies have an edge in international competition because they have capable states that have harnessed their autonomy in creative interaction with the private sector. As the preceding discussion sought to show, so-called 'intervention' has worked more often than not in East Asia because of the intersection of three disciplinary mechanisms, which we can summarise as state, market and networks. First, governments have set the larger goals concerning which industries and technologies ought to be promoted; but they have done this increasingly in combination with industry organisations, leaving the major details to firms. Second, with the goals established, firms are then expected, and given every assistance, to prepare for intense competition, whether with local firms or in export markets. Finally, public–private networks serve to discipline capital and build in public accountability through performance conditions set by the state.

4. Implications and conclusion

This chapter has advanced the proposition that a capable state is a key component of international competitiveness. In this new era of international, innovation-driven competition, East Asia's advantage resides in institutions that have enabled and encouraged a coordinated and cooperative approach to economic change. Two important implications follow.

'Anglo-Saxonisation' or 'East Asianisation'?

First, capable states are likely to be more rather than less important as markets are internationalised, production is globalised, and regimes democratised, although the manner of their involvement in the industrial economy changes over time. The key issue, then, for the East Asian economies is not how to weaken (i.e. 'Anglo-Saxonise') the state's role in economic coordination, but how to strengthen business cooperation with government (while of course minimising opportunities for rent-seeking). Far from declining in importance as democratisation and internationalisation proceed, the need for cooperative coordination is being emphasised more than ever in this region as the new round of competition intensifies the pressure to develop and upgrade technology.

The clearest test case to watch here is Korea. In Korea, there is a much greater potential for 'business failure' than in Japan. This is in large part because the Korean *chaebol* have not developed the leadership capacities of the Japanese *keiretsu* in coordinating intra-industry agreement. The resulting crisis of surplus capacity in the petrochemical industry towards the end of the 1980s is a case in point. If the present prognosis is correct, any further weakening of government coordination will significantly retard the process of industrial upgrading that is so essential to Korea's ability to remain ahead of the second-tier NICs.[41]

If this general point applies to the high-performing economies, it surely applies with even greater force to the relatively uncoordinated Anglo-American economies where the standard of living has for many years stagnated or fallen and, in Australia's case, where technological capacity now lags behind that of the East Asian NICs. Unless these countries can match the economic coordination capacities of the East Asian Three, they are unlikely to develop the strong manufacturing base on which rising living standards and a more equitable income distribution ultimately depend.

Obstacles to institutional emulation?

The issue, then, turns in the first instance on institutional emulation. Three observations are worth making in this regard. First, there should be no reason why one country may not learn from another's institutional strengths, as it may from its weaknesses. It is an obvious point that learning of this kind cannot mean 'copying', but rather 'adapting'.

Second, in spite of all the well-known caveats recited by many different commentators—from so-called 'historically specific' conditions to sociopolitical obstacles—institutions do change, and not necessarily with glacial speed. Ronald Dore[42] is right to remind us of the relative youth of some of Japan's more famous institutions, including the *keiretsu's* mutual security cross-shareholding and lifetime employment. In fact, all the institutional features examined for Taiwan and Korea—from bureaucratic insulation to encompassing industrial representation—are barely three or four decades old.

Third, there is no single recipe for effective bureaucratic organisation. This ranges from the highly insulated and hierarchical EPB to the more flexibly organised bureaus of MITI. But core elements in common include the relative insulation from direct client groups, in-house expertise, and the ability to set and monitor performance outcomes in exchange for support.

What then are the key obstacles to instituting such a production-oriented agency in Australia and are they insurmountable? We can best approach this issue by first considering and rejecting two common presuppositions. First is the assumption that the operation of such an agency would not sit well in a democratic political environment. The grounds for this assumption, however, are not at all established. In an important respect, East Asia's pilot agencies have been more accountable for their policy outcomes than their Australian (or, indeed, American) counterparts. The ability and willingness to *discipline* capital in exchange for public support have been central to that accountability, and indeed to policy success more generally. As Amsden[43] has observed, all late industrialising countries have been noted for disciplining labour; what makes the East Asians *distinctive,* however, is that they have also disciplined *capital*.

It is here that history has left its mark. The more extensive nature of disciplined support in Japan, Taiwan and Korea owes much to the timing of development and to the sequencing of state–industry intervention. In late industrialising nations, relatively 'strong' states helped to develop relatively weak business sectors by pursuing catch-up strategies in the national interest. Under such conditions, disciplining capital in exchange for support has become the standard means of achieving developmental goals. By contrast, in the Anglo-American economies, state support has grown in the context of an already constituted industrial sector, and has developed more recently as a reactive, *ad hoc* response to the growing challenges of international competition. It is not that democracy militates against such disciplining of capital (i.e. the monitoring of specified performance outcomes), for there are many instances of democratic governments stipulating performance standards in exchange for support. On the whole, however, these instances tend to be the *exception* rather than the rule. This suggests that the differences in question owe more to historical contingency than to a political logic.

The lack of public sector competence is another factor that is frequently assumed to block any effort to implement East Asian-style development strategies. While the problem of administrative competence should not be underplayed, the point is that competence is not something fixed for all time. In any given setting, it has varied over time and across different agencies. In recent years, the establishment of agencies like Sematech in the USA shows what can be done to reverse the decline of an industry. Similarly, in Australia, the establishment of Austrade as a means of promoting exports and linking companies with overseas market opportunities has demonstrated the coordinating potential of the public sector. In this particular case, it has also revealed that the capacities of such an agency to provide crucial services can very often outrun the capacities of the private sector to respond to them.

The main obstacles to institutional learning along East Asian lines would seem to be two. One is the absence in Australia of a perception of vulnerability that elsewhere played a vital role in generating the political willingness and legitimacy necessary to the adoption of a developmental project. But even in the presence of severe decline and perceived vulnerability, it is doubtful that anything resembling an Asian-style development strategy would ensue. For while we may now consider ourselves, geographically at least, part of Asia, by ideological temperament we are still much closer to neo-liberal Britain and America. Both countries show that one can decline very far indeed in the industrial order of things without seeking to change the domestic rules of the game. There is, of course, little prospect of addressing the institutional issue (government–industry relations) while the 'in principle' case for strategic trade and technology policy cannot even be discussed.[44] Moreover, as long as influential groups continue to counterpose industrial competitiveness and social welfare as necessary trade-offs, political parties will continue to wage the electoral struggle and structure popular expectations in terms of what are largely false alternatives.

Whatever current institutional weaknesses and political 'obstacles' may exist in the Australian context, there is nothing peculiarly East Asian or uniquely situational about the ability of the state to set performance conditions for whatever level of support it provides. There are already examples of this in the public arena, notably in the area of procurement policy.[45] If that disciplinary principle were to be extended to *all* public programs for industry, this would not only enhance policy success but also create an institutional platform for a more comprehensive system of governed interdependence.

'Liberalisation' versus 'governed interdependence'?

Is governed interdependence just another way of opposing liberalisation? On the contrary, governed interdependence is liberalisation-neutral. If anything, it is an important condition of successful liberalisation rather than an obstacle. This is because it furnishes a country with alternative means other than simple protectionism in order to meet international competition and pressures for change.

The important point is that countries lacking the institutional capacity for coordinating change and upgrading their industry and technology are more likely to turn to protectionist solutions. Institutional weakness means that the state repeatedly seeks 'solutions' to industrial performance problems in *illiberal* measures, such as protective tariffs, quotas, and so forth, for a whole range of special interests. This has long been the case in the USA where protectionist policies have ranged widely from motor cycles, cheese, and textiles, to automobiles, steel, machine tools and semiconductors.[46] It is worth reiterating the point that such actions are not simply the luxury effects of size (i.e. being big enough to shift the costs of change on to other countries), as Katzenstein[47] has noted. Rather, they are the manifestations of institutional weakness. Protection is the most likely option when state capacity for coordinating change is weak and, in direct contrast to the East Asian experience, is given without any strings attached.[48]

This was of course Australia's position for most of this century. Recent changes suggest the beginnings of an effort (by no means concerted) to build coordinating capacity at bureaucratic level. Austrade is perhaps at the forefront of this emerging, though far from conclusive, shift in national objectives. The real test of course is whether the impulse can be directed to the agencies responsible for industry and technology. The recognition that the Department of Industry, for example, has neither 'policy skills' nor 'intellectual clout' has not stimulated any significant effort to enhance government 'learning' in that context.[49] Even without a sea change, however, a vital start can be made by holding business to a higher standard, ensuring that no public resources are given away without securing in exchange a developmentally oriented performance standard that can be monitored.

The immediate lesson from the East Asian experience suggests it is time to discard the false polarities that have guided debate over our developmental options. The choice is not between 'free markets' and 'state intervention', or between *laissez-faire* and industrial policy, but between *ad hoc* and reactive support without strings attached on one hand, and greater emphasis on governed interdependence on the other.

In conclusion, the dominant school of neo-classical economics has for quite some time commanded much of the ideological airspace and most of the policy discussion in Australia. That it has prevailed for a much longer period in Britain and the USA, two countries that have thus far failed to decisively reverse their industrial slide and falling standards of living, should make our policymakers sit up and take notice. There are as many lessons to be gained from the relative slide of former industrial giants and their unsuccessful attempts to reverse this process, as there are from the newly ascendant industrial powers to our north.

Notes

1 While the whole issue of the relationship between democracy, equity, welfare and economic performance demands systematic comparative research, there is substantial evidence to suggest that equity in income distribution and decent welfare systems are friends not enemies of growth, a pattern strikingly clear for Japan, Taiwan, Hong Kong, Korea and Singapore where equity and growth have gone hand in hand. See World Bank. Also of relevance is the fact that while industrially powerful Germany has a generous welfare system, Britain and the US, both with depleted welfare systems, have become notable for the highest rates of poverty and income inequality in the advanced democracies, combined with the failure to arrest their industrial slide.

2 This distinction is of course highly misleading since some of the East Asian countries (notably Singapore, and to some extent Hong Kong) provide extensive welfare programs in public housing, health, education and subsidised transport. In so far as Singapore maintains a relatively sophisticated social policy while rejecting political liberalisation, it bears a striking resemblance to Germany under Bismarck.

3 In the British case, both insulation and insularity are combined to the detriment of the state's coordinating capacity. See Stephen Wilks' excel-

lent analysis of government's role in the British motor industry in 'Institutional Insularity: Government and the British Motor Industry Since 1945', *Government, Industries and Markets*, ed. M. Chick, Edward Elgar, London, 1990.

4 Between 1962 and 1986, per capita income in Korea and Taiwan leapt far ahead of the Brazilian and Mexican levels, even though they began from a much lower base. While Mexican per capita GNP increased from US$340 to $1839 and Brazil's from $240 to $1811, the Taiwanese and Korean changes were, respectively: from $170 to $3480 and from $110 to $2372. See Wade, Robert, *Governing the Market: Economic Theory and the Role of Government in East Asian Industrialization*, Princeton University Press, Princeton, 1990, table 2.1.

5 See especially Johnson, Chalmers, *MITI and the Japanese Miracle: The Growth of Industrial Policy: 1925–1975*, Stanford University Press, Stanford, 1982, and 'Political Institutions and Economic Performance: The Government-Business Relationship in Japan, South Korea and Taiwan', *The Political Economy of New East Asian Industrialism*, ed. F. Deyo, Cornell University Press, Ithaca, New York, 1987; Amsden, Alice, *Asia's Next Giant: South Korea and Late Industrialization*, Oxford University Press, New York, 1989; and Wade, op. cit.

6 Hughes, Helen, Policy Lessons of the Development Experience, Occasional Paper no. 16, Group of Thirty, New York, 1985, p. 16.

7 Contrary to the claim that Korea and Taiwan failed to experience growth until the economic reforms of the 1960s, all the evidence points to periods of decent growth already under way before the alleged reforms. Taiwan's manufacturing output actually doubled between 1952 and 1958, recording an annual growth rate of around 12 per cent (see Wade, Robert, 'State Intervention in "Outward-looking" Development: Neo-classical Theory and Taiwanese Practice', *Developmental States in East Asia,* ed. G. White, St Martin's Press, New York, 1988, p. 40.). Even war-devastated Korea saw GNP grow in real terms at about 5 per cent annually. It is correct to note that Korean growth rates 'stagnated' in the 1958–60 period, but neo-classical accounts neglect to mention that stagnation followed directly upon the adoption of a stabilisation program in 1957, which was imposed as a condition of US aid (see Sakong, I., *Korea in the World Economy*, Institute for International Economics, Washington, DC, 1993, pp. 2–3). This of course does not help the free-market case. Perhaps even more damaging is the well-documented finding that the scope of the reforms during the high-growth period was severely limited, especially with regard to trade liberalisation (cf. Wade op. cit.; Luedde-Neureth, Richard, *'Import Controls and Export-Oriented Development, A Reassessment of the South Korean Case'*, Westview Special Studies on East Asia, 1986; Weiss, Linda & Hobson, John M., *States and Economic Development: A Comparative Historical Analysis*, Polity Press, Cambridge, 1995, chapter 5). As to the claim that industry was left to its own devices, even revisionist neo-classical analysis disputes this, as the following discussion makes clear.

8 It must be emphasised that 'intervention' is a dismally inappropriate term

for the kind of state activity prominent in East Asian economies; the notion of 'coming between' betrays the prejudices of Anglo-Saxon economic thought: the idea that the market is natural and the state is artificial. The pioneering work that lays that notion to rest is Karl Polanyi's *The Great Transformation*, Octagon, New York, 1944/75.

9 World Bank, *World Development Report 1987*, Oxford University Press, New York (for the World Bank), 1987; Krueger, Anne O., 'The Developmental Role of the Foreign Sector and Aid', *Studies in the Modernisation of the Republic of Korea: 1945–1975*, Council on East Asian Studies, Harvard University Press, Cambridge, 1979.

10 For details see Alam, M. Shahid, *Governments and Markets in Economic Development Strategies: Lessons from Korea, Taiwan and Japan*, Praeger, New York, 1989; also Luedde-Neurath, op. cit.

11 Wade, 1990, op. cit.; Luedde-Neurath, op. cit.

12 Chu, Wan-Wen, 'Import Substitution and Export-Led Growth: A Study of Taiwan's Petrochemical Industry', *World Development*, vol. 22, no. 5, 1994, pp. 781–94.

13 cf. Wade, Robert, 'The Visible Hand: The State and East Asia's Economic Growth', *Current History,* vol. 92, no. 578, 1993, p. 435.

14 See e.g. Chang, H.-J., 'Political Economy of Industrial Policy in Korea', *Cambridge Journal of Economics*, vol. 17, no. 2, 1994, pp. 131–57; Woo, Jung-En, *Race To The Swift: State and Finance in Korean Industrialization,* Columbia University Press, New York, 1991; Sakong, op. cit.

15 In this regard, GMT tends to err on the side of caution rather than overstating its case. It readily concedes, for example, the difficulty of demonstrating with any precision just how much policy A contributed to the success of industry B. But if it is possible to attribute 'failure' or 'damaging effects' to a particular policy, as economists readily attempt to do, then surely it is equally possible to indicate 'beneficial' outcomes and policy 'success'. An increasing number of sectoral studies do just that (e.g. Fransman, Martin, *The Market and Beyond: Information Technology in Japan,* Cambridge University Press, New York, 1990; Meaney, Constance S., 'Approaches to High-Tech Competitiveness: The Role of the State in the Development of Taiwan's Semiconductor Industry', unpublished paper, 1990; Okimoto, Daniel I., *Between MITI and the Market: Japanese Industrial Policy for High Technology,* Stanford University Press, Stanford, 1989; JETRO (Japan External Trade Organization), *'Industrial Policy in East Asia'*, JETRO, Tokyo, 1993; Chu, op. cit.

16 For an earlier elaboration see Weiss, Linda, 'Government-Business Relations in East Asia: the Changing Basis of State Capacity', *Asian Perspective*, vol. 18, no. 2, 1984.

17 Wade, op. cit., Amsden, op. cit. and 'Asia's Industrial Revolution: "Late Industrialization" on the Rim', *Dissent*, vol. 40, Summer 1993, pp. 324–32; Johnson, op. cit.; Lim, L.Y.C., 'Singapore's Success: The Myth of the Free Market Economy', *Asian Survey*, vol. 23, no. 6, 1983, pp. 752–64; Rodan, Garry, *The Political Economy of Singapore's*

Industrialisation: National State and International Capital, Macmillan, London, 1989; Luedde-Neurath, op. cit.; Alam, op. cit.; Schiffer, J., 'State Policy and Economic Growth: A note on the Hong Kong model', *International Journal of Urban and Regional Research*, vol. 15, no. 2, 1991, pp. 180–96; Scott, Bruce R., *Economy Strategy and Economic Performance*, Harvard Business School, 1992, note 792–086; Matthews, Trevor & Ravenhill, John, 'Strategic Trade Policy: The East Asian Experience', *Working Paper 1993/2*, Department of International Relations Canberra: Research School of Pacific Studies, ANU, 1993.

18 See e.g. World Bank, 1991, op. cit. and *Government, Policy and Productivity Growth: Is East Asia an Exception?* The Lessons of East Asia series, World Bank, Washington, DC, 1993; *The East Asian Miracle: Economic Growth and Public Policy*, Oxford University Press, New York (for the World Bank), 1993.

19 Titles include: *Korea: A Case of Government-Led Development; Thailand: The Institutional and Political Underpinnings of Growth.*

20 World Bank, *Government, Policy and Productivity Growth*, p. 18. But there are still serious inconsistencies in this report. For instance, it continues at various points to confuse the act of 'doing less to hamper growth' with that of actually 'generating growth', which is tantamount to saying that not standing in the way of an act is the same as causing it to happen!

21 Leipziger, Danny M. & Thomas, Vinod, 'Roots of East Asia's Success', *Finance & Development*, vol. 31, no. 1, 1994, p. 9.

22 A label to refer to that body of work loosely unified by an explicit emphasis on strategic policies and, more or less implicit, on government capacities and institutions as a major component of East Asia's strong economic performance. See e.g. Johnson, op. cit., 1982, and 'The Institutional Foundations of Japanese Industrial Policy', *The Politics of Industrial Policy,* eds C.E. Barfield & W.A. Schambra, Oxford University Press, Oxford, 1986; Amsden, op. cit., 1989; Wade, op. cit., 1990; Evans, Peter, 'The State as Problem and Solution: Predation, Embedded Autonomy, and Structural Change', *The Politics of Economic Adjustment,* eds S. Haggard & R. R. Kaufman, Princeton University Press, Princeton, New Jersey, 1992.

23 Leipziger & Thomas, op. cit.; Page, John, 'The East Asian Miracle: Building a Basis for Growth', *Finance & Development*, vol. 31, no. 1, 1994, pp. 2–5; Vittas, Dimitri & Cho, Yoon Je, 'The Role of Credit Policies in Japan and Korea', *Finance & Development*, vol. 31, no. 1, 1994, pp. 10–12.

24 Lubeck, Paul M., 'Malaysian Industrialization, Ethnic Divisions, and the NIC Model: The Limits to Replication', *States and Development in the Asian Pacific Rim*, eds R. Appelbaum & J. Henderson, Sage, London, 1992.

25 Johnson, op. cit. 1982; Choi, Byung Sun, 'The Structure of the Economic Policy-Making Institutions in Korea and the Strategic Role of the Economic Planning Board (EPB)', *The Korean Journal of Policy Studies*,

vol. 2, no. 1, 1991, pp. 1–25; Gold, Thomas, *State and Society in the Taiwan Miracle*, M. E. Sharpe, Armonk, 1986.

26 Interview 1, Ministry of Trade, Industry and Energy, Technology Policy Division, Industrial Technology Bureau, Seoul, 1994; Interview 2, Ministry of Economic Affairs, Industry Development Bureau, 2nd Division, Taipei, 1994.

27 cf. Johnson, op. cit. 1986.

28 cf. Jones, Leroy P. & Sakong, I., *Government, Business, and Entrepreneurship in Economic Development: The Korean Case*, Harvard University Press, Cambridge, 1980; Interview 3, Korea Trade Promotion Corporation (KOTRA), Seoul, 1994.

29 Interview 2, see note 26, and Interview 4, Industrial Technology Research Institute, Electronics Research & Service Organization (ERSO), Hsinchu, Taiwan, 1994; Interview 5, Taiwan Electrical Appliance Manufacturers' Association (TEAMA), Taipei Hsien, 1994.

30 Choi, op. cit., pp. 7–8. In Korea, interministerial conflicts have increased in recent years as ministries have jockeyed for policy leadership; jurisdictional conflicts between the EPB and individual ministries have also mounted in conjunction with the EPB's efforts to quicken liberalisation in the financial sector and in imports, in the (mistaken) belief that this would weaken the excessive power of the *chaebols*.

31 e.g. Evans, Peter, 'Predatory, Developmental and Other Apparatuses: A Comparative Political Economy Perspective on the Third World State', *Sociological Forum*, vol. 4, 1989, pp. 233–46; and op. cit. 1992.

32 Johnson, op. cit., 1986.

33 Okimoto, op. cit., p. 73.

34 See e.g. Sone, Yasunori, 'Structuring Political Bargains: Government, *Gyokai* and Markets', *Political Dynamics in Contemporary Japan*, eds D. Allinson & Y. Sone, Cornell University Press, Ithaca, New York, 1993, pp. 300–03.

35 Recent initiatives are aimed at technical and management upgrading. Central to this strategy is the TTF Design Centre and computer-assisted design service for member companies. In 1992, the Industrial Development Bureau agreed to a TTF proposal to upgrade the industry, which emphasised the value-adding potential of design. Of the funding for the upgrading program, 60 per cent came from government and 40 per cent from TTF.

36 For a more extended theoretical discussion and illustration of the various forms of governed interdependence, see Weiss, Linda, 'Governed Interdependence: Rethinking the Government-Business Relationship in East Asia', *The Pacific Review*, 1995.

37 For the original exposition see Mann, Michael, 'The Autonomous Power of the State: Its Origins, Mechanisms and Results', *States, War and Capitalism*, ed. M. Mann, Basil Blackwell, Oxford, 1984/1988.

38 Weiss, 1995 op. cit.

39 Amsden, op. cit.

40 Interview 7, Secretary to the President for Trade, Industry, Energy and

Communications Affairs, Office of the President, Republic of Korea, Seoul, 1994.

41 Johnson, Chalmers, 'What Is the Best System of National Economic Management for Korea?', *Korea's Political Economy*, eds Lee-Jay Cho & Yoon Hyung Kim, Westview Press, Boulder, Colorado, 1994; Amsden, Alice, 'The Specter of Anglo-Saxonization is Haunting South Korea', *Korea's Political Economy*, eds Lee-Jay Cho & Yoon Hyung Kim, Westview Press, Boulder, Colorado, 1994.

42 Dore, Ronald, 'What Makes the Japanese Different?', *Ethics and Markets*, eds C.Crouch & D. Marquand, Basil Blackwell, Oxford, 1993, p. 79.

43 Amsden, op. cit. 1989.

44 Carter, Colin, 'The Industry Policy Debate: a Business Strategy Perspective', *Australian Business in the Asia Pacific Region: The Case for Strategic Industry Policy*, ed. I. Marsh, Longman Professional, Melbourne, 1994, p. 98.

45 Capling, Ann, 'The "Partnerships for Development" program in Australia', *Journal of Industry Studies*, vol.1, no. 2, 1994, pp. 1–22.

46 cf. Thurow, Lester, 'The Case for Industrial Policies in America', *Industrial Policy and Technological Change,* eds T. Shishido & R. Sato, Croom Helm, London, 1985, p. 230; Tonelson, Alan, 'Beating Back Predatory Trade', *Foreign Affairs*, vol. 73, no. 4, 1994, p. 123.

47 Katzenstein, Peter J., *Small States in World Markets: Industrial Policy in Europe*, Cornell University Press, Ithaca, New York, 1985, p. 23.

48 Nonetheless, one should not underestimate the incidence of government–business cooperation even in the American setting where much has been made of the 'arms-length', low-trust nature of the government–business relationship. In the USA, for example, some sectors such as agriculture, defence, and certain defence-related, high-tech sectors like semiconductors, the relationship more closely resembles the governed interdependence of East Asia. The larger reality, however, is that of the continuing pre-eminence of Congress and the subservience of the state bureaucracy to special interests. Thus the total of $250 billion or so in government lending and loan guarantees recorded in the mid-1980s was allocated to firms with Congressional pull (see Thurow, op. cit., pp. 255–6). This may be a form of pork-barrel democracy at work, but its outcomes are not publicly accountable.

49 As reported by the Minister for Industry (*The Australian*, June 7, 1993).

Further References

Gold, Thomas, 'Changing Relations Between the State and Private Sector in Taiwan and Mainland China', *Taiwan: a Newly Industrialized State*, eds Hsin-Huang Michael, Hsiao, Wei-Yuan Cheng & Hou-Sheng Chan, National Taiwan University, Taipei, 1989.

Interview 6, Taiwan Textile Federation (TTF), Taipei, 1994.

Jenkins, R., 'The Political Economy of Industrialization: A Comparison of Latin American and East Asian Newly Industrializing Countries', *Development and Change*, vol. 22, 1991, pp. 177–94.

Samuels, Richard J., *The Business of the Japanese State: Energy Markets in Comparative and Historical Perspective,* Cornell University Press, Ithaca, New York, 1987.

Soskice, David, 'Reinterpreting Corporatism and Explaining Unemployment: Co-ordinated and Non-coordinated Market Economies', *Labour Relations and Economic Performance,* eds R. Brunetta & C. Dell'Aringa, Macmillan, London, 1990.

Wade, Robert, 'East Asia's Economic Success: Conflicting Perspectives, Partial Insights, Shaky Evidence', *World Politics*, vol. 44, no. 2, 1992, pp. 27–320.

Yin, K.Y., 'The Development of the Textile Industry in Taiwan', *Industry of Free China*, January, 1954, pp. 5–18.

Part IV

Strategies for engagement: industry policy and labour policy

8

Exploring economic integration with Asia: the Australian food industry and global change

Robert Fagan

A reassessment of Australia's relationships with Asian nations is long overdue. This chapter considers the vexed question of closer economic integration with Pacific Asian countries and what it may mean for Australian policies seeking to bring about industrial change. By the early 1980s, the pillars that supported industry policy in Australia during the previous three decades had crumbled. Within the powerful policymaking culture ascendant in Australia since this time, 'Keynesianism', with its legitimation of direct state intervention in the economy, has been cast as protectionist and out of kilter with moves towards deregulation and increased competition taking place throughout industrialised countries. By the mid-1980s, the degree of international integration of national commodity and money markets in these countries had become vastly different from the experiences during the relatively stable period of industrial growth between 1950 and about 1970. In Australia, this growing *globalisation* has been expressed politically as the requirement that domestic economic activity meet international standards of cost structure, price and profitability.[1] This has limited the possible scope of industry policy initiatives since the mid-1980s, lest they should damage Australia's international competitiveness.

During the past decade, the federal Labor Government has received contradictory advice from its advisers and think-tanks. The Garnaut Report[2] crystallised the 'level playing field' school of thought with its firm support of financial deregulation, minimal controls on capital inflow and outflow, the removal of *all* tariff protection by 2000 and anti-inflation policies. It linked microeconomic reform to the international competitiveness of industry. Garnaut argued that by these means, Australia would become more integrated with 'the North Asian ascendancy'. By contrast, the Pappas Carter Report[3] rejected the zero tariff position, recommending phased reductions in protection according to a timetable reflecting the degree of success in other industry policies designed to foster increased competitiveness and new markets in Pacific Asia. The Report was more interventionist, recognising both the key role of transnational corporations (TNCs) and government policies (including the widespread use of non-tariff protection, especially by Japan and the European Community). According to the Pappas Carter consultants, Australian governments should: create a new financial environment for investment in production; carry out microeconomic reform directed at state utilities and infrastructure; support the key exporting firms; and foster a 'new workplace culture' in the manufacturing sector. The Pappas Carter rejection of Garnaut's stance on removing tariffs proved too much for the local financial press and, ultimately, for the Hawke–Keating Government. Lumped in with so-called new protectionism, the expensive study disappeared almost without debate.

Both of these inquiries identified industries like Australia's food-processing sector as having great potential for building new export-oriented manufacturing, directed particularly at new Asian markets. Australia was seen to have a competitive advantage in land-based production over vastly more densely populated East Asian economies. It was further assumed that rapid growth of new, urban middle classes in Pacific Asian countries would create new markets for processed foods. Food processing has long been Australia's most export-oriented manufacturing sector, has internationalised rapidly during the 1980s, and local production is dominated by branch plants of food and agribusiness TNCs, most of which have major operations in Asian countries. By drawing on the results of a five-year research project into globalisation and restructuring in these industries, this chapter aims to shed light on the possibilities and pitfalls facing closer economic integration with Asia.

Yet the chapter also develops a broader argument. The idea of globalisation itself is examined as part of the discourse about closer integration with Asia since the mid-1980s. The Pacific Asian Region has been central both to Australia's experience of globalisation since the early 1970s and to the political debates about deregulation. There are two main reasons. First, a key feature of the more integrated global economy of the 1980s and 1990s has been the rise of Japan, Australia's principal trading partner, as the world's most powerful exporter of industrial goods and finance. Second, one of the central features of this new system has been the dramatic rise of Asian newly industrialising countries (NICs). To influential voices in the discourse, Japan and the NICs provide models of the benefits of deregulation and closer integration with globalised markets and production systems. According to this thesis, Australia has little choice but to seek closer integration of its production, trade and financial systems with this dynamic region to secure its long-term economic future. To other voices, often marginalised by the dominant neo-liberal orthodoxy, the growth of Asian NICs epitomises the perils for local workers and manufacturing regions of the move towards a new international division of labour (NIDL), dominated by TNCs and bringing about new forms of dependent development in low-wage economies to the north while accelerating domestic deindustrialisation and social polarisation in Australia.

The broad outlines of this debate are well known by now. This chapter seeks to extend the debate in a more constructive direction. Theoretical and empirical research into globalisation since the mid-1980s shows that both the neo-liberal position and the NIDL thesis are fundamentally flawed. During the early 1980s, social scientists analysing the economic, social, political and cultural impacts of TNCs produced a much better grasp of processes seeming to operate beyond the level of nation-states, the economic spaces still assumed unproblematically by economic orthodoxy. Yet this upsurge in research coincided with, and partly created, a proliferation of *global metaphors*—global market, global village, global factory, the 'world car', and so on. Despite the popular appeal of these ideas, it remains difficult to conceptualise 'global' change. The metaphors are abstractions which bury the continued importance of other scales of analysis (including national, regional and local). They exaggerate both the degree of economic integration and the determination of the system from the top down.

The chapter introduces briefly an attempt to reshape the pervasive metaphor of 'globalisation' and then illustrates the processes at work with examples from the corporate behaviour of major players in Australian food-processing industries. The framework is then used to reassess prevailing government policies which envisage Australian food production sailing into new Asian markets on a tide of competitive advantage and 'international best practice'.

Global and national restructuring

A thorough review is beyond the scope of this chapter.[4] It is important, however, to draw attention to two discourses about global restructuring that approach the phenomenon from fundamentally different directions. To economic rationalists, globalisation is about international competitiveness—a return to the canons of the marketplace in establishing the most appropriate relationships between national economic units. It provides a rationale for governments to abandon regulatory structures of the long boom while sharply reducing the (unsustainable) growth rates of expenditure on welfare and social infrastructure. According to this paradigm, the need for a return to less constrained market forces is highlighted by three things: first, periodic episodes of stagflation and recession in Australia since the mid-1970s; second, the build-up of massive current account deficits; and third, increased competition in both domestic and international markets from low-cost goods from NICs manufactured with state-of-the-art technology and 'best practice'. In this orthodoxy, NICs around the Asia-Pacific rim are held to be examples of the triumph of market forces over state intervention.

Since about 1980, however, the majority of research into global restructuring undertaken outside the confines of this neo-classical orthodoxy has rejected this market framework and been situated instead within alternative discourses about the internationalisation of capital. One of the most influential counter-theses during the 1980s was based around the idea that a new international division of labour (NIDL) had emerged. According to this thesis, the long boom in industrialised countries from about 1950 to the early 1970s was brought to an end by capital accumulation crises accompanying widespread downturns in profits among manufacturing firms, steady increases in a variety of production costs and problems of market saturation.[5] Transnational manufacturing firms responded by moving production to new sites around the world which could offer cost advantages such as cheap labour and state subsidy in specially designated zones for new manufacturing exporters. Imports from these newly industrialising countries (NICs) further undermined production in the world's major mass consumption markets. Hence, the NIDL thesis directly linked the growth of NICs such as the 'four tigers' of East Asia (South Korea, Hong Kong, Taiwan and Singapore) to the decline of manufacturing as an employer of labour within developed capitalist countries. Far from reflecting the interplay of new international market forces, these sites of growth and decline were held to be linked directly through TNCs and the emergence of a new competition between places, embraced by authoritarian nation-states, for their investments.

In this view, internationally competitive production in countries like Australia could be maintained only through severe rationalisation, widespread technological change and concentration on competitive sectors such as those based on resources (minerals, food, tourism) or information-rich services. The resulting competition between places would reduce costs, help restore profits and compel both the trade union movement and Australian governments to introduce comprehensive changes to the social relations developed during the long boom.

The NIDL thesis showed that restructuring is about profits and power relations not markets. It highlighted the emergence of a *global* economic system transcending the links between nation-states still central to neo-classical economic orthodoxy. Yet flaws in the NIDL thesis had become well known by the 1990s. It is worth remembering four of them.

1 The search for cheap labour by TNCs was seriously overstated as a reason for rapid industrialisation of NICs. The role of strong government intervention and the role of growing entrepreneurial classes in all Asian NICs was crucial. Indeed, while bringing the globalising nature of economic change to the forefront of analysis, the NIDL thesis played down major geographical, social and cultural differences between the NICs[6] and their crucial role in shaping the kinds of industrialisation which took place.

2 A 'spatial fix' to problems of profits and accumulation was far from a universal corporate strategy, especially during the 1980s. NIDL theorists paid much attention to global networks of production which could link corporate hierarchies and the R&D advantages of key industrialised countries, with new standardised production in NICs of components for export to developed country markets, including Australia. This provided some explanation of trends in the motor vehicle and electronics industries, but was less common in most other sectors of production and has nothing to say about food processing.

Changing relations between capital, labour and state *within* Australia have had greater overall impact on restructuring. These have included political pressures to deregulate labour markets, continued automation of production and casualisation of the industrial workforce. Only in certain sectors (and places) can these changes be linked to the growth in imports from Asian NICs or the flight to those countries of TNC branch plants.

3 The most widely neglected dimension (in both discourses) has been the growth of a genuinely global financial system during the 1980s, accompanied by widespread abandonment of financial regulation. In many key sectors of industrialised countries, restructuring became driven primarily by rapid changes in global flows of money perhaps reaching a crescendo before the stockmarket crashes of 1987. 'Debt-overhang' arising from this period is still a potent factor in the restructuring of Australian productive enterprises during the 1990s.

4 The NIDL thesis, like the neo-classical market orthodoxy, severely understates the continuing importance of international politics, the break-up of US political hegemony within the global economic system, the continued rise of Japan as a world economic power, and the moves towards greater European integration. Trade, production links and political negotiation between the leading nation-

states of this Triad[7] still dominate the global economy, notwith-standing the premises of trade theory. These links are forged by state policies, massive flows of money and the competitive behaviour of TNCs.

The research project on the food industry has been based on an alternative conception of integration in the global economy.[8] The basis of this alternative thesis is summarised in Table 8.1 which shows some of the most important relationships between production within a national economy and the emerging global system. Throughout the history of capitalist economies, capital has always moved through circuits of *production, trade* and *investment* in the search by firms for future markets, profits and growth. The internationalisation of production, trade and investment has played an important part in reproducing the system. Table 8.1 represents the emergence of a more integrated global economy through *all* three circuits rather than according privileged status to either international trade, as in neo-classical models of competitive advantage, or internationalised production through TNCs, as in the NIDL thesis.

The circuits of trade, financial flows and transnational production give rise to a variety of links with global capital accumulation but these must be determined empirically in actual times and places rather than being simply read off from abstract ideas. Table 8.1 divides total capital within an economy according to the different ways in which firms become inserted into global accumulation through their patterns of production, trade and investment. Firms in the *national* division, for example, produce, sell their commodities, raise capital and reinvest largely within the territorial space of their home nation. By contrast, the *global* division comprises firms for which local production takes place within global networks of TNC branch plants; goods and services are sold on world markets (international trade), and investment capital is obtained globally (e.g. from the profits of their overseas production or by borrowing from transnational banks). This global division in any country is not based on the *nationality* of enterprises but on the ways in which they plug into the global economy.

Investment-constrained firms produce and reinvest locally but sell a significant proportion of their output on world markets. These firms include large domestic exporters (other than TNCs) whose integration with the global economy is constrained by their producing and investing largely inside a particular nation. By contrast, firms in the *market-constrained* division obtain finance outside the nation-state (as foreign investment) but, in addition, can invest domestic surpluses internationally. The complete integration of these firms with the global economy, however, is constrained because most of their output is sold to the

Table 8.1   Circuits of capital and links with the global economy

Division	International circuit of capital			Links with global economy
	Production	Trade	Investment	
National	N	N	N	import competition; competition from TNCs; global finance technology, licences
Investment-constrained	N	G	N	imports/exports; competition from TNCs; global finance technology, licences
Market-constrained	N (G)	N	G	TNC branch plants; import competition; global finance technology, licences
Global	N (G)	G	G	TNC branch plants; imports/exports; global finance technology, R&D

Source: Fagan & Webber, 1994
N = national; G = global

markets in which they are located. This division contains foreign-owned branch plants of TNCs serving national markets which may be protected by tariff barriers. In recent years, TNCs primarily adopting this strategy have been called 'multi-domestics' and they remain common in the food and clothing industries.

Restructuring since the late 1970s has seen genuinely global corporations added to the multi-domestics of the long boom. These TNCs do not simply produce, market and invest in many nations, but integrate the three circuits of capital inside global corporate organisations. Such integration lies outside the market framework of competitive advantage which cannot deal adequately, if at all, with intra-corporate trade and money flows. Table 8.1 indicates links with the global economy for each division. Notice that even firms in the national division are linked increasingly to the global economy through: relationships with international banks (even when borrowing 'locally'); technology imports, franchising and the payment of patent royalties; subcontracting with global firms; and increased competition for local markets either from TNC branch plants or imports. This framework suggests three additional things about globalisation.

1   Nation-states are still central to capitalist development because capital, labour and state interact in specific nation-states (rather than 'globally'). These national relationships are not subordinate to globalised accumulation but simultaneously shape the way it happens. The idea of a two-way flow between local and global is difficult for politicians to grasp, perhaps most obviously because

it undermines the 'steam-roller' metaphor that there is no alternative
for countries like Australia but accommodation to global change.

2   Nation-states cannot intervene on behalf of all divisions at once.
    Indeed, their patterns of intervention are determined in both formal
    and informal political spheres and may be resisted strongly within
    some divisions while supported (pressured?) by others. During the
    long boom after 1950, for example, Australian governments intro-
    duced a triad of policies to underwrite industrial growth and dis-
    tribute the outcomes through society: first, tight control of the
    financial system; second, a high tariff regime; and third, rising real
    wages passed quickly through the labour market by the centralised
    wage-fixing system. The triad worked alongside encouragement of
    high rates of immigration to expand further both the domestic
    market and the labour force. These policies were specific interven-
    tions on behalf of national and market-constrained divisions but
    were frequently contested by the investment-constrained firms
    (major exporters).

3   Since the early 1980s, the state has moved towards a new accumu-
    lation strategy[9] involving financial deregulation, substantial tariff
    reduction (opening the economy to global market forces), strategies
    to encourage exports of goods and services in which Australia
    should have international competitive advantage, and moves to
    deregulate the labour market, all underpinned by a series of
    'Accords' between the state and organised labour. The imperatives
    of globalisation have been employed as a rationale for the direction
    of much of this change. Yet policies designed to encourage new
    connections with globalised accumulation have resulted from polit-
    ical processes at national and local levels within Australia. These
    have been carried out *in the context of* dramatic changes in the
    Asia-Pacific region and, especially, the relationship with Japan. Yet
    the United States and the European Community also remain crucial
    to this global context, especially for Australian mining and manu-
    facturing firms, and financial institutions. Table 8.1 suggests that
    the resultant deregulation is just as much an intervention by the
    state as was the policy regime it has been designed to replace but
    on behalf of different divisions, encouraging different connections
    with old and new trading partners.

In these situations, local agents of globalised firms are often crucial
in developing corporate strategies for change but these are often
represented by such agents as reflecting global imperatives, such as
'Asianisation', in their efforts to control bargaining over restructuring
with the state and local communities. Similarly, national or global
processes can be *constructed* as local—for example moves to encour-

age localities and regions to take responsibility for their own employment development strategies[10]—to suit the purposes of the most powerful stakeholders in change.

Social sciences have generally taken too mechanical a view of links between global and local. The dominant discourse about globalisation has implied its hegemony. Yet globalisation must be seen as an uneven and contested process. There is no single path to restructuring either globally or locally since paths are constructed contingently by stakeholders. Further, these various agents construct images of both past and future to sell their contemporary restructuring strategies to others. Representatives of capital, politicians, bureaucrats and academics all employ such discourses—the discourse about integration with Asia is just one. From this, it is easy to see how the concept of globalisation can be used to legitimise state deregulation or a business push for greater 'flexibility' in domestic workplaces. It is also clear how the 'global leviathan' imagery of the NIDL thesis can be locally or regionally disempowering.

The Australian food industry and global change

Australian food and beverage processing constitutes the largest (remaining) sector of domestic manufacturing employing about 170 000 people in 1992 or 17 per cent of the national manufacturing workforce. Perhaps of more relevance is its export orientation. The mineral booms of the 1970s radically restructured Australian exports and completed their reorientation to the Asia-Pacific region. Yet throughout the 1980s, foodstuffs (both raw and processed) have constituted between one-fifth and one-quarter of total exports. Four-fifths are traded as unprocessed or semi-processed commodities leaving some one-fifth as processed foods (valued at $A2.2 billion in 1990). While Australian government policy has been keen to encourage exports of higher value-added foodstuffs, by the 1990s most still receive only relatively simple processing such as slaughtering, freezing, canning or other packaging.

The value of processed food exports has increased steadily since 1980, but the growth has not kept pace with other sectors. As a result, the share of processed food exports in Australia's total trade was nearly 10 percentage points lower in 1990 than it was in 1980. Absolute growth of exports has been very significant for some sectors, while volumes exported have increased significantly between 1991 and 1993. This has been most noticeable in the wine industry where exports are targeted at the European Community and North America. In addition, increasing quantities of processed cereals and vegetable products have been sold recently in Asian markets. While recent trends give some encouragement to the hopes of both state and labour for the food industry, the export performance has been disappointing considering the quantities and qualities of foodstuffs potentially available for export and the government's strong embrace of the concept of comparative advantage.

Restructuring of Australian food processing, including technological change and rationalisation, began more slowly than in manufacturing as a whole. While forms of non-tariff protection are important in some food sectors, effective rates of protection have always been among the lowest in manufacturing. Yet once restructuring began in earnest in food processing during the 1980s, it moved more quickly than in many other sectors. Total employment has stabilised since the mid-1980s but this disguises very major job-shedding from larger plants in key sectors supplying both domestic and export markets. Processed food imports have increased steadily over the last five years but the growth has *followed*, not preceded, the restructuring of the 1980s. Changing trade patterns, a major plank in the neo-classical arguments about the benefits of removing impediments to trade, have not been a principal cause of restructuring in the Australian food industry—perhaps least of all, in the 1980s, the changes springing from trade with Asia. The reasons for restructuring must be found elsewhere.

A large number of small businesses manufacture food and beverages in Australia, and there has been much discussion about the rise of boutique producers cultivating niche markets. Yet all key sectors remain dominated by large companies, often subsidiaries of TNCs, most of which arrived in Australia during the 1960s, attracted to the rapid population growth and relative affluence of the market to enter the market-constrained division of Table 8.1. The 30 largest food manufacturers in 1992 (Table 8.2) accounted for 70 per cent of total industry turnover and the vast proportion of processed food exports. By 1992, 11 of these 30 largest producers were subsidiaries of foreign owned TNCs including six of the largest ten firms.

The behaviour of these corporate groups is a key to understanding food restructuring. There has been an epidemic of mergers and takeovers with some of Australia's largest business acquisitions in the heady days of the 1980s made in this sector. Four overall types of corporate strategy underpin the new geographies.

1   Fierce struggles for market power developed nationally in brewing and the production of wine, chicken-meat, confectionery, biscuits and frozen foods. In some sectors, this reflected competition for domestic markets growing much more slowly than they had during the long boom.

Table 8.2   Australia's thirty largest food and beverage companies, 1992

Rank	Company	Ownership	Pacific Asian countries with operation*	Exports ($A million), 1992	Turnover ($A million), 1992
1	Foster's Brewing	Aust.	–	40	10 371
2	Goodman Fielder	Aust. (NZ)	6	59	4210
3	Coca-Cola Amatil	USA*	1		1866
4	Southcorp	Aust.	1	135	1500(est.)
5	Aust. Meat Holdings	USA*	–	750	1185
6	Unilever	UK/Neth*	p	51	1158
7	Nestlé	Switz.*	p	141	1113
8	Pacific Dunlop	Aust.	2		1000(est.)
9	Lion Nathan (C-T)	NZ*	–		1000(est.)
10	Cadbury-Schweppes	UK*	1	26	988
11	George Weston	UK*	1	13	930
12	National Foods	Aust.	1		845
13	Effem Foods (Mars)	USA*	p	90	714
14	Arnotts Ltd	USA*	–		710
15	Bonlac	Aust.(co-op)	1	267	694
16	Inghams	Aust.	–		662
17	Metro Meat	Japan*	p		630
18	Murray Goulburn	Aust.(co-op)	–	260	560
19	Angliss Group	UK*	–	363	550
20	Pepsico	USA*	–		535
21	Kraft	USA*	p		534
22	Burns Philp (food)	Aust.	2	80	500(est.)
23	Bunge	UK/Arg.*	2	25	465
24	CSR (sugar)	Aust.	–	13	450
25	Aust. Co-Op. Foods	Aust.	–		434
26	Nippon Meat	Japan*	p		366
27	Ricegrowers' Co-op	Aust (co-op)	–	210	357
28	Kellogg	USA*	p		309
29	Bundaberg Sugar	UK*	–		297
30	QUF	Aust.	–	38	280

* numbers refer to plants controlled by the Australian HQ
p overseas parent has Asian plants

2   Established food corporations diversified away from food, often with poor results (sugar, agribusiness, brewing).

3   The 1980s saw a massive shift *into* food by corporations which, under the Australian government's new deregulated financial environment, had raised large amounts of foreign debt to finance restructuring. After 1985, food processing became most attractive to highly geared companies because of the steady cash flows that result from dominant domestic market shares. This has been especially significant in Australia where, by 1990, a single firm con-

trolled more than half of domestic market share in 13 out of the 40 4-digit food manufacturing categories.

4   Some Australian companies attempted to reconstruct themselves as food TNCs during the mid-1980s often with loans raised from transnational banks. Australian firms made major offshore investments although, until very recently, these were dominantly made in North America and the EC. Investments in the Asian NICs grew slowly in the 1980s; indeed some of the largest agribusiness organisations actually reduced their role in the Asia-Pacific region between 1985 and 1990. None of these offshore developments is explained by the NIDL thesis with its focus on low-cost labour.

The categories in Table 8.1 can be used to summarise the results of the food industry study which show that there has been no inexorable shift towards the *global division* since 1980. Through a spate of mergers and takeovers, many national and investment-constrained firms were welded into global groups, especially in cases where the acquisitions were made by TNCs or finance was provided by transnational banks. Heavy domestic rationalisation followed to maintain cash flows and some product divisions were sold off to national firms or other TNCs to quickly restructure debt. There was some shift of production to overseas markets after 1980 but a major retreat after 1987. By 1990, the debt burdens being carried by larger food and agribusiness enterprises, such as Elders IXL Ltd, and by corporate raiders such as Adelaide Steamship and Bond Corporation, brought about massive changes among the food producers listed in Table 8.2. While much of the shake-out was oriented towards securing power within the Australian market, virtually all of it was financially driven as companies struggled to restructure debt. Very little of this huge investment in food processing has been related to new technology, innovative product strategies or the development of new markets in the Asia-Pacific region.

Recent restructuring has seen major disposals of food assets, often at fire-sale prices, some of which had been owned for only a short time. The takeovers and divestments had impacts that can be traced to factory level in the main food-processing regions, especially Sydney and Melbourne where job-shedding was greatest. For many firms, the financial uncertainties at the top caused productive investment strategies to become stalled. Firms have attempted to develop simpler structures based on fewer commodities, epitomised by Elders IXL divesting most of its agribusiness divisions since 1991 and renaming itself Fosters Brewing around one of Australia's cultural icons.

In the *investment-constrained* division, the major changes after 1980 were increased vertical integration and attempts to control the export of unprocessed foods. Debt problems caused some withdrawal of firms from this strategy after 1987 and the incorporation of some leading exporters into global food enterprises after 1990. TNCs have snapped up some of the divested assets in their own global strategies which focus on brand name power and differentiated markets, including Japan and East Asian NICs. As a result all five of Australia's largest red-meat processors and exporters are now foreign-owned, dominated by the purchase in 1992 of Australian Meat Holdings from Elders by the giant US corporation, Conagra. By contrast the *market-constrained* division has experienced a resurgence despite the predictions of the theoretical model that it would remain simply as a relic from the long boom period. While there has been heavy rationalisation of employment in TNC branch plants, foreign ownership has increased again with a resurgence of concentration in the domestic market around key brand-name products (e.g. in soft drinks, confectionery, margarine and oils, general foods). The importance of multi-domestics has risen sharply since 1990 as processed foods from globalised corporations are marketed through local brand names.

Finally, the *national* division has experienced major restructuring in several sectors usually around the replacement of regional marketing by struggles for *national* market share (notably in dairy products). With the near financial collapse of organisations such as Adelaide Steamship, whose path towards globalisation was blocked by unsustainable foreign debt and an audit by the Australian Taxation Office, new national firms have been spawned in the 1990s (epitomised by National Foods Ltd). This restructuring of Adelaide Steamship also brought into frozen foods, ice cream and convenience foods Pacific Dunlop, one of Australia's largest TNCs with an aggressive global rationalisation strategy first developed in the TCF industries. Rapid growth of 'boutique' producers also occurred during the 1980s but problems in raising local finance, and the costs of maintaining market share against the scale economies of the top 30 (Table 8.2), caused several 'success stories' to become absorbed into the large firm sector by the 1990s (notably in brewing and wine-making).

Major changes in food marketing and consumption habits have strongly influenced these patterns of restructuring. The old debate about how much of this reflects consumer choice, and how much is constructed by advertising and brand-name strategies, now contributes little. Rather, we should note that for both reasons 'localised' marketing has become crucial in food company strategies. Food manufacturers have begun to promote food as entertainment or healthy lifestyle. Some of the key changes include: increased production of fast foods which supposedly add 'value'; shifts to forms of protein other than red meat; moves towards fresh and packaged frozen foods and away from canned and processed foods; so-called 'green' foods where marketing emphasis is placed on nutritional value and hygiene; and the growing health- and 'real' food market, especially among the new urban service classes in Australia's largest cities. Here, value is added by 'naturalising' rather than homogenising the food product but the naturalised product is a cultural and industrial construct.

As markets have become locally differentiated, new technologies of product design, transport and warehousing have allowed production from large firms exploiting scale economies to be targeted at niche markets. Faced with a renewed struggle for national (and international) market share, large firms have resorted increasingly to brand consciousness. Brand names allow companies to cash in on the cultural icon status of many food products. Indeed, the *construction* of these icons has become a major strategy for food companies. Sometimes, companies have literally cashed in the brand names, disposing of them as they withdraw from certain products or markets following leveraged buy-outs. Brand names help to create barriers to entry and protect market share. They have also become crucial in the growing struggle between Australian retailers and manufacturers for a share of the profits from domestic food markets where branded products compete with the supermarkets' generic brands. Finally, ignored by most corporate watchers, brand name loyalties allow companies to obscure product origins (notwithstanding labelling regulations: if the product is an Arnott's SAO biscuit, it must be the good old recipe). This helps to construct a barrier between the final consumer and the place and conditions under which the food was produced, a further demonstration of the localisation of globalising products.

To summarise: the food case-study shows that global restructuring is far from being a smooth process. Globalisation is uneven and *contested;* it cannot be captured by a focus on either the circuit of trade, as in the competitive advantage models, or the circuit of production, as in the NIDL thesis. Detailed analyses of production, trade, financial flows and the relationships between them, are all essential in understanding restructuring. Since the early 1980s, Australian food manufacturers have 'moved' in both directions in Table 8.1 rather than simply towards global structures. With the prevalence of financially motivated restructuring, it is not surprising that development of new food export markets has been unspectacular. For all divisions, however, the connections with globalised capital accumulation processes in 1994 were much more complex than in 1984. The influence of global processes such as trade negotiations and market changes, the circulation of finance capital by transnational banks, and the behaviour of TNCs has steadily increased. Yet these processes cannot be decoupled from the national and local spaces in which Australian and Asian food consumption, processing and food agriculture take place. The national and local spaces still have to be negotiated by global food companies.

The so-called logic of globalisation is both enabled and contested by national regulatory environments and local events. The continued volatility of corporate structure in the Australian food-processing industries is illustrated well by the decision by Pacific Dunlop Ltd, announced in May 1995, to sell its food-processing division because of dissatisfaction with returns on this investment made just four years previously. The so-called poor returns reflect a combination of national and international factors in the markets for the company's other production divisions and a re-assessment of longer-term corporate strategy. Because of the size of these food assets, the stockmarket immediately anticipated that control would fall to a TNC such as H.J. Heinz or Nestlé.

The push for competitive advantage: Australian food in Asia

All of these findings have major significance for evaluating the government's strategy of boosting Australian food exports to Asian Pacific countries. They also expose some serious flaws in the prevailing wisdom about how to achieve closer economic integration with Asia. The food case-study shows that determinants of international competitiveness are complex. Australia's penetration of promising export markets has not been enhanced by the decade of deregulation; nor has the food industry's decade of sustained globalisation put it in a better position to take advantage of Asian opportunities. Indeed, export-orientation has gone backwards. This has little to do with the quality of raw materials, the productivity of Australian agriculture or even the costs of local labour in processing plants. It has much to do with: levels of R&D in process technologies, product development and marketing; patterns of state intervention; and the strategies of food corporations driven partly by international finance.

The discourse about competitive advantage also makes major cultural assumptions about the new middle classes in the Asia-Pacific region. There is no doubt that food markets will grow in Asia, and liberalised trade regimes will help to produce new commodity flows to serve them. Changes in basic demography, family structures, the economic role of women, and further rapid growth of an urban middle class, all ensure this. Yet major assumptions are being made both in government and industry circles about the kinds of demands these new food shoppers will have. Australian regulatory bodies such as the Foreign Investment Review Board (FIRB), under tight rein by the Australian government, have often placed themselves in contradictory positions arguing, for example, that the national interest could be served through the acquisition of Australian food companies by TNCs with 'know-how' to help them penetrate markets that are in their infancy[11], are highly differentiated between countries, and are still largely unknown even (especially?) to the world's major food TNCs with their feet planted firmly in North America and the EC.

Australian food manufacturers face strong competition from other potential suppliers also targeting these growing markets. Since the late 1980s, all of the world's largest TNC food processors have begun to position themselves to supply these markets from existing production bases around the Pacific Rim—for example, on the west coast of the United States—and by opening new plants, often as joint-ventures, in China and the NICs. Production is targeted not only at newly developing markets but, primarily, at Japan which is by far Australia's largest export market for processed foods.

A good illustration is provided by the case of Arnotts Ltd, Australia's largest biscuit manufacturer with control over two-thirds of the domestic market. In 1992–93, a hotly contested takeover bid for Arnotts Ltd resulted in the company passing under the effective control of Campbell Soup (USA). The Australian Government's role in the bid demonstrates the confusion inherent in its position on deregulating the economy to foster both a domestic export-oriented manufacturing sector and further economic integration with the Asia-Pacific Region. The FIRB approved Campbell moving to a controlling interest after a protracted debate both in the media and on the stock exchanges. Supporters argued that Campbell had the technical expertise and marketing contacts to take the famous Arnott's brand names into Asian markets. The Australian company, they argued, had botched an earlier attempt to gain market share in the United States. Opponents argued that the brand names, some of which have cultural icon status, should not be allowed to fall under foreign control, and that Campbell, through its own US biscuit brands, had contributed to Arnott's poor North American result.

While the importance of brand names in food globalisation was recognised, the debate was narrow and nationalistic. There is little doubt that Campbell was seeking to use Australian biscuit production as a base for a position in Pacific Asia. Yet there are at least four ways in which this could happen:

1 Australian biscuits could be exported into Asian markets, reflecting Australia's raw material advantages and marketable brand names. This was the government's preferred outcome, accepted implicitly by the FIRB.

2 Products using Arnott's brand names and technologies could be

manufactured from Australian raw materials inside the major Asian markets, reflecting lower labour costs in those countries, but also taking advantage of state incentives and the advantages of localising food marketing.

3 A controlling share of the Australian market could be used simply as a secure cash flow for Campbell seeking to penetrate the more risky Asian markets with its range of other brand names and production sources.

4 Campbell–Arnotts could use imports from such offshore sources, including new plants in Asia, to increase pressure for cost reductions in existing Australian processing plants.

The problem for the government's strategy is that the first option is no more likely than any of the others; all of them would increase the integration of the Australian economy with the Pacific Rim, but only the first would contribute towards local revitalised, export-oriented manufacturing.

A poor profit result for Arnotts in 1994 caused them to shelve plans to build a new biscuit factory in Sydney's outer suburbs and to threaten locating it offshore[12], a public confirmation of option four. In addition, the lower profits have almost stalled the company's strategy to increase its export drive into Asia. The company has blamed much of its poor result on the Prices Surveillance Authority's refusal to sanction domestic price rises, further illustrating the importance of domestic market sales in corporate strategy.

The focus on trade, explicit in the government's international competitiveness strategy, diverts attention away from these other factors that determine patterns of exports and the location of production. Politicians from all Asian Pacific economies take a domestic political agenda to the negotiating tables to discuss trade and future development issues. The Australian food industry is affected strongly by the crucial social and political role of agriculture in potential markets such as South Korea, Thailand and Indonesia, and especially the emergence of more 'industrialised' contract farming in which members of ruling political structures have major commercial and political interests. Asian processed food industries, encouraged by interventionist state policies and already installing highly automated production systems[13], will become important outlets for these agricultural developments, contributing to employment growth and reducing the need for food imports.

Hence, Australia must expect that greater economic integration with Pacific Asia during the next decade will not simply open up food markets but sources of imports as well. Rapid growth in imports of processed foods from Southeast Asia since the late 1980s has been mentioned. In Thailand, the state remains strongly interventionist in agriculture and has encouraged export-oriented food processing especially in seafoods, canned vegetables and processed chickens. Thailand is a very low-cost source of these processed foods, but trade patterns with Australia are conditioned strongly by corporate strategies and the role of the state at both ends. Since the late 1980s, Australian imports from Thailand of tinned tomatoes and pineapples have increased sharply. These have been staple products for Australian fruit and vegetable processing cooperatives such as Letona-SPC and Golden Circle which have been affected seriously by imports.

In both cases, the imports have come through offshore sourcing by Australia's supermarket chains (Coles and Franklins) to provide price competition for local branded products and to support their own generic brands. This is part of an on-going struggle between the largest manufacturers in Table 8.2 and the major retailers for a share of profits available from domestic food markets. Coles returned to local purchasing in 1991–92, following a successful anti-dumping case brought by local canneries, but began to source low-cost Thai tomatoes again in 1993. This demonstrates an increasing trend for offshore sourcing of processed foods to be used by both retailers and manufacturers as a lever to bring about 'international best practice' in local processing plants—code words for price-competitiveness with the lowest-cost sources in the Asia-Pacific Region. In 1994, Pacific Dunlop, Australia's largest manufacturer of ice cream, purchased a controlling interest in one of Thailand's major ice cream producers.

The emergence of agribusiness TNCs based in Asia also has major implications. A good example is Charoen Pokphand (CP) of Thailand, a conglomerate with interests in stockfeed, rice, pork and chicken products, prawn aquaculture, brewing and retailing.[14] During the 1980s, processed poultry has become one of Thailand's main food exports. Companies like CP, controlling all aspects of chicken production, provide stiff competition in Asian markets for Australia's two domestic producers, Goodman Fielder and Inghams (neither of whom has shown any real interest in exporting chicken meat: see Table 8.2). Yet CP could also target the growing Australian market as local diets shift further away from red meat. The role of Australian government regulation will be crucial. While quarantine regulations have insulated Australia from chicken imports, the government is considering a recommendation from the Quarantine Inspection Service that these be relaxed, according with the moves to liberalise regional trade under APEC. Such a scenario could cause either of the Australian companies to consider divesting their poultry operations which, in the case of Goodman Fielder, have been under-performing compared with other food divisions. CP would be an interested buyer of assets which would bring not only production bases inside Australia but locally accepted brand names for poultry products sourced offshore.

Conclusion

The dominant discourse of the 1980s on economic integration with Asia is showing some signs of breaking down under the weight of evidence about its flaws. Yet it remains powerful among the Australian Government's principal policy advisers and think-tanks. Implicit in the discourse has been the 'steam-roller' model of globalisation; changes take place 'out there', for example in the Asia-Pacific Region, and must be accommodated 'in here'—Australia's workplaces, cities, manufacturing and exporting regions. Yet connections between global and local are either simply assumed or ignored. They remain poorly understood, partly because they must be determined empirically for specific sectors, times and places. We urgently need more of this understanding so that more constructive notions of integration can be pursued.

The metaphor of globalisation now occupies a powerful place in the discourse about Australia and Asia. The steam-roller model can be used to support beliefs widely held that Asian countries, dominated by notions of hierarchy, authoritarianism and 'leadership', provide new cultural underpinnings to economic success and international competitiveness. Australians face little alternative than to get their acts together or get left behind. On the other hand, those celebrating moves towards a 'level playing field' argue that microeconomic reform and further deregulation (usually at a faster pace than in our major regional trading partners) are demanded by globalisation. In many ways, this standpoint has been epitomised by pronouncements emanating from the APEC summit in November 1994. It is a matter of urgency that the debate be lifted from these cul-de-sacs.

Macroeconomic policy changes to stimulate 'international competitiveness' are being aimed at too many desired policy outcomes, some of which are mutually incompatible. Simply attempting to level the playing field, to the exclusion of understanding corporate restructuring behaviour and the relationships between production, trade and finance, seems to put Australian production at a disadvantage relative to key players controlling both Triad markets and the NICs. The example of the food industry shows that massive investments during the 1980s were not directed towards improving Australia's export base in value-added products. Research and development expenditures in this sector by 1990 remained among the very lowest in Australian manufacturing.[15]

A revitalised food manufacturing sector will not result from simply joining the alchemy of competitive advantage with the magic of Asian dynamism. Industry plans are now out of favour with the Federal Labor Government despite evidence that some of the most significant increases in exports of higher value-added manufactured goods since 1990 have been from industries subject to plans introduced during the 1980s (notably the motor vehicle sector). Yet adoption of a clear food industry strategy by the Government would be more constructive than simply relying on domestic restructuring to make food exports competitive in new Pacific Asian markets. Such a strategy should recognise that local political and economic decisions determine the kind of 'globalisation' Australia will experience and, especially the social distribution of both its benefits and costs. Otherwise, the discourse of globalisation provides a smokescreen for stalling or delaying fundamental national and local restructuring within Australia which is just as much, if not more, likely to result in fruitful economic and social ties with Pacific Asian economies.

Acknowledgments

The author is grateful to Phillip O'Neill and Richard Le Heron for constructively critical debates about globalisation and what it might mean. Sherrie Cross researched much of the empirical information on which the case-study is based and Bill Pritchard provided useful insights into recent changes in the food industry.

Notes

1 Bryan, R. & Fagan, R.H., 'Industry Policy: Is it a Matter of Patriotism?', Institute of Australian Geographers, Study Group on Industrial Change, Conference, September 1992, Newcastle.
2 Garnaut, R., *Australia and the Northeast Asia Ascendancy*, Australian Government Publishing Service, Canberra, 1989.
3 Australian Manufacturing Council, *The Global Change: Australian Manufacturing in the 1990s*, The Pappas Carter Report, Australian Manufacturing Council, Melbourne, 1990.
4 The arguments are developed further in: Fagan, R.H. & Le Heron, R. B., 'Reinterpreting the Geography of Accumulation: The Global Shift and Local Restructuring', *Environment and Planning D: Society and Space*, vol.12, 1994, pp. 265–85; Fagan, R.H. & Webber, M., *Global Restructuring: The Australian Experience*, Oxford University Press, Melbourne, 1994.
5 The evidence is reviewed by Harvey, D., *The Condition of Postmodernity*, Basil Blackwell, Oxford, 1989.

6 Much greater in the Asia-Pacific region than in Latin America. See Daly, M. T., 'The Road to the Twenty-First Century: The Myths and Miracles of Asian Manufacturing', *Money Power and Space*, eds S. Corbridge, R. Martin & N. Thrift, Blackwell, Oxford, 1994, p. 179.

7 See Ohmae, K., *The Borderless World*, Fontana, London, 1989; and Daly, op. cit., p. 167.

8 Developed in Fagan & Le Heron, op. cit.

9 O'Neill, P. M., 'Working Nation, Economic Change and the Regions', *Australian Geographer*, vol. 25, 1994, pp. 109–15; Fagan, R.H. & O'Neill, P. M., 'The New Regional Policy: What Chance of Success?', *Australian Quarterly*, vol. 67, 1995, pp. 55–68.

10 See Fagan, R.H., 'Working Nation and the Outer Suburbs: The Example of Western Sydney', *Australian Geographer*, vol. 25, 1994, pp. 115–20.

11 Goldstein, C., 'Asia's Rich Promise', *Far Eastern Economic Review*, 17 May 1990, pp. 28–9.

12 *Australian Financial Review*, 2 March 1994.

13 Tsuruoka, D., 'Using their Noodle', *Far Eastern Economic Review*, 17 May 1990, p. 45.

14 East Asia Analytical Unit (Department of Foreign Affairs and Trade), *Subsistence to Supermarket: Food and Agricultural Transformation in South-East Asia,* Australian Government Publishing Service, Canberra, 1994, p. 298.

15 Department of Industry, Technology and Commerce, *Australian Processed Food and Beverages Industry*, Australian Government Publishing Service, Canberra, 1991, p. 4.

Further References

Tabakoff, N., 'Arnotts Threatens to Build Offshore if Prices Held Down', *Australian Financial Review*, 2 March 1994, p. 14.

9

Asian trade and Australian labour market restructuring

Rob Lambert

Australia's pattern of trade with Asia has been shaped by the nation's change of status from one of the world's most protected economies to its present position as arguably the most open.[1] This trade strategy sought to address the severe structural imbalances that had emerged from the mid-1970s which were reflected in declining competitiveness, growing external debt and a reliance on commodity exports that were falling in value. The proposed solution to these structural problems was the deregulation of the financial markets, the dollar float and the radical reductions in tariff protection. These were intended to renew Australian manufacturing that Paul Keating referred to as 'a completely uncompetitive lump of industrial archaeology'.[2] This 'uncompetitive lump' was to be transformed into a sleek, competitive, globally integrated manufacturing system that could contribute to Australia's trading position through a strong export focus.

These strategic initiatives were taken at a time of the most significant restructuring of the global economy for more than a century. The World Bank predicts that China will overtake the United States as the world's biggest economy within the next twenty-five years and seven of the world's fifteen largest economies will be from the Asian region.[3] This global change clearly has implications for the Australian economy and society.

Asian growth, predicated heavily upon low-priced exports, is having an impact on Australia's pattern of trade and investment, the structure of its manufacturing sector, real wages, employment patterns and the distribution of income. During the period of economic deregulation from the mid-1970s, the manufacturing sector has contracted in relative terms with important segments relocating all or part of their production into Asia; unemployment has ratcheted upwards independently of economic cycles; real wages for the unskilled and semi-skilled have declined; part-time, casual work has expanded; income disparities have widened and the external debt has grown significantly.[4] The structural problems identified by these researchers underlie the current debate on labour market reform in which there are essentially three positions:

1   The neo-liberal perspective, led by the Coalition and the major representative organisations of Australian business such as the Business Council of Australia (BCA) and the Australian Chamber of Commerce and Industry (ACCI), all of whom argue that only a bold, extensive deregulation of the labour market will resolve this structural crisis.

2   The Labor Government contends that these problems are best addressed via a social democratic variant of labour market deregulation, centred on a partial, socially controlled deregulation, implemented within a corporatist framework that seeks to achieve a balance between decentralisation and controlled wages outcomes.

3   There is the emerging critique of both policy positions that derives from European and North American analyses of the present form of globalisation[5] and from research on the Australian manufacturing sector and Asian labour markets.[6] Essentially, it argues for greater control over capital mobility, an interventionist industry policy that focuses on the issue of imports as well as the promotion of exports and finally, a greater policy awareness of the impact of Asian labour standards on trade patterns and investment flows.

This policy debate on labour market strategies relevant to globalisation has a wider social and political significance because arguments focus on the legal status and role of trade unionism and the character of state labour market intervention via the industrial relations' apparatus. A high degree of state intervention in these areas has been the cornerstone of social democracy's political evolution, both in Europe and in Australia. Restrictions impelled by global competitive pressures are likely to have significant social and political impacts. Robison alludes to this in his introduction to this book when he poses the question: Can social democracy 'be combined with achieving a new competitiveness in the world economy and engaging with Asia'?[7]

This chapter seeks to provide insight into this central question through analysing the three positions in the Australian labour market debate. Before proceeding, an overview of Australian labour market restructuring and the changing role of the state arising out of globalisation and Asian trade will be presented.

Asian trade and the Australian labour market

Forsyth[8] has analysed the impact of the changing pattern of Asian trade on the Australian labour market. Drawing on the Factor Price Equalisation

Theorem[9] which states that trade results in a shift in resources from goods that use expensive factors intensively towards those that use the relatively cheap factors intensively, Forsyth argues this means that Australian production of labour-intensive goods will be reduced, given the low cost of Asian labour. Hence Asian trade will decrease the demand for labour in Australia, causing a fall in its relative price. This problem has been exacerbated by the entry of Asian nations into trade with focused export strategies that have resulted in a substantial drop in the price of labour-intensive commodities.

In the early phase of Asian growth when Japan played a dominant role, its impact on the labour markets of other countries was not very significant because Japanese wages, while lower than those of the developed economies, were not significantly discrepant. In any case, Japanese wages soon rose to comparative levels. In the early postwar period, other Asian economies had little impact on the labour markets of the developed economies as they had not yet come to rely on an export industrialisation strategy. Only when they had become heavily dependent on trade did they have some influence. The expansion of labour intensive manufactures from Singapore, Hong Kong and Taiwan had a limited effect because of the relative size of their economies and their own rising wage levels. However, the rapid industrialisation of Korea, Thailand, Malaysia, the Philippines and Indonesia has the potential to have a major impact on the labour markets of the older industrialised societies, especially Australia, given the latter's proximity. In Forsyth's view, the structural adjustment problems of the developed economies relate directly to the entry of these economies into the global marketplace over the past two decades. Furthermore, the entry into global markets of the 'awakening giants', China and India, is likely to further exacerbate labour market problems in the developed economies, given the large reserves of unskilled labour in both these countries. Considering their low wage structure, their impact is likely to be substantial.

Given the relatively unprotected Australian economy, the consequence of these changes is the increasing import penetration of Asian labour-intensive commodities. Indeed, the pattern of Asian exports has been to concentrate first on countries like Australia, then on the United States, presently their dominant market. Asian productive efficiency has advanced as manufacturers from the industrialised countries, including Australia, relocate offshore, combining their advanced technologies and design skills with cheap Asian labour. This results in commodities being placed on world markets at comparatively low prices.

Forsyth argues that these changes have had a consequential impact on the Australian labour market. Closures and relocation have resulted in the contraction of the manufacturing sector in relative terms and several industries have contracted sharply in absolute terms. Consequently, manufacturing employment has fallen. Labour-intensive Australian industries could only compete if flexibility were introduced into the wages system and real wages were lowered to competitive levels with Asian workers, a move essential to the reduction of structural unemployment. There are two obstacles to this possible response: labour market institutions and the social security system. In regard to the former, the award system and the unions obstruct such a response. As for the social security system, the provision of income and other benefits to the unemployed constrains wage flexibility, for were wages to fall below this income, workers would have little incentive to work. Lowering wages would also further undermine the pattern of income distribution and this would have to be accepted by Australian society. These are the dilemmas posed by attempts to adjust the labour market to the changing trade patterns.

The changing trade pattern also appears to have had a negative effect on the external debt. A goal of the tariff strategy was to transform 'this lump of industrial archaeology' into a world class, export-oriented manufacturing system, capable of contributing to reducing, rather than exacerbating, past structural imbalances in Australia's trade relationships. In fact, the opposite seems to be occurring. For example, the 1993 breakdown of Australia's merchandise exports and imports by Standard International Trade Classification (SITC) category shows that the merchandise trade deficit for manufactured goods (SITC categories 5 to 8) for the financial year was a record $32.6 billion. This new record for manufacturing trade has occurred despite the rapid growth in manufactured exports since 1987 (14% p.a. compound) and despite a growing proportion of elaborately transformed manufactures. Figure 9.1 reveals the levels of manufacturing trade deficit from 1964 to 1993. Two features can be observed. First, the serious deterioration in this series began in 1974, the year following the unilateral 25 per cent tariff reduction of the Whitlam Government. Second, the continued deterioration in manufacturing trade roughly follows the decline in the level of average effective manufacturing protection and the consequent rise in the import penetration ratio shown in Figure 9.2.[10]

Asian trade and the Australian state

This changing pattern of trade and investment has been facilitated by a notable shift in the role of the state from that of regulating corporate

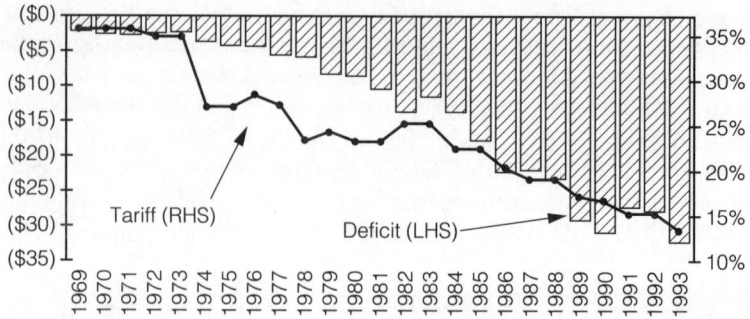

Figure 9.1   Manufactures trade deficit v. average effective manufacturing tariff

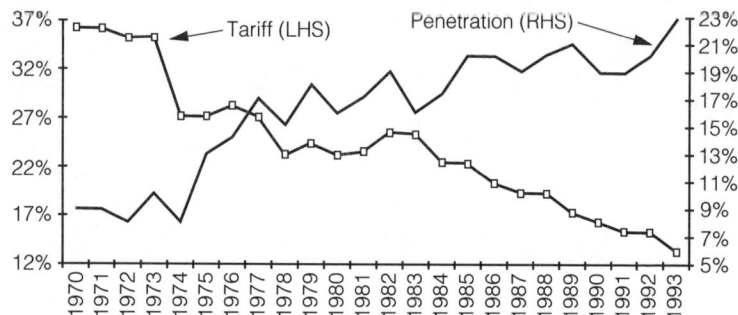

Figure 9.2   Import penetration ratio v. average effective manufacturing tariff

capital, protecting domestic investors, and securing wage outcomes to that of the enforcer of global competitive conditions on the domestic economy. Given the unparalleled mobility of capital facilitated by financial deregulation and the new communications and transportation technologies, the state's strategic options appear to be severely constrained. Financial deregulation has meant that companies can now move at will, without the constraints previously imposed by central banks.[11]

In this new competitive environment, states of the developed OECD economies such as Australia, are under pressure from the low wage and low corporate tax regimes of the Asian states to retain their investment base. All avenues of possible competitive edge are constantly being explored. Aside from competition via corporate tax rate changes, the labour market is one of the key terrains within which competitive struggles between states is now being waged. The state is under intense pressure to develop internationally competitive wage rates and more highly productive work forces to stem the tide of 'off-shoring'. While existing labour market institutions have become involved in the productivity issue, they are resistant to the pressures for wage flexibility arising out of the changing trade patterns. There are political demands for the state to withdraw from its present institutional intervention in the labour market through the Industrial Relations Commission, the award system and through its emphasis on the centrality of trade unionism in the bargaining process. However, such a withdrawal is not without its own set of social and political constraints. These institutions were a reformist response to late nine-teenth century working-class militancy. In order to incorporate the belligerent unionism of the 1890s, the state positioned itself as the champion of working-class interests, constantly 'watching over their welfare and prosperity'.[12] The closed economy bounded by high tariffs delivered a wages system that resulted in significant real wage gains. Between 1939 and 1974, workers' real wages rose by an average of 2 per cent per annum, which was exceptional when compared to other industrialised countries. Unemployment averaged less than 2 per cent and the 40-hour working week was common by the late 1930s.[13]

These gains deeply entrenched lifestyle expectations and a sense that all working people were entitled to a 'fair go', as a matter of right. This culture, which the state played a pivotal role in creating and sustaining through protection and through the wages system, now places social and political constraints on the state's attempts to fully deregulate the labour market and allow wages to find a market level driven solely by global labour market forces. Yet here lies the set of conundrums: if the state fails to restructure the labour market towards wage rates competitive with Asia, achieved via a combination of productivity gains and declining real wages, then off-shoring will continue apace, exacerbating unemployment and the external debt. The neo-liberal position is that this process of disinvestment is a sign of a more rational and efficient allocation of resources. Labour-intensive commodities are best produced in Asia's low-waged economies, leav-ing the way open for the expansion of high value-added industries based on greater knowledge and skill, more advanced technologies and sophisticated niche-marketing strategies. While the trade statistics reveal that the proportion of elaborately transformed manufactures (ETM) exports have grown, they have been outpaced by manufactured imports from Asia. Furthermore, these new factories are not labour intensive and therefore contribute only marginally to the resolution of the labour market problems produced by off-shoring.

While the political and economic pressure on the Australian state to withdraw from labour market regulation is intensifying, the interventionist role of Asian states has not yet entered the policy equations. Whereas the Australian state intervenes so as to mediate the conflicting interests of labour and capital through recognising trade unions and employer organisations as representative, independent forces in civil society and through creating the structures of negotiation and conflict resolution, Asian states have sought to develop a variety of instruments to restrict independent labour organisation, while at the same time developing the state institutions to discipline and control labour. Such disciplining is a part of the export-oriented industrialisation strategy, the belief being that foreign investors will only be attracted if they can be certain that labour will be pliant. So, for example, this is a major reason why the Malaysian state refuses to recognise union activity in the electronics sector. Hence wages and working conditions in Asia are not simply an outcome of surplus labour market conditions. Low wages and poor conditions are sustained by the restrictive role of the state which wishes to ensure that newly urbanised workers do not combine in a way that would expand their horizons and stimulate a sense of relative deprivation as they compare their experience of industrialisation with that of other social classes.[14]

This labour market role of Asian states has contributed to the competitive demands that the Australian state faces. Given the liberal democratic character of the state, Asian-styled labour market interventions are constrained, although the West Australian state is now proceeding down this route in a legislative sense.[15] These competitive pressures confront the Labor Government with dilemmas it has yet to acknowledge. The new role of the Australian state means that Labor is striving for two apparently contradictory objectives: those of enforcing conditions of global competition on the domestic economy while simultaneously striving to retain a social democratic agenda. Consequently, the Keating government has refused to abandon the state system of labour market regulation, choosing instead to introduce a degree of what they perceive to be socially controlled deregulation. In contrast, the Coalition is not so constrained, aiming instead at dismantling the state industrial relations system to achieve a consistency with other deregulatory policies and new potential for competitiveness with the Asian economies. These two major political positions are now analysed.

'Freedom to choose'

Neo-liberal labour market deregulation

Theoretically within this paradigm, labour market deregulation is an integral and logical component of the wider process of economic deregulation essential to securing a more rationally ordered global economy. Within this framework, open economies, and the resultant increased specialisation in production and trade, represent a rational and efficient allocation of the factors of production. Efficiencies are gained because an open global trading system allows for the more effective operation of the law of comparative advantage. Hence labour market institutions, particularly trade unions and the state institutions that underpinned them, were integral to the past era of closed, regulated national economies. Their persistence into the new phase of open globalism limits the efficiencies that derive from free trade, thereby undermining the law of comparative advantage. These antiquated institutions therefore lie at the heart of the structural imbalances presently being experienced in countries such as Australia.

Within this model it is contended that the abundant supply of cheap labour in Asia is an asset since it provides low-priced commodities to the industrialised economies, allowing consumers in the developed world to benefit from obtaining 'the best and the cheapest products' sourced from 'anywhere in the world'.[16] The only concern of the new 'nationality-less' consumers is product quality, price, design, value and appeal. These imports into the developed economies have stimulated the rapid industrialisation of Asian societies and hence the development of the middle class that in turn opens up new opportunities for sophisticated exports to Asia. In this way free trade benefits both the developed and the new industrialising societies.

Current application of neo-liberal labour market arguments are best captured in the recent OECD report (1994) on employment and unemployment. Here it is again argued that adjustment problems exist in the developed economies; hence improvements in the rational efficiencies of the trade system should be sought in policies designed to improve the competitive efficiency of the developed industrialised economies in the global marketplace. The 'root cause' of widespread unemployment in the developed economies resides in their 'failure to adapt satisfactorily' to the rapid changes ushered in by the increasingly complex process of globalisation.[17]

A range of policies that had been put in place over the past 30 years had 'contributed to ossifying the capacity of economies and the will of societies to adapt' (p. 27). A more effective adaptation to globalisation depended upon change in two essential areas. First,

OECD countries needed to accelerate the switch from low-waged labour products in industries where they could not meet 'the competition from low wage countries' (p. 31) to high technology, high productivity, industries using advanced manufacturing processes and flexible production systems that need highly educated and skilled workers (p. 32). High technology manufacturing sectors include aerospace, computer and office equipment, communications equipment and semiconductor, electrical machinery, pharmaceutical and scientific instrument industries. Jobs created in these industries would serve to offset the 20 per cent drop in employment in the traditional low technology industries.

Second, the labour market rigidity that prevented these societies from adapting needed to be addressed. During the 'tumultuous period' of globalisation 'when so many forces were testing the flexibility of economies, policies to achieve social objectives were extended' (p. 25). This had the effect of further entrenching labour markets' inflexibilities. Low-waged jobs were 'disallowed' as were 'precarious conditions and poor health or other benefits' (p. 26). 'Disincentives' to greater employment needed to be removed. This meant allowing for 'flexible working time arrangements' that might contravene standardised working time that was the 'outcome of historical developments' that had 'remained enshrined in legislation and collective agreements' (p. 33). New working time arrangements could reduce unit production costs. The other key measure to resolve the unemployment crisis was the widening of wage differentials, thus allowing 'the market clearing role of wages' (p. 35). Minimum wages should be allowed to vary between regions and between occupations. All these measures would require institutional changes in the fields of social policy and collective bargaining. This labour market flexibility would contribute towards overcoming the substantial decline in investment in OECD countries (p. 28). This was essential if these countries wished to remain 'at the head of the pack' (p. 2).

The report also noted that while trade in manufactured goods with non-OECD countries remained in surplus, the developed economies moved into a trade deficit in manufactured goods with the industrialising countries of Asia. Apart from labour-intensive manufactured products, these countries had also increased their market shares in the knowledge-intensive sectors such as office equipment and telecommunications (p. 14). While still relatively small compared to trade flows between OECD countries, trade with these Asian countries was growing rapidly. The number of markets that they were contesting was greater and their effect on the intensity of competition was increasing (p. 23).

The Coalition and Australian employers have argued in similar fashion.[18] Institutional rigidity in the labour market, it is argued, are the source of Australia's worsening trade position, its high unemployment, declining living standards and growing external debt. Consequently, labour market deregulation has been a key feature of the Coalition's political agenda. Their position is consistent with the arguments advanced by the BCA since the late 1980s. The 'highest possible productivity' of Australian enterprises could only be achieved if there was a 'fundamental reorientation' away from the existing structure of regulation based on an 'adverse' industrial relations system. This system should be replaced by 'direct relationships between employers and employees'.[19] The industrial relations system 'reflected the prevailing Australian values in the earlier part of this century, but those values have changed' (p. 5). Australia had become an increasingly diverse society in which 'a strong streak of individualism' prevailed. While Australians 'still put a high value on a fair society', they are increasingly seeking a society in which there is more scope for individual talent for Australians had become 'the most individualistic people in the world' (p. 19). A shift towards an enterprise focus would best express these values, this new culture and the rising individual aspirations associated with the change. It was claimed that were Australia to jettison industrial relations for this individualised approach, productivity would increase by 25 per cent (p. 8). While the report allowed for the possibility of trade union involvement at enterprise level, union-free workplaces was the preferred option. Here parties could develop their 'own working arrangements that override awards' (p. 103).

In the 1993 election campaign, Shadow Industrial Relations Minister Howard proclaimed, 'the dramatic and radical deregulation of Australia's industrial relations system is now clearly an idea whose time has come'. Howard proposed a system of direct workplace agreements between employers and employees that marginalised trade unionism through insisting that workplace agreements could only be concluded between 'individual employers and one, some or all of their employees. Unions or employer organisations . . . cannot be parties to a workplace agreement'.[20] Under the proposed system, unions were to lose legal privileges so as to 'remove their stranglehold'. 'People' were to be restored to the heart of the process. Compulsory arbitration was to end and the role of the Industrial Relations Commission was to be 'substantially reduced'. An award stream would be preserved, but workers could only remain within awards if their employer consented. Hence employers were given an effective veto over award provisions.[21] While the ensuing election defeat froze the strategy at Federal level, the election of conservative state governments in Victoria and in Western Australia gave some scope to this agenda.[22] In the present build-up to the 1996 election, Howard is promising a softer version of his 1993 proposals, allowing workers to opt out of the award system, rather than forcing them out, and allowing for a return if they so choose.

Hard on the heels of its election victory, Labor focused on industrial relations reform, hoping to neutralise this radical push. Given their relationship with the labour movement, further labour market deregulation was never going to be an easy path to hoe.

Labor's triumphant pragmatism

From the mid-1980s the Labor Government evolved a vastly different program of labour market reform to that espoused by the Coalition in the 1990s. Labor believed that a resolution of the structural problems besetting the Australian economy mentioned in the introduction, such as persistent unemployment and burgeoning external debt, lay, at least in part, in the improved efficiency and productiveness of Australian labour. A key issue for Labor's strategists was how could these efficiencies be retained without at the same time undermining Labor's social commitments and the basic institutions and programs of social democracy. In Robison's terms, can the latter be combined with the rigours and policy demands of global competitive pressures? This section explores Labor's attempt to grapple with the inherent contradictions in this dual commitment. That is to say, Labor's socially constrained form of labour market deregulation may well have heightened the contradictions rather than resolving them.

Labor's labour market reform strategy differed markedly from Coalition policy in that it centred on an attempt to resolve this global efficiency/social democracy dilemma. Unlike the Opposition, their strategy centred on the notion that organised labour was a partner in labour market reform and was not an obstacle to efficiency, *per se*. Arguing that global change had ushered in a new era of industrialisation that provided scope for upgrading manufacturing technologies and seizing new global market opportunities, a form of corporatism was forged that emphasised the trade union role in promoting efficiencies. This strategic unionism represented a deep cultural shift as unions moved from an 'adversarial' emphasis to participatory and cooperative relations with management.[23] Unions set about transforming the inefficient craft structures that they had inherited and became deeply immersed in the restructuring process. Success in this venture is mixed.[24] However, these measures did not abate the political pressure on Labor to deregulate the labour market. These arguments were persuasive because Labor had adopted the economic and trade policies of neo-liberalism outlined above, with the exception of the labour market prescriptions. The contradiction in such a position was constantly emphasised in the media. Faced with these pressures as well as being committed to the logic of neo-classical free trade, Keating signalled a major change in labour market policy soon after the 1993 election when he gave a major policy speech setting out the ALP's blueprint for the 1990s. His speech was characterised as outlining 'a plan of attack on the last great bastion of the old order: Australia's highly regulated labour market' in which, at long last, the Labor Government 'was moving towards divorcing Labor's interests from those of the ACTU'.[25] This was a bold, 'vision splendid' that spelt out 'the effective death warrant for the centralised wages system and the role of the tribunal as a main player'.

Keating's radical change signalled that the role of trade unionism, the Commission and awards would be scrutinised. He declared: 'Completing industrial relations reform is another link in the chain of reform which began a decade ago. It is important now that we accelerate the reform so that all the other elements of flexibility in the economy can work in greater harmony'.[26] 'A new model of industrial relations' that would 'overcome the shortcomings' of the existing system was required.[27] Two months later, Industrial Relations Minister Brereton confirmed that the Government was about to break with the past. He enthused that a 'new, all encompassing concept of industrial relations was in the process of emerging in Australia' in which flexibility, team building and consultation would be maximised, in contrast to the old adversarial system centred on strikes and lockouts.[28] He warned that the future package could only be achieved through the unions reaching 'painful decisions'. These centred on the 'means of spreading agreements in the non-union sector'. Employer organisations welcomed this 'sweeping program, this epochal change in Australian industrial relations'.[29] The *West Australian* editorialised:

> After attacking the Opposition's industrial relations policy relentlessly during the election campaign, Prime Minister Paul Keating has changed tack towards bipartisanship on labour market reform . . . Mr Keating has committed the Government to labour market deregulation that differs from the Opposition's plan only in degree.[30]

These initial agenda-setting pronouncements drew a sharp response from the union movement. Non-union enterprise agreements would open the way for the exploitation of workers and were unnecessary because the system was flexible enough to achieve productivity gains.[31] However, only days later ACTU expressed public support for the 'sweeping reform agenda' having received assurances that the award system would be maintained. A working group of key unions was convened to develop the union's proposals. The Federal Government worked closely with this group, so much so that employer organisations complained that they were not being properly consulted.

Finally, after eight months of negotiations, the *Industrial Relations Reform Act* was passed in December 1993. Labor viewed this as an historic moment in the reform process, one that captured the ALP's willingness to boldly extend and refine the labour market reforms of the past decade. For Keating the reforms were 'a sea change in one of the most difficult and intractable areas of reform' and represented 'an important structural change that is permanent'.[32] The Act is seen to achieve a vital balance between efficiency and worker protection, in stark contrast to the Coalition's drive to impose a New Zealand styled individual contract system. The following statement by the Department of Industrial Relations captures the notion of reconciling economic demand and social need.

> The legislation provides employers with the flexibility they need to improve productivity and compete internationally, while recognising that employee protection is crucial to the success of enterprise bargaining.[33]

This is deemed to be a further instance of triumphant pragmatism, of the political capacity to steer straight down the middle of contesting social forces, thereby achieving this near perfect balance in the national interest. There is a belief that lies at the heart of Labor's variant of social democracy that the efficiencies of global market forces can indeed be harnessed, while the powerless are protected. In this practical and realistic politics, it is claimed there are only winners. So the Act creates a framework and a process whereby productivity is enhanced, translating into higher profits, higher wages and secure employment, as Australian companies move towards world best practice. This seemed to be an instance of Australian social democracy in full cry, where 'strong economic policy' could be wedded to 'programs that produce not just social justice but social cohesion and strength' thereby fostering 'a creative, innovative, manufacturing nation in the front rank of trading nations and the front rank of social democracies'.[34] The Act was a cornerstone of Keating's 'compact for competition' wherein the reconciliation is attained.

Were both capital and labour to view the reforms thus, convinced their real interests had been secured, then Labor might have felt that the magic balance had indeed been struck. However, the partial labour market deregulation compromise has intensified the conflict. Employer organisations are on the offensive. They have launched a relentless campaign to reform the Act. Employers sense that the Act represents the first real chink in the armour of union-centred, labour market regulation. On the other hand, unions have supported the Act since they played a significant role in its formulation. However, anxiety has crept in. Will the Government succumb to the employers' campaign? Certain interpretations the Commission has placed on the Act's provisions have only served to heighten the fears. The Act has thus become a fiercely contested terrain and the question of labour market reform is unlikely to fade.

Pragmatists in the Labor Government argue that the Act has secured the union role within workplace bargaining to the maximum possible degree, given the current circumstances. A counter view, which has no real political base, would contend that despite affirmation of the trade union role in the bargaining process, the state has also legitimated a non-union-based industrial relations system for the first time in Australian history and that this has vast ramifications for the future. In a real sense, both interpretations appear plausible because the Act has both undermined *and* secured the union role, introduced flexibility into the labour market *and* placed defined boundaries on that flexibility. In allowing some scope for union involvement and a continuing role for awards as a benchmark, as well as strengthening the unfair dismissal laws, Labor would argue that the flexibility that the Act introduces is also socially constrained.

From the perspective of the BCA, the ACCI and the Coalition, this partial deregulation solution is an improvement. However, in their view, the provisions are still far too constraining, thus placing Australian business at a disadvantage in a highly competitive region. There is insufficient scope in the new laws to introduce the degree of labour market flexibility essential to a successful economic relationship with Asia. Furthermore, this partial deregulation is out of synchrony with the broader deregulation measures already adopted by Labor. Australia's persistent structural deficiencies reflected in falling living standards and growing external debt are caused by Labor's inability to accept the inevitability of a full deregulation of the labour market. Labor is limited by its close relationship with the ACTU, hence only the Coalition can deliver the reforms so essential to enhancing Australia's trade position with Asia and other regions. Labor counters that the labour market reforms have consolidated and further stimulated the competitive changes now occurring in Australian workplaces. Higher rates of productivity and flexibility have been achieved through a participatory process that has involved the unions and that has guaranteed security through the award safety net. Labor contends that the labour market reforms have advanced both the goal of global competitiveness and the essence of social democracy. Their reforms have skilfully resolved the dilemma posed by Robison.

These positions will remain highly contested. However, this

political debate has tended to isolate labour market reforms from the broader deregulation measures and thereby present these reforms, or the lack of them, as a panacea to the structural problems arising out of trade with Asia. This rather narrow focus fails to critically assess the impact of the other deregulatory measures such as tariffs and industry policy more generally on the process of Asian economic integration. In this final section, we briefly consider an emerging critique of both policy positions that centres on a more assertive, planned industry policy, meshed into a greater regulation of financial markets; a competitive tariff program that takes cognisance of Asian tariff levels and the high degree of state intervention in the labour market in Asia; and finally, an aid program that accelerates the growth of independent unionism in the Asian region.

Towards a critique of labour market deregulation

Markets don't give a tinkers damn about fundamentals: they are mainly driven by charts and follow-the-leader mentality.[35]

Were the critiques of neo-liberal deregulation merely to have emerged from radical analyses of globalisation, they might be tersely dismissed, given the current intellectual climate. However, a critique is evolving, tentatively and unevenly, from within the mainstream, as some of the major policy players reassess outcomes. Fred Argy, the secretary of the Campbell Committee and signatory to the report it produced in 1981, which set the stage for major changes such as the dollar float, the lifting of foreign exchange controls and deregulating the banking sector, has now produced a study *'Financial Deregulation: Past Promise—Future Realities'*[36] which calls for a reassessment. He argues that while they had claimed in early 1980s that such policies would end currency speculation and would stimulate productive investment in Australia, financial markets had instead become more volatile and destabilising of the real economy, thereby constraining the ability of governments to pursue social goals. Australia had in fact become dangerously exposed to world financial markets and destabilising speculation, while control of economic policy had shifted from governments to the financial markets. Free markets were supposed to have produced superior results to those of governments, yet ratings agencies and fund managers attach little importance to 'low unemployment and social justice. This means that governments are going to find it increasingly difficult to pay for welfare, health, education, labour market programs for disadvantaged workers and social and community infrastructure'. Establishment figures overseas such as Sir James Goldsmith have developed a similar critique.[37]

Social inequality has increased most in countries that have deregulated most rapidly.[38] In a recent study of some 900 areas covering 8 million Australians, labour market economist Bob Gregory provided empirical evidence that the social inequality between different areas in Australia was worsening inexorably.[39] Between 1976 and 1991, the poorest areas of Australian cities had lost one-third of their employment and a quarter of their household incomes. Average incomes in neighbourhoods with socioeconomic status ranking in the bottom 10 per cent slumped $7000 over the period, measured in 1995 dollars. In contrast the average incomes in the top 10 per cent of neighbourhoods climbed about $10 000 in current dollars. In the top 1 per cent of suburbs, the gain was $20 000 in real terms. The income gap has widened 92 per cent. In the poorer neighbourhoods, 60 per cent of men and 80 per cent of women were not working, whereas in 1976 the poor from these areas had jobs. Women from well-off areas have increased their share of work and income, whereas males from the poorer areas had either lost jobs or had been banished to low paid work. Gregory stated that the deterioration over the last fifteen years where there was now widespread male unemployment in these poor areas was startling. Neighbourhood employment patterns for men were now reminiscent of the 1930s when there were substantial ghettos of non-employment. He warned that a deregulated labour market would further entrench income inequality.[40] It is possible that the trend of off-shoring production facilities into Asia and into New Zealand may be impacting quite severely on these poorer regions. Furthermore, where are the new ETM factories being located? These are important questions that require further research. For example, Campbelltown in Sydney's south-west has been affected by companies moving production off-shore.[41]

These social outcomes raise pertinent questions regarding the efficacy of neo-liberal deregulation in general and labour market flexibility in particular. The perspective developed in Pollert's[42] edited collection provides a starting point for a more rigorous analysis. The book focuses on the concept of flexibility, which is a central organising principle of labour market deregulation. Within neo-liberal discourse, flexibility is synonymous with competitiveness and efficiency. In Pollert's view, the literature on flexibility is highly prescriptive rather than being rigorous and analytical. The concept gained hegemony with the revival of neo-classical economics and the preoccupation with market efficiencies and became a material force in the policy language of government and employers, and has therefore had a huge ideological influence. Theoretically, the concept draws on functionalist sociology and centres on a model of social integration that reflects a harmonious, pluralist, stable economy, that moves smoothly from one stage of social equilibrium to another. Flexible systems are deemed to be functional to these transitions. Hyman[43] contends that the concept is little more than a rhetorical slogan and has therefore tended to obscure, rather than illuminate, the massive changes in the deployment of labour in the 1980s. These include the influence of Japanese lean production techniques in the intensification of labour; the changing nature of employment contracts; the core/periphery structuring of workforces; and the demands for labour versatility and mobility. The concept has also masked the growth in unemployment; the expansion of low-paid, intermittent, non-permanent forms of work; the increased polarities within the working class; and finally, growing social inequality.

The issue of the labour market cannot be addressed without also addressing these questions of changing labour deployment flowing out of the globalisation process itself. These have to be analysed in terms of both their economic and their social impacts. Furthermore, labour market change cannot be analysed independently of the vexed issue of financial deregulation. While it is sensible to acknowledge the immense power of international finance capital and therefore the difficulty of meaningful reform without some form of capital strike, it is nevertheless important to consider the social implications of the high capital mobility the system now facilitates. Current policies smooth the way for the rapid transfer of capital between countries. This is a powerful influence in moulding global and regional labour markets that bring the Factor Price Equalisation Theorem into play, reflected in a tendency for the long-term equalisation of wage rates and conditions, modified only by differential productivity rates, or by deliberate state intervention. Such a trend has social consequences, given the state-controlled low wages and poor conditions across Asia. Under such conditions, labour market deregulation will continue to be pursued with vigour since any state-sponsored institutional constraints will create a situation of competitive disadvantage, making it difficult to retain reasonable levels of investment. Such a trend has further work and income consequences for Australia, given the competitive advantage countries in Asia have with their low corporate tax rates, state-controlled low wages and poor conditions.

Thus far this chapter has elaborated three positions on labour market reform. The first two propound policies that purport to create an alternative to the two-nation slide that Gregory alludes to, claiming their labour market strategies will ameliorate the high levels of joblessness in poor areas and reduce the growing social inequality. The above critique would need to shift from critical discourse to policy propositions, if an alternative is to enter into contention as a realisable and practical possibility in the longer term. It is beyond the scope of this chapter to elaborate all the dimensions of such an alternative, except to say that it includes an interventionist industry policy; a degree of regulation of the financial markets and exchange controls; a greater balance between exports, global trade and inward industrialisation; strategic intervention on the labour standards issue in Asia; and finally, labour market regulation and the reorientation of the trade union role towards what has been termed 'the democratic development of capacities'.[44] In the following section, an alternative industry policy and an Asian labour standards strategy are briefly considered as possible key elements to addressing the social dislocations identified by Gregory more effectively than solutions proposed by the market.

Australia's manufacturing challenge

Elsewhere in this volume, Fagan has highlighted the complex global impacts on the Australian food sector, arguing against a too mechanical view of the links between global and local manufacturing and the need to take account of the interconnected dynamics of production, trade and investment as firms searched for future markets, profits and growth. Globalisation is an uneven and contested process in which 'there is no single path to restructuring either globally or locally since the paths are constructed contingently by the stake holders'[45]. Fagan contends that in this process the concept of globalisation can be used to legitimate deregulation and greater flexibility in domestic workplaces.

The restructuring of the Australian home appliances sector is a pertinent illustration of points Fagan raises. Transformations in the industry following deregulation also serve to highlight the contradictions in Australian industry policy, problems surrounding the integration process with Asia, and the relative merits of the contending labour market positions outlined in this chapter.

There was certainly no single path to restructuring companies in this sector. This is a labour-intensive, assembly-line manufacturing sector—the perfect example of a sector certain to relocate into Asia's cheap labour havens once tariffs dropped to a negligible 5 per cent. Neo-classical theory holds that such a restructuring would represent an efficient and rational allocation of resources. However, of the three dominant producers, the two foreign-owned companies followed this pattern. They closed their manufacturing base, set up in Asia, and imported back into Australia. The only fully Australian-owned company decided to retain as much production as possible inside Australia, while also globalising its operations by setting up joint ventures in China and in New Zealand. The Australian plant has continued to produce for the local market and is facing fierce competition from the Asian-produced imports of the other two companies. Its Chinese joint venture produces for global markets.[46]

In confronting these global competitive pressures from the perspective of its Australian base, the company faces systemic obstacles.

1 Financial markets appear to have made a judgement against what they regard as low-technology, labour-intensive manufacturing remaining in Australia. The large institutional investors appear not to be backing this type of venture to the degree that would advantage the company. The company's share price has been reduced by more than 60 per cent over the past year, despite record profits.

2 Exchange rate fluctuations and the upward movement in the dollar has placed the company's locally produced commodities at a competitive disadvantage in relation to the companies that have chosen to produce in Asia and import.

3 The company's direct competitors that now produce from Asia are able to gain comparative advantage from their Asian production sites where state labour market intervention has sought to pre-empt any form of independent unionism, thereby maintaining production regimes based on ultra-low wages, long working hours and poor working conditions in contrast to Australia's regulation in these areas and its observance of ILO labour conventions.

4 High Asian tariffs have precluded the company from exporting to Asia.

5 Ultra-low Asian corporate tax rates provide Asian based plants with a competitive advantage.

Interestingly, from the perspective of the debate over labour market policy outlined in this chapter, the regulated Australian labour market is not perceived as the main impediment to competitiveness, although there is a view that the company could become even more competitive were Australia to deregulate the labour market. However, there is an equally strong counter view in management ranks.[47]

In reality, innovative management, particularly in the areas of human resource strategies, research, design and production have combined creatively with plant-level union leadership in an effort to try and secure the company's competitive position, despite the abovementioned difficulties. This productive and cooperative relationship between management and labour has led to workplace restructuring that has seen productivity leap by a massive 320 per cent in certain lines over the past 14 months so that the unit labour cost of producing commodities in the Australian plant is now equivalent to that in Asia, despite the vast difference in wage rates and conditions. This has meant that the plant can compete with imports into Australia. The Labor

Government's partially deregulated labour market does not appear to have been a barrier to achieving this outcome, although the view is held at senior level, but not shared by all, that a deregulated labour market would be advantageous.

Despite the competitiveness of this plant, there are no guarantees that production will remain in Australia. A second joint venture is currently being established in Asia and the company is increasingly evaluating its situation in Asian regional rather than Australian terms. Much depends on the unfolding of the relatively unpredictable and volatile external factors specified earlier. If manufacturing remains in Australia, this will be a sign that labour-intensive manufacturing can survive, despite the pressures from low-waged Asian production. Sydney jobs in one of the city's largest manufacturers will be retained as will the market for home appliance components. Closure would signal that productive efficiency alone will not save this sort of production in Australia. Job losses would exacerbate the trends Gregory identified, with little indication as yet that the new breed of ETM companies can in any way compensate the scale of these job losses.

The challenges locally based manufacturing in the remaining labour-intensive production face raise a number of complex policy issues. From a neo-liberal perspective, the survival or otherwise of such plants is of little consequence, since Asian relocation is viewed as a rational market choice. The difficulties that the company faces highlights the unresolved dilemmas of Labor's marriage of market rationalism to their traditional social agenda. If a company that has proved its competitiveness eventually has to close and import from Asia, then there is no future for any other relatively labour-intensive manufacturing. This admission would have enormous consequences for the labour market and for immigration policy. If this fate for labour-intensive manufacturing in Australia is accepted, then the Industry Commission advising government would have to be relatively certain, given present trends, that the new high-technology industries and the growing service sector would make up the collapse in these manufacturing jobs. There appears to be little empirical evidence to support this contention at present, although the Industry Commission study due out in 1996 might fill this information void.

Apart from these employment and income consequences, the character of the process of Asian integration and restructuring of this sector raises another issue—that of Australian manufacturing's contribution to resolving the growing external debt. In this case study we see a situation where economic deregulation has led to manufacturing closures and the familiar 'produce in Asia and import into Australia' scenario, a scenario made possible by Australia's negligible levels of tariff protection. Yet the company that chose to produce locally cannot export to Asia because of the high tariff barriers. So here we have a sector restructuring that contributes to the growing external debt rather than reducing the burden through export growth. There are no exports, only high levels of imports which will be 40 per cent higher if the remaining manufacturer also chooses to produce in Asia. In this instance, the present tariff policy discriminates in favour of the interests of foreign-owned companies that now produce in Asia, while discriminating against a wholly Australian-owned company that has evidenced some degree of commitment to jobs in Australia.

The argument against the reintroduction of some degree of tariff protection is that such measures protect inefficiencies and force consumers to subsidise such Australian-based manufacturing, instead of having the choice of purchasing cheaper commodities produced in Asia. Yet here we have an instance of the evolution of a world-class manufacturing plant in terms of its cost and price competitiveness that would not burden consumers in any way. Furthermore, it is a plant that has now reached the border zone of efficiency in that it is difficult to see any further advances in assembly speed or quality. The imposition of a degree of tariff protection relative to disadvantages faced would secure the future of this plant, thereby contributing to employment and income, while also reducing the debt by reducing imports. In debating such a policy shift it is important to note that some neo-liberal writers in extolling the benefits of free trade policies have argued that the success of the East Asian NICs is proof of the superiority of these policies.[48] Yet these same writers find it difficult to acknowledge that while the East Asian states promoted exports, they also maintained high levels of protection. In acknowledging this dimension of these regimes' successful industrialisation strategy, there is a case to be made from the Australian side for penalising the exports of those Asian countries that prohibit the entry of Australian exports through high tariff regimes. In all of this, there is a need to rethink the way the current strategy is *actually* unfolding as against theoretical prescriptions as to what might happen at some future point, other things being equal. A national interest needs to be defined in a way that the conflicting interests of foreign-owned companies and Asian states are recognised and factored into the policy equation.

The Asian integration and restructuring of this sector raises afresh the issue of industry policy, the role of financial markets and Asian labour standards, and the degree to which state interventions in these areas could secure the future of companies wishing to manufacture in Australia. There are contending views on all three issues. For neo-liberals, interventionist industry policy has the potential to misallocate resources whereas deregulated product markets promote efficiency and competitiveness, and hence economic welfare.[49] Like protection, an interventionist industry policy involves forsaking the gains of trade since it would inevitably emphasise assistance to labour-intensive industries that are best located in Asia's cheap labour havens.[50] Forsyth does, however, acknowledge that an assertive industry policy could secure jobs as well as creating jobs in new industries, thereby addressing the unemployment issue.

Arguments for greater state intervention in promoting the growth of manufacturing can draw on historical precedent. Apart from the European economies and Japan, Taiwan, South Korea and Malaysia are examples of industrialisation through extensive state intervention to protect and promote strategic industries through the provision of economic infrastructure and through the channelling of resources to particular locations and uses.[51] An alternative to a passive stand-off in Australian industry policy has been advanced by Sicklen where he argues that such policy should 'no longer be considered to be the poor relation to economic policy'.[52] The state's role in promoting the manufacturing sector should not be understated considering that the majority of the growth in manufactured exports that has occurred over recent years has come from industries that have been subject to some form of industry policy. From 1986–87 to 1991–92 the top five manufacturing classifications that received some form of government assistance accounted for 45.6 per cent of total manufactured exports growth. The objectives of industry policy should be the reduction of unemployment through higher investment; encouraging investment into areas that will improve Australia's international and national competitiveness and reduce exposure to external shocks such as changing terms of trade; financing investment expansion domestically as far as possible; encouraging private sector research and development expenditure; using government purchasing policy more widely as an instrument of industry policy; and finally, ensuring that foreign takeovers meet industry policy objectives.

Sicklen proposes institutionalising a *Strategic Priorities Program* (SPP) that would aim at motivating local and foreign business to expand investment in Australia through offering a range of special investment incentives. This is not completely new as many of the incentives and conditions Sicklen proposes already apply in certain programs. The proposed SPP merely extends their depth and coverage. A broad range of incentives would be available for new investment by members of the SPP, each of which would have specified time periods. These would include: reduced tax rates, in some cases to zero to high scoring applicants; dramatically accelerated research and development and capital expenditure write-offs; targeted government infrastructure expenditure; special government procurement preference; tax breaks for other companies who purchase products or services from the firms in the program; selective import protection in the form of quotas, tariffs, licences; special government export marketing assistance; and finally, export subsidies. These SPP policies fall into the same category of techniques that the Japanese used in the 1950s and 1960s to reindustrialise. The major difference in Sicklen's proposal is in the process of gaining access to the scheme. With the Japanese model, MITI identified specific industries by *product* and then provided the incentives. In contrast to this 'picking winners' Sicklen's proposal is based on economic characteristics rather than products. Companies are ranked according to whether or not they possess desirable industrial characteristics. They can then tender for the incentives.

In Sicklen's submission, the problem of financing capital expenditure from offshore sources is also addressed. He proposes that the offshore investment of Australian superannuation funds should be reduced and the supply of loan capital to small and medium sized business should be increased through the expansion of the Commonwealth Development Bank. There should also be a temporary halt to Australia's unilateral reduction of import protection. Australia, he argues, has created one of the lowest import protection regimes of any developed economy. More than 70 per cent of manufactured goods enter the country absolutely free of duty, while many Australian based companies face massive Asian tariff and other trade barriers. The state should pressure Australia's top thousand importers to switch to local production.

This brief summary of Sicklen's proposals is presented to further stimulate debate around the issues the case study raised for it is possibly in the area of creative industry policy that the structural imbalances in the economy are best addressed, rather than focusing *solely* on yet another wave of labour market reform, for as the case study shows, labour can be hyper-productive to the point of out-competing cheap Asian labour, yet the companies can still relocate.

The other contentious area of much needed debate is the impact of Asian labour standards on trade and investment flows and the possibility and desirability of some form of intervention in this arena.[53] Fagan has summarised the critiques of the NIDL thesis of the relocation of production from high-waged to low-waged regions so there is no need to repeat the arguments here, except to emphasise that low wages and conditions are only one factor, albeit an important one in the process of investment choice.

Other factors include market access, raw material inputs costs, low corporate tax rates and union-free workplaces. Given the intensity of global competition where costings influencing investment choice are precisely calculated, marginal shifts can alter the pattern of investment flows between countries and regions. In the longer term, the growing power of independent labour organisation in Asia is likely to have an impact on the structure of the global economy and could possibly become a key component reducing the pressure to deregulate the developed economy's labour markets. Australian government policy to accelerate this trend through indirect forms of assistance to Asia's emerging labour organisations is a potentially important element in the armoury of trade strategies.

Conclusion

In the introduction to this chapter, attention was drawn to the pertinent question posed by Robison: 'Can social democracy be combined with achieving a new competitiveness in the world economy and engaging with Asia?' The current debate over labour market reform elaborated in this chapter has a bearing on this vexed question. The two political dominant labour market strategies both claim to provide a solution to the structural imbalances in the Australian economy. In claiming to address the problem of declining living standards, unemployment, growing social inequality and rising external debt, both would also claim that their strategy has the potential to balance competitive efficiency and social need.

This chapter has sought to move beyond the party political ideological debate and has situated these differing degrees of labour market deregulation within an analysis of the wider deregulation measures adopted in the 1980s that have so shaped the character of Australia's trade relationships with Asia. The critiques of these measures that are now emerging from within the policymaking establishment might be a more fertile starting point for evaluating the economic and social outcomes of trade with Asia than simply viewing labour market reform as the panacea. The case study of restructuring in the home appliances sector indicates that the process of economic integration with Asia is complex and contradictory. In the present circumstances, a case can be made for at least opening further debate on the merits or otherwise of a more interventionist industry policy and the indirect promotion of labour market regulation in Asia, given the present gap between the promise and the fulfilment of neo-liberal free trade. If the differing policy positions are to be debated rationally, rigorous research on the changing pattern of Asian trade and investment and its relationship to the changing structure of Australian manufacturing needs to be continued.

Notes

1 See Derek Sicklen (*National Industry Policy: The Key to Job Growth and Industry Structure*, A document of Australian Economic Analysis Pty Ltd, Sydney, Nov. 1993, p. 19) where he argues that Australia's trade weighted average tariff of less than 5 per cent means that Australia has created one of the lowest import protection regimes in the world. (Data sourced from the Industry Commission.) Tariff reductions since 1987 exceeded those required by GATT by 50 per cent, a rate of reduction unmatched by our trading partners. See also Sicklen, *Industry Policy Briefing Note*, no. 2, December 1993.

2 *Australian Financial Review*, 27 July 1995.

3 Woodall, P., 'The Global Economy: War of the Worlds', *The Economist*, 1–7 October 1994.

4 The degree to which these structural problems have been exacerbated by the current pattern of global trade relations in general, or Asian trade relations in particular, has yet to be fully researched. However, the World Bank projections of the shift of the centre of the global economy to the Asian region would seem to indicate that the impact of Asian trade on Australian economic trends is likely to be fairly substantial. See Forsyth, P., *Trade Patterns and Labour Demand: International Influences on Wages and Unemployment in Australia,* Policy Paper no. 293, Centre for Economic Policy Research, Australian National University, 1993; Raskall, P., 'Widening Income Disparities in Australia', *Beyond the Market: Alternatives to Economic Rationalism*, eds S. Rees, G. Rodley & F. Stillwell, Pluto Press, Sydney, 1993; Gregory, R. & Hunter, B., *The Macro-Economy and the Growth of Ghettos and Urban Poverty in Australia*, Centre for Economic Policy Research, Working Paper no. 325, Australian National University, 1995.

5 Barnett, R. & Cavanagh, J., *Global Dreams: Imperial Corporations and the New World Order*, Simon & Schuster, New York, 1994; Bienefeld, M., 'Capitalism and the Nation State in the Dog Days of the Twentieth Century', *Between Globalism and Nationalism*, eds R. Milliband & L. Panich, Merlin Press, London, 1994; Panich, L., 'Globalisation and the State', *Between Globalism and Nationalism,* eds R. Milliband & L. Panich, Merlin Press, London, 1994; Pollert, A. (ed.), *Farewell to Flexibility*, Blackwell, Oxford, 1991. Albo, G., 'Competitive Austerity and the Impasse of Capitalist Employment Policy', *Between Globalism and Nationalism,* eds R. Milliband & L. Panich, Merlin Press, London, 1994.

6 See Lambert, R.V., 'International Labour Standards: Challenging Globalization Ideology', *The Pacific Review,* October 1995., for an attempt to analyse the possible impact of internationally recognised labour standards on the future structure of the global economy. The author is presently researching the globalisation of the Australian home appliance sector.

7 See introduction, page xii.

8 Forsyth, op. cit.

9   Dixit, A. K. & Norman, V., *Theory of International Trade*, Cambridge University Press, Sydney, 1980, ch. 4.

10 The data in this paragraph and the two tables are drawn from Sicklen's 1993 research.

11 Barnett & Cavanagh, op. cit., Kennedy, P., *Preparing for the 21st Century*, Harper Collins, London, 1993; Reich, R. B., *The Work of Nations: Preparing Ourselves for 21st Century Capitalism*, Simon & Schuster, Sydney, 1991.

12 Alfred Deakin, one of the founding fathers of the Australian Federal State. Quoted in Pusey, M., *Economic Rationalism in Canberra: A Nation Building State Changes its Mind*, Cambridge University Press, Sydney, 1991, intro chapter.

13 Gruen, F.H., *How Bad is Australia's Economic Performance and Why?*, Discussion Paper no. 127, Centre for Economic Policy Research, Australian National University, 1985, p. 4.

14 Runciman, W. G., *Relative Depravation and Social Justice: A Study of Attitudes to Social Inequality in Twentieth Century England*, Routledge Kegan Paul, London, 1966.

15 Productivity and Labor Relations Minister Kierath plans to introduce what he refers to as his 'second wave' legislation into State Parliament this September. This is a package of laws that will restrict trade unions' right of access to workplaces; restrict union finance and other organisational capacities. Asian states go a step further in backing their restrictive labour laws with the full force of the state's repressive apparatuses—the intelligence service, police force and the military.

16 Ohmae, K., *The Borderless World: Power and Strategy in the Interlinked Economy*, Fontana, London, 1990, p. 11.

17 The information in the following paragraphs comes from OECD, Employment–Unemployment Study, Paris, 24 May 1994.

18 Chief Executive Officers of companies I am currently researching on the impact of global competition have emphasised what they view as the contradiction of de-regulating everything except the labour market, thereby causing competitive problems for Australian industry.

19 Business Council of Australia, *Enterprise Bargaining: A Better Way of Working*, 1989, p. ix. The following page numbers refer to this.

20 Liberal Party of Australia, *Jobsback*, 1993, 2.7.

21 Industrial awards would automatically terminate within a year, unless both parties notified the Commission that they wished the award to continue. Workplace agreements had to comply with a set of minimum conditions. These included an hourly rate for adults that could not be less than the minimum award rate, excluding penalties, allowances and loadings under the award; a minimum youth wage; four weeks annual leave; two weeks non-cumulative sick leave and twelve months unpaid maternity leave after twelve months of service. One area where there would be total flexibility was in working hours.

22 See the Western Australian *Workplace Agreements Act* of 1993. Under the new legislation, unions are prevented from being a party to an agreement, unless the employer consents.

23 Australian Council of Trade Unions and Department of Foreign Affairs and Trade, *Australia Reconstructed*, Australian Government Publishers, Canberra, 1987; Mathews, J., *Tools for Change*, Pluto Press, Sydney, 1989, and *Riding the Wave*, Pluto Press, Sydney, 1994; Ewer, P., Hampson, I., Lloyd, C., Rainford, J., Rix, S. & Smith, M., *Politics and the Accord*, Pluto Press, Sydney, 1991.

24 Botsman, P., *Unions 2001: A Blueprint for Trade Union Activism*, Evatt Foundation, Sydney, 1995; Lambert, R V., 'State of the Union: An Assessment of Union Strategies', *The Economic and Labour Relations Review*, vol. 2, no. 2, December, 1991.

25 *Australian*, 24–25 April 1993.

26 Speech to Institute of Company Directors, Melbourne, 21 April 1993.

27 Foreshadowing the essential content of the new legislation, he listed the shortcomings. First, the present system had failed to extend enterprise bargains to workers who 'don't have a union to represent them'. Second, the status of enterprise agreements relative to the award system needed upgrading. In a statement strongly supported by employers organisations and opposed by the ACTU, he held that enterprise agreements should become 'full substitutes for awards'. Third, the role and powers of the Industrial Relations Commission should be recast from the 'adversarial system' of the past to fit 'the system we are creating', that is, a system of 'cooperative workplace relations'.

28 Speech to British Chamber of Industries, May 1993.

29 *Australian*, 22 April 1993.

30 *West Australian*, 23 April 1993. It is interesting to note that Keating's speech reflected the precise concerns expressed by ACCI in their survey of 240 enterprise agreements approved during the first quarter of 1993.

31 *Australian*, 22 April 1993.

32 Prime Minister's answer during question time. *Hansard*, 1 February 1994.

33 *The 1993 Industrial Relations Reforms*, Department of Industrial Relations, December 1993.

34 *Australian*, 22 April 1993.

35 F. Argy, *Australian*, 29–30 April 1995.

36 Argy, F., *Financial Deregulation: Past Promise—Future Realities*, Working Paper, Centre for the Economic Development of Australia (CEDA), Melbourne, April 1995.

37 Goldsmith, J., *The Trap*, Carroll and Graf, New York, 1994; Harvey, R., *The Return of the Strong*, MacMillan, London, 1995.

38 Response by Professor Hohn Neville, University of NSW, to the report by Argy.

39 Gregory & Hunter, op. cit.

40 Professor Gregory commenting on the research findings at the National Press Club, *Australian*, 27 April 1995; *Australian Financial Review*.

41 I have conducted field work in this area and have listed the closures.

42 Pollert, op. cit.

43 Hyman, R., ' "Plus ca change?", The Theory of Production and the

Production of Theory', *Farewell to Flexibility,* ed. A. Pollert, Blackwell, Oxford, 1991.

44 Gindin, S., 'International Competitiveness and the Democratic Development of Capacities', *South African Labour Bulletin,* vol. 19, no. 3, 1995, p. 37; Albo, op. cit.; Bienefeld, op. cit.; Lambert, op. cit. 1995; MacEwan, A., 'Globalization and Stagnation', *Between Globalism and Nationalism,* eds R. Milliband & L. Panich, Merlin Press, London, 1994.

45 See Chapter 8.

46 Lambert, R. V., 'Globalization and the Restructuring of the Australian Home Appliances Sector' (forthcoming)

47 ibid.

48 World Bank, *World Bank Development Report,* Oxford University Press, New York, 1981; Balassa, B., 'The Newly Industrializing Developing Countries after the Oil Crisis', *The Newly Industrializing Countries in the World Economy,* Pergamon, New York, 1981; Bradford, C. & Branson, W. H., *Trade and Structural Change in Pacific Asia,* University of Chicago Press, Chicago, 1987; Keesing, D.B., 'Outward-Looking Policies and Economic Development', *The Economic Journal,* vol. 77, no. 306, 1967; Kreuger, A. O., 'Export-Led Industrial Growth Reconsidered', *Trade and Growth of the Advanced Developed Countries in the Pacific Basin,* eds W. Hong & L.B Krause, Korea Development Institute, Seoul, 1981; Little, I. M. D., 'The Experience and Causes of Rapid Labour Intensive Development in Korea, Taiwan Province, Hong Kong and Singapore; and the Possibilities of Emulation', *Export Led Industrialization and Development,* ed. E. Lee, ILO, Geneva, 1981; Riedel, J., 'Trade as the Engine of Growth in Developing Countries, Revisited', *Economic Journal 94,* 1984.

49 Green, R., *Industry Policy and Jobs,* Policy Paper no. 299, Centre for Economic Policy Research, Australian National University, 1993, p. 14.

50 Forsyth, op. cit., p. 23.

51 Amsden, A., *Asia's Next Giant: South Korea and Late Industrialization,* Oxford University Press, Oxford, 1989; Haggard, S., *Pathways from the Periphery: The Politics of Growth in the Newly Industrializating Countries,* Cornell University Press, Ithaca, 1990; Rodan, G., *The Political Economy of Singapore's Industrialization: National State and International Capital,* Forum, Kuala Lumpur, 1989.

52 Sicklen, op. cit., p. 6.

53 Lambert, op. cit. 1995.

Further References

Bell, S., *Australian Manufacturing and the State: The Politics of Industry Policy in the Post-War Era,* Cambridge University Press, Melbourne, 1993.

Blandy, R. & Niland, J., *Alternatives to Arbitration,* Allen & Unwin, Sydney, 1986.

Burrows, R., Gilbert, N. & Pollert, A., *Fordism and Flexibility: Division and Change,* MacMillan, London, 1992.

Business Council of Australia, Avoiding Strikes: A Better Way of Working, 1991.

Campling, A. & Galligan, B., *Beyond the Protective State: The Political Economy of Australia's Manufacturing Industry Policy*, Cambridge University Press, Melbourne, 1992.

Carroll, J. & Manne, R., *Shutdown: The Failure of Economic Rationalism*, Text Publishers, Melbourne, 1992.

Cockett, R., *Thinking the Unthinkable: Think Tanks and the Economic Counter-Revolution*, Harper Collins, London, 1994.

Department of Industrial Relations, *The 1993 Industrial Relations Reforms*, Australian Government Publishers, Canberra, 1993.

Deyo, F. C., *Beneath the Miracle: Labour Subordination in the New Asian Industrialism*, University of California Press, Berkeley, 1989.

Donaldson, M., *Time of Our Lives: Labour and Love in the Working Class*, Allen & Unwin, Sydney, 1991.

Frenkel, S., *Organized Labour in the Asia-Pacific Region: A Comparative Study of Trade Unions in Nine Countries*, ILR Press, Cornell, 1993.

Garnaut, R., *Australian Protectionism*, Allen & Unwin, Sydney, 1987.

Hancock, W. K., *Australia*, Ernest Benn, London, 1930.

Harvey, D., *The Condition of Postmodernity*, Basil Blackwell, London, 1989.

Hawkins, E. D., 'Labour in Transition', *Indonesia*, ed. R. McVey, Yale University Press, New Haven, 1963.

Hewitt, P., *About Time: The Revolution in Work and Family Life*, Rivers Oram Press, London, 1993.

Jessop, B., *Nicos Poulantzas: Marxist Theory and Political Strategy*, Macmillan, London, 1985.

——*State Theory: Putting Capitalist States in their Place,* Polity, London, 1990.

Kelly, P., *The End of Certainty: The Story of the 1980s*, Allen & Unwin, Sydney, 1992.

Macintyre, S. & Mitchell, R., *Foundations of Arbitration: The Origins and Effects of State Compulsory Arbitration 1890–1914*, Oxford University Press, Melbourne, 1989.

Muller, W. & Neussuss, C., 'The Illusions of State Socialism and the Contradictions Between Wage Labour and Capital', *Telos*, vol. 25, 1970, pp. 13–90.

Munck, R., *The New International Labour Studies: An Introduction*, Zed Books, London, 1988.

Potter, D., 'Democratization in Asia', *Prospects for Democracy: North, South, East, West,* ed. D. Held, Polity Press, Cambridge, 1993.

Richard, J., *H. B. Higgins*, Allen & Unwin, Sydney, 1984.

Rueschemeyer, D., Stephens, E. H. & Stephens, J. D., *Capitalist Development and Democracy,* Polity Press, Cambridge, 1992.

Stewart, J., *The Lie of the Level Playing Field: Industry Policy and Australia's Future,* Text Publishers, Melbourne, 1994.

Urry, J., *The Anatomy of Capitalist Societies: The Economy, Civil Society and the State,* Macmillan, London, 1981.

Index

255

Pathways to Asia